Perpetual
Adolescence

Perpetual Adolescence

Jungian Analyses
of American Media,
Literature, and Pop Culture

EDITED BY
Sally Porterfield
Keith Polette

AND

Tita French Baumlin

SUNY
PRESS

Published by State University of New York Press, Albany

For information, contact State University of New York Press, Albany, NY
www.sunypress.edu

Production by Ryan Morris
Marketing by Fran Keneston

Library of Congress Cataloging-in-Publication Data

Perpetual adolescence : Jungian analyses of American media, literature, and pop culture /
edited by Sally Porterfield, Keith Polette, and Tita French Baumlin.
    p. cm.
  Includes bibliographical references and index.
ISBN 978-1-4384-2799-7 (hardcover : alk. paper)
ISBN 978-1-4384-2800-0 (pbk. : alk. paper)
1. Adolescent psychology—United States. 2. Adolescence—United States. 3. Jung, C. G.
(Carl Gustav), 1875–1961. I. Porterfield, Sally F. II. Polette, Keith, 1954– III. Baumlin, Tita
French.
  BF724.2.P47 2009
  150.19'54—dc22
                                        2008051873

10 9 8 7 6 5 4 3 2 1

Contents

Acknowledgments

We express our personal gratitude in particular to Craig A. Meyer for his generous compilation of the index for this volume.

In addition, our thanks go to James Peltz and Ryan Morris of SUNY Press for their expert guidance, and to James S. Baumlin for his assistance with early versions of the draft.

Introduction to the Puer/Puella Archetype

GEORGE H. JENSEN

The psychological context of dream contents consists in the web of associations in which the dream is naturally embedded. . . . [C]areful analysis will never rely too much on technical rules; the danger of deception and suggestion is too great. In the analysis of isolated dreams above all, this kind of knowing in advance and making assumptions on the grounds of practical expectation or general probability is positively wrong. It should therefore be an absolute rule to assume that every dream, and every part of a dream, is unknown at the outset, and to attempt an interpretation only after carefully taking up the context.

—C. G. Jung, *Psychology and Alchemy*

The fantasy we call "current events," that which is taking place outside in the historical field, is a reflection of an eternal mythological experience. . . . Nothing can be revealed by a newspaper, by the world's *chronique scandaleuse*, unless the essence is grasped from within through an archetypal pattern. The archetype provides the basis for uniting those incommensurables, fact and meaning.

—James Hillman, "An Aspect of the Historical and Psychological Present"

All schools of criticism—at least, those with some staying power—ebb and wane. They begin with a brilliant and original thinker who breaks through habitual, routine interpretations to offer an entirely new way to view texts. A first generation of followers emulates the great thinker, and the new method becomes a school. As the school grows, methods become rules, interpretations sound like recitations, and insight reduces to mimicry. The school loses its luster until a fresh thinker—or a generation of them—stretches the theory, alters the methods, and surprises us once again. Jung understood this, and he often warned his readers against mapping his thought process into a series of steps. Interpretation should never be based on "technical rules." Every text has its context—its "web of associations," a remarkably postmodern phrase—and context is always a shifting ground.

If interpretation evolves from context, as Jung certainly believed, then all context is important, including popular culture. We bring our complete selves to the texts we write, and, whether we realize it or not, we draw from our complete selves as we interpret texts. As context shifts, so too should interpretations. This belief in the totality of self, culture, and text drew Jung to look for psychological insights in both high and low art, history and politics, myth and fads. Even the most highly developed individuals, he believed, could not entirely rise above the mass-mindedness of their times.[1] Thus, analyzing popular culture, looking for a collective trauma that might soon erupt into political upheaval, is potentially even more important than finding some truth about the psyche in Greek tragedy.

Jung, for example, wrote an extended essay on UFOs. Even during his lifetime, many who did not bother to read more than the title of Jung's work assumed that he was a "saucer-believer." He was not. As in all things, Jung was a skeptic in the best sense of the term. Without adequate evidence, he doubted. When confronted with radical ideas, he kept an open mind. Jung was not a believer in little green men, but he was interested in the "tendency all over the world to believe in saucers and to want them to be real" (*CW* 10: 309). He argued that the tendency to believe in UFOs was related to a remnant trauma from World War II and the "increasing uncertainty" of the early cold war, "the strain of Russian policies and their still unpredictable consequences" (*CW* 10: 319, 324). Such events "arouse expectations of a redeeming supernatural event" (*CW* 10: 328), leaving individuals vulnerable to mass-mindedness, charismatic leaders, and totalitarianism. Jung wrote about UFOs "to sound a note of warning" (*CW* 10: 311). He believed that it was "difficult to form a correct estimate of the significance of contemporary events," yet analyzing contemporary expressions of archetypes could lend some distance and objectivity. In a similar vein, the essays in this volume examine contemporary expressions of the puer archetype—the eternal youth—to understand our own times.

The Collective Unconscious and Archetypes

Jung is often discussed and rarely read. Even when read, he is typically encountered piecemeal. Many know enough about concepts such as the collective unconscious and archetypes only to dismiss them. However, if understood within the context of Jung's theory of self, the notion of a collective unconscious is not so difficult to accept.

It is interesting that even those who accept a rather mechanistic version of the unconscious often question the idea of a *collective* unconscious. To understand why so many find the collective unconscious and archetypes problematic, we should begin with what they *believe* Jung wrote. The common (mis)understanding of Jung's theory is that archetypes are universal images that are passed on genetically and stored in an area of the brain called the collective unconscious. A host of questions arise at this point that, even in the asking, indicate the categories of archetype and collective unconscious have already been reified: Can any image be universal? Can images be passed on genetically? Is there an area of the brain that could serve as the collective unconscious? Another reaction to this (mis)understanding of Jung's theory is to dismiss it without any thought at all, a gut response that this theory conflicts with fundamental—perhaps even unspoken—beliefs: *Animal behavior is ruled by instincts and drives, but humans learn and change. Animals do not really feel. Animals do not solve problems. Humans are the products of language, history, culture.*

Of course, we could avoid such problems by bracketing the collective unconscious. In *Anatomy of Criticism* (1957), Frye chooses to "not speak" of the collective unconscious as the source of archetypes. Instead, he emphasizes the literary tradition: "Poetry can only be made out of other poems; novels out of other novels" (97).[2] For him, an archetype is a "recurring image" or a "social fact" that "helps to unify and integrate our literary experience" (99).[3] In contrast, Hillman, who founded the school of archetypal psychology with the publication of *Re-Visioning Psychology* in 1975, brackets the collective unconscious by emphasizing the subject. For Hillman, an archetype—a term that he prefers to avoid—is not so much an archetype either because it emerges from the collective unconscious or because it is a "social fact" in the literary tradition; rather, Hillman argues that we experience the "archetypal"—his preferred term—because we view it archetypally ("Inquiry into Image"). Jung might say that Frye's approach is extraverted, and Hillman's is introverted. He might add that they both fail to explain the power of archetypes, which comes from a momentary unity of outer and inner, material reality and perception, culture and body, history and experience. As Erich Neumann says, archetypes are powerful because they represent a "unitary reality." The material world, culture, being, meaning all become "transparent" (174–75).

But perhaps we need not dance around the collective unconscious. What Jung actually wrote is not so problematic. He wrote that archetypes are ideas *in potential* that are fully realized only once they have emerged and taken on the content of a particular culture and historical epoch.[4] The influence of culture on archetypes, Jung says, is so great that the spirit archetype as it manifests itself in France cannot be substituted for the same archetype as it manifests itself in India. We cannot adopt the archetypes of another culture in the same way that we put on a new suit of clothes: "If we now try to cover our nakedness with the gorgeous trappings of the East, . . . we would be playing our own history false" (*CW* 9.1: 14). Archetypes develop historically and they can be interpreted only historically:

> The forms we use for assigning meaning are historical categories that reach
> back into the mists of time—a fact we do not take sufficiently into account.
> Interpretations make use of certain linguistic matrices that are themselves
> derived from primordial images. From whatever side we approach this ques-
> tion, everywhere we find ourselves confronted with the history of language,
> with images and motifs that lead straight back to the primitive wonder-world.
> (CW 9.1: 32–33)

Contrary to essentialist views of his theory, Jung argues that our knowledge
of archetypes is anything but pure. Archetypes, which Jung says evolve over
time, are constantly being transformed and reinterpreted by the individual's
consciousness, and they are inseparable from language, history, and culture.

Rather than conceive of archetypes as fixed for millennia, we might
consider that history is to archetypes as jazz is to melody. We might think
that we know the melody to "Stormy Weather" or some other standard, until
a remarkable jazz artist transforms it. Indeed, one might even argue that what
jazz has taught us is that we can never know the melody; we can, however, be
surprised. We can be repeatedly and endlessly surprised to find what we knew
assume a new form.

Certainly, female archetypes are most in need of exploration. Jung
himself encouraged Toni Wolff, Marie-Louise von Franz, and his wife in this
task. More recently, in her study of mythic patterns in novels authored by
women, Pratt writes of the female imagination—which is "not escapist but
strategic"—as it rediscovers a means of transformation that patriarchy pushes
into the unconscious:

> [F]or three centuries women novelists have been gathering around campfires
> where they have warned us with tales of patriarchal horror and encouraged
> us with stories of heroes undertaking quests that we may emulate. They
> have given us maps of the patriarchal battlefield and of the landscape of our
> ruined culture, and they have resurrected for our use codes and symbols
> of our potential power. . . . They have dug the goddess out of the ruins and
> cleansed the debris from her face, casting aside the gynophobic masks that
> have obscured her beauty, her power, and her benefice. (375)

Pratt and other scholars rightly demonstrate that archetypes are primordial
and ever new (see also Elias-Button). Artists, often in consort with scholars,
rework archetypes of a previous age and discover archetypes that can emerge
only in a new age (Neumann 90).

Unlike most theories of symbols or signs, however, Jung explains why
archetypes carry such enduring power: although they are a part of a cultural

tradition, they are more than mere cultural creations. When archetypes function as cultural signs, they are meaningful because they connect with the archetype (as part of our heritage) that remains within (*CW* 12: 11). This statement will not surprise those who have read Jung's essays—read "essays" in the sense of *tries* or *attempts* here—to explain archetypes, but I would like to suggest that everything we need to know about archetypes and the collective unconscious is in a simple poetic phrase, a style rare in Jung's works: "Hunger makes food into gods" (8: 155). Let us unpack this metaphor and see where it leads. For *hunger*, we could substitute the body in the broadest possible sense, not as reduced to biology or genetics.[5] For *food*, we can substitute the body's relation to its context. Any human who is denied food will experience hunger, which is an emotion, what Jung calls a "feeling-toned" instinct. But would it be accurate to say that we inherit hunger or that emotions are genetic? Not entirely. These emerge as the body *lives* in its material context.[6] However, once we do experience something like hunger, we make *food* into *gods* or archetypes, a transaction that occurs within a historical and cultural context. As we follow this explanation of the development of an archetype, we can see how it can be both universal (emerging from hunger, the body) and variable (contingent on the material, historical, and cultural context).[7] And, equally important, we can understand why archetypes are so powerful. They do not simply come to us as socially constructed symbols from outside; they also connect with some emotionally charged aspect of our body. Indeed, when we experience the archetypal, there is no inner and outer or split between mind and history (Samuels, *Plural Psyche* 27). As Neumann writes, we experience "a unitary image" of the "unitary world" (173). Jungian criticism that ignores history is not very Jungian (for an example of the blending of archetypes and history, see Emma Jung and von Franz's *The Grail Legend*).

Jung's theory of archetypes, I have been arguing, needs to be viewed more fluidly, and Jung's emphasis on history, language, and culture needs to be acknowledged. We also need to recognize that Jung developed a model of the psyche that was dynamic and holistic, perhaps an unacknowledged debt to Hegel (see Kelly's *Individualism* and Jensen's *Identities*). Jung wanted to embrace positions that, in current academic debates, are often considered irreconcilable: cognition and social construction, structure and history, mind and body, stability and fragmentation, idealism and materialism, form and culture.

Puer, Senex, and Mother

In the *Apocryphon of John*, one of the so-called Gnostic texts found near Nag Hammadi in 1945, John flees the harassment of Pharisees by turning "away from the temple to a desert place." It is there that Jesus appears before him:

Straightway, while I was contemplating these things, behold, the heavens opened and the whole creation which is below heaven shone, and the world was shaken. I was afraid and behold I saw in the light a youth who stood by me. While I looked at him he became like an old man. And he changed his likeness again becoming like a servant. There was not a plurality before me, but there was a likeness with multiple forms in the light and the likeness appeared through each other, and the likeness had three forms.

He said to me, "John, John, why do you doubt, or why are you afraid? You are not unfamiliar with this image, are you?—that is, do not be timid!—I am the one who is with you always. I am the Father, I am the Mother, I am the Son. I am the undefiled and incorruptible one. Now I have come to teach you what is and what was and what will come to pass, that you may know the things which are not revealed, and those which are revealed, and to teach you concerning the unwavering race of the perfect Man.

As Jesus speaks to John of the "perfect Man," he assumes the form of the Father (the Senex, or wise old man), the Mother, and the Son (puer, or youth).

Had Jung lived long enough to read this passage when it was eventually published, I think he would have liked it, for Jung believed that archetypes formed constellations of three. Recognizing the constellation can mean the difference between being unconsciously under the power of an archetype and becoming more conscious of the reasons we are being drawn into the same pattern repeatedly, even when we are harmed in the process. When we move to an awareness of the constellation, we are more likely to move through the process of individuation (Jung's term for personal development, which includes exploring the potential of the individual and one's connection to others) and gain some separation from a potentially dangerous pattern. It is all a matter of perspective. As Hillman writes, "In analytical practice, we have learned that an archetypal understanding of events can cure the compulsive fascination with one's case history. *The facts do no change, but their order is given another dimension through another myth.* They are experienced differently; they gain another meaning because they are told through another tale" ("An Aspect" 34).

Hillman goes so far as to claim the polarities of puer and senex "provide the psychological foundation of the problem of history" (35). Or, to paraphrase, to say that history repeats itself is to say that history is an expression of human nature. I would add that the polarity is foundational to personal development. In the simplest terms, puer is potential and senex is experience, or the wisdom that should come with experience. In terms of personal development, the key is to gain wisdom without losing potential. At a broader societal level, puer is the element of chance and the embrace of change; senex is the accumulated wisdom of a culture as embodied in its institutions and laws. In *The Birth of*

Tragedy, Nietzsche described these forces as Apollonian and Dionysian. As with all things Jungian, we are better to avoid becoming "one-sided" and seek a unity of opposites.

The essays in this volume explore the presence of the *puer aeternus* in popular culture. The archetype could be describes as eternal youth, which makes it sound rather pleasant, the fountain of youth that so much advertising sells us along with a multitude of products. Yet *puer aeternus* embodies, according to Marie-Louise von Franz, "all those characteristics that are normal in a youth of seventeen or eighteen continued into later life" (7). She continues:

> The one thing dreaded throughout by such a type of man is to be bound to anything whatever. There is a terrific fear of being pinned down, of entering space and time completely, and of being the singular human being that one is. There is always the fear of being caught in a situation from which it may be impossible to slip out again. Every just-so situation is hell. At the same time, there is a highly symbolic fascination for dangerous sports—particularly flying and mountaineering—so as to get as high as possible, the symbolism being to get away from reality, from earth, from ordinary life. If this type of complex is very pronounced, many such men die young in airplane crashes and mountaineering accidents. (8)

Thus, this archetype, when split from its constellation, deals more with arrested development than eternal youth. We are drawn to the puer. As Terry Eagleton points out, "Most of us would prefer a spree with Dionysus to a seminar with Apollo" (2). Yet, for all the appeal of the puer, do we want to rely on reckless teenagers to solve the significant problems facing us?

I wanted to begin with a discussion of the puer archetype within a constellation—a whole—to raise the following question: Why is the *puer aeternus* stalled in adolescence? Marie-Louise von Franz, in her classic study of the *puer aeternus* as manifested in *The Little Prince*, argues that the male is a homosexual who is fixated on the mother. We are all probably ready to move past this explanation, so I want to encourage readers to view the splitting of *puer aeternus* from a constellation with the senex and the mother-wife as traumatic, a reality borne of violence. As Greg Morgenson wrote, "Whenever a sacral form splits—be it a theological dogma, a scientific theory, a politic of experience, or a social role—it splits like an atom. The imagination explodes. Possibilities inflate the ego, and the puer flies" (55).

Jung believes that we experience individual trauma *as well as* trauma at social and cultural levels. He wrote extensively about the trauma of childhood *as well as* the trauma of Nazism, Stalinism, world war, and atomic bombs. He realized that even those outside of Germany were affected by Nazism, those outside of Russian were affected by Stalinism, those outside of Europe or Asia were affected by World War II, and those outside of Hiroshima and Nagasaki were affect by the bomb.

Because we live in a media-saturated culture, we are even more vulnerable to societal and cultural trauma than were Jung and his peers. Reading a book about the Holocaust is not the same as watching it on television. With the speed and presence of current mass media, we experience *pan*traumatic events even more intensely. The entire world watched the World Trade towers collapse, and we watched it over and over, twenty-four hours a day, seven days a week, for months. How has mass media brought trauma from the other side of the world to our living room? How has mass media made us more vulnerable to trauma? How has mass media altered our memory, making it more difficult to heal? The examples of *puer aeternus* discussed in this volume explore these questions and offer insights into how we need to adapt to recent technological changes. By understanding current manifestations of the puer, we can learn more about the trauma that affects us all and how we might heal. We need to be more aware that archetypes had a role in terrorists flying airplanes into the World Trade towers and that archetypes had a role in the wars that followed.

Conclusion

At a small, four-screen cinema, which usually screens documentaries and artsy independent films, I recently watched *An Inconvenient Truth*, the documentary about Al Gore's campaign to convince the world that global warning is a real danger. I was impressed by Gore's ethos, the range and depth of his scientific data, and the effectiveness of his visual rhetoric. As I watched, I asked myself, "How could anyone ignore Gore's message?" About two weeks later, I walked into *Unidentified*, playing at the same cinema. I had not read reviews of this film, and I knew only that it had something to do with UFOs. I expected an artsy independent film, maybe something like Spielberg's *Close Encounters of a Third Kind* on a small scale, but *Unidentified* was anything but artsy. The film was grainy, the dialogue was stilted, and the acting was stiff. I probably should have walked out and asked for a refund, but I was curious. I wanted to know why the theater was full of people intently watching a horrible movie about two reporters as they investigated UFO incidents. Early on, one of the characters talked about going to church, and another scene ended with a perplexingly long close-up of the Bible on a bookshelf. Then, about an hour into the film, I learned UFOs, which appear from behind dark clouds, are actually demons that control our thoughts. As I watched *Unidentified*, I asked myself, "How could people believe such rubbish?"

How could people ignore the scientific evidence in *An Inconvenient Truth*? How could people believe that UFOs are demons that control our thoughts and tempt us to sin? The answer to both questions, Jung would say, is the same. Despite millennia of cultural evolution, we are still creatures with instincts. For better or worse, we still lead lives that are, to a large extent, irrational and unconscious. To improve our understanding of such irrational and unconscious forces, the essays in this volume analyze expressions of a single archetype—the puer.

The early articles in this volume examine the puer archetype from the perspective of psychotherapy or mental health. Anodea Judith's "Culture on the Couch" argues that the planet is facing enormous problems, such as global warming, that will require a mature response, yet Western Civilization has thus far reacted as if stagnated in adolescence. She asks, "What if Western Civilization were a client that came in for analysis?" Her answer is a fascinating case study of W.C., the culture seeking therapy. Susan Rowland's "Puer and Hellmouth" examines the TV show *Buffy the Vampire Slayer* as an example of popular culture with a "positive ensouled mission": to heal the split between the senex and the puer. Rinda West ("Puer in Nature") analyzes two polarities of the puer as responses to the natural world: the slacker, whose utilitarian approach to nature expresses itself in cynicism and gratuitous violence (examined here in John Gardner's novel *Grendel*); and the purist, expressed in isolation from human culture in the name of protecting nature (analyzed here in Werner Herzog's documentary *Grizzly Man*). Dustin Eaton's "Grounding Icarus" discusses the urge to suicide in brilliant artists; he focuses on the life and death of Kurt Cobain, lead singer and songwriter for the rock band Nirvana.

The volume next moves into an analysis of developmental issues related to the puer archetype. John A. Gosling's "Protracted Adolescence" argues that the American collective psyche is developmentally retarded, characterized by a "fear of Other." Luke Hockley's "Shaken, Not Stirred" analyzes Agent 007 as our contemporary culture's Peter Pan and ties this image to British culture's "shadow of Empire and World War II consciousness." Darrell Dobson's "A Crown Must Be Earned Every Day" is a self-analysis of the role of aesthetic experience in the formation of personal identity. Keith Polette's "Senex and Puer in the Classroom" claims that the American educational system, despite its claims to encourage maturation, prevents students from becoming adults.

Finally, the volume addresses the puer archetype as it impacts broader cultural issues. Sally Porterfield's "The Puer as American Hero" discusses our fascination with "celebrity" as a media substitute for authentic heroism. Susan Schwartz's "Little Lost Girl" looks to Sylvia Plath's life as an example of the puella woman who wants "to excel and to be loved but not to be known intimately." Marita

Delaney's "Provincials in Time" examines midlife passage among puer-possessed Americans. Chaz Gormley's "The Marriage of the *Puer Aeternus* and Trickster Archetypes" investigates early trauma as the prime indicator of the creation of the puer personality. Craig Chalquist's "Insanity by the Numbers, Knowings from the Ground" ties our culture's obsession with quantitative research to a childish insistence on factism, which is ultimately a denial of our humanity.

The essays in this volume acknowledge that we are inspired by archetypes to make heroic sacrifices *and* that we are also driven by archetypes toward mass-mindedness. It is as important, Jung would say, for us to be critical of all of the forces that shape our lives, whether these forces be science or myth. It is equally important for us to understand the trauma that affects our times.

Notes

1. Certainly, the central example of "mass-mindedness" during Jung's lifetime was Nazi Germany. From the early 1930s to the beginning of World War II, Jung was involved with German psychoanalysis. This connection as well as some of Jung's comments about national character brought charges of anti-Semitism that have never been entirely resolved. In *Jung: A Biography*, Deirdre Bair devoted her longest chapter to this issue, drawing heavily upon material in the Jung archives (431–63). While it certainly could be argued that Jung made questionable decisions that drew him into the Nazi propaganda machine, Bair's thorough analysis makes it difficult to view Jung as a Nazi sympathizer or an anti-Semite. As Bair points out, Jung felt that he was maintaining contact with the German psychoanalytic community to work on behalf of Jewish colleagues. For example, in the years leading to World War II, Jung sponsored the immigration of a number of Jewish psychoanalysts to Switzerland, agreeing to support them if they were unable to support themselves. In citing this example, however, I do not want to close debate on this period of Jung's life. As Baer points out, we will know more as restricted archives, including the Freud archives, are opened to scholars.

2. In *Anatomy of Criticism*, Frye wanted to create a systematic, even scientific, approach to criticism (7–8). He also opposed the Romantic notion of originality: "Originality returns to the origins of literature, as radicalism returns to its roots" (97–98). Jung's explanation of the collective unconscious struck him, no doubt, as too mysterious and too Romantic to be scientific.

3. Much of the appeal of Frye's work should be viewed within the context of the 1950s. Whereas New Critics tended to stay within the borders of single works, Frye's work was intertextual. He drew the idea of archetypes from Jung to catalog literature, that is, to articulate a grammar of literary themes in a way that was not so scientific (though he, at times, claims that criticism is a science) or reductive. Frye was not a psychologist. He did not tie archetypes to the mind of the writer or reader. Similar to New Critics, formalists, and structuralists, Frye's approach to literature traverses a terrain that might include literary characters but is rather devoid of human beings.

4. Joseph Campbell has presented the most articulate defense of a traditional reading of Jung's theory of the collective unconscious and archetypes in "The Imprints of Experience," a chapter in *Primitive Mythology: The Masks of Gods* (50–131).

5. By using the term *body* rather than *brain*, *mind*, or *biology*, I hope to convey the sense of the collective aspects of humanity that account for the unity or permanence of our experience. I mean the body as Kenneth Burke uses the term in *Permanence and Change*, a book written when Burke was reading Jung. Burke writes: "Insofar as the individual mind is a group product, we may look for the same patterns of relationship between the one and the many in any historical period. And however much we may question the terminology in which these patterns were expressed, the fact that man's neurological structure has remained pretty much of a constant through all the shifts of his environment would justify us in looking for permanencies beneath the differences, as the individual seeks by thought and act to confirm his solidarity with his group" (159). Burke argues that it is the body that accounts for permanence and culture that brings about change.

6. While Jung did not believe that the mind is a *tabula rasa* at birth, he does not subscribe to the notion that we can ever speak of anything such as genetically driven behavior. In *Psychological Types*, Jung stresses repeatedly that modes of thought or patterns of behavior emerge historically. The Romantic movement, for example, developed a new world perspective and its own approach to understanding identity. Even though the Romantic movement is long past, some individuals, given their psychological type, might be still be prone to adopt Romantic views, but he hardly espouses anything close to a deterministic or purely genetic model.

7. One of the problems with a more traditional approach to archetypes is Jung's separation of "form" and "content." If we recognize that what Jung calls the "form" of an archetype might as easily be labeled as "emotions" or "affect," then the "form" and "content" of archetypes do not seem so separate. A complex of emotions comes together with a social scene, what Jung on a few occasions referred to as archetypal constellations, and distinctions between the "inner" and "outer" dissolve. The world, as Neumann describes it, becomes "transparent" (175).

Works Cited

Bair, Deirdre. *Jung: A Biography.* Boston: Little, Brown, 2003.

Burke, Kenneth. *Permanence and Change: An Anatomy of Purpose.* 3rd ed. 1935. Berkeley: California UP, 1984.

Campbell, Joseph. *Primitive Mythology: The Masks of Gods.* 1959. New York: Penguin, 1969.

Eagleton, Terry. *Holy Terror.* Oxford: Oxford UP, 2005.

Elias-Button, Karen. "Journey into an Archetype: The Dark Mother in Contemporary Women's Poetry." *Jungian Literary Criticism.* Ed. Richard P. Sugg. Evanston, IL: Northwestern UP, 1992. 355–66.

Frye, Northrop. *Anatomy of Criticism: Four Essays.* Princeton: Princeton UP, 1957.

Gore, Al. *An Inconvenient Truth.* Dir. David Guggenheim. Paramount, 2006.

Hillman, James. "An Aspect of the Historical Psychological Present." *Senex and Puer.* Ed. Glen Slater. Putnam, CN: Spring 2005.

———. "An Inquiry into Image." *Spring* (1977): 62–88.

Jensen, George H. *Identities across Texts.* Cresskill, NJ: Hampton Press, 2001.

Jung, C. G. *The Collected Works of C. G. Jung.* 20 vols. Trans. R. F. C. Hull. Ed. H. Read, Michael Fordham, and Gerhard Adler. Princeton: Princeton UP, 1953–1989.

Jung, Emma, and Marie-Louise von Franz. *The Grail Legend.* 1960. Trans. Andrea Dykes. 2nd ed. Princeton: Princeton UP, 1970.

Kelly, Sean. *Individualism and the Absolute: Hegel, Jung, and the Path toward Wholeness.* New York: Paulist Press, 1993.

Morgenson, Greg. *A Most Accursed Religion: When Trauma Becomes God.* Putnam, CN: Spring 2005.

Robinson, James. *New Hammadi Library in English.* New York: Harper and Row, 1977.

Samuels, Andrew. *The Plural Psyche: Personality, Morality, and the Father.* London: Routledge, 1989.

Unidentifed. Dir. Rich Christiano. *Five and Two Pictures,* 2006.

von Franz, Marie-Louise. *The Problem of Puer Aeternus.* Toronto: Inner City, 2000.

Culture on the Couch

Western Civilization's Journey from Crisis to Maturity

ANODEA JUDITH

> The only myth that is going to be worth talking about in the immediate future is one that is talking about the planet, not this city, not these people, but the planet and everybody on it. . . . And what it will have to deal with will be exactly what all myths have dealt with—the maturation of the individual, from dependency through adulthood, through maturity, and then to the exit; and then how to relate this society to the world of nature and the cosmos. . . . And until that gets going, you don't have anything.
>
> —Joseph Campbell, *The Power of Myth*

Sooner or later, we all have to grow up. We've heard this a thousand times, as if it were a fact as certain as death and taxes. Continue to put one foot in front of the other and you will eventually get there, wherever "there" might happen to be. Ideas of what constitutes maturity vary widely, but most people assume that it will just happen by itself, like ripening fruit, with time as the only necessity.

If only it were that easy! Would that we could endlessly play in the sun for our ripening, hanging passively on the vine, waiting for the day when we finally let go and return to the earth. Would that we could play innocently in the Garden of Eden, with benevolent parents to protect and guide us, as we imagine it might have been in times of old. Or would that we didn't have to grow up at all and could live in the endless pursuit of our pleasures, following our whim from moment to moment, without limitation or responsibility. These are longings of a former time.

The world of our ancestors was indeed simpler. People grew up, but, with fewer choices, their paths held more certainty. Follow your duty, do as you're told, and everything will work out. There were challenges, of course, but the external world was expected to continue, just as it always had. Mother Earth would provide for our needs, and the Father would set the rules. Growing up meant that we surrendered gracefully to authority and became obedient members of society. Conformity became more important than doing the grueling work of finding our true Self. "Maturity" in these times, at least for most people, lacked authenticity and meaning.

Today we face a far different reality, and facing this reality squarely may indeed be the first of our many tasks of maturation. The parental free ride that has given us the abundance of resources that we have enjoyed since our earliest infancy is, alas, coming to an end. We who are alive today are saddled with a responsibility far greater than any our ancestors have faced: the task of saving four billion years of evolution from the possibility of extinction—no less than the task of caring for an entire planet.

Most people know the litany: global warming that could cause worldwide famine and displace hundreds of millions from their homes; war and terrorism that escalate with ever more dangerous weapons in the hands of power-driven leaders; disappearing oil reserves that threaten economic collapse; rampant consumption that exhausts resources; environmental decline polluting our air, water, and land; and politics expected to govern an exponentially growing population with unsustainable energy. A grim situation indeed.

We also know that these dire circumstances reveal a deeper crisis of morals, meaning, and maturity. Depression and chronic illness are epidemic. The World Health Organization states that 450 million people worldwide suffer from mental health problems, with 120 million complaining of chronic depression (*Signposts*), while 10 percent of children have psychological symptoms severe enough to cause impairment (*Agenda for Children's Mental Health*, qtd. in Goode). Economic values serve self-interest above the public good, with the dollar being the deciding factor in newscasts and voter pamphlets. Meanwhile, our public media distract us with sensationalist broadcasting of "Reality TV" shows that have nothing to do with reality—certainly not the reality that is crying for our attention.

The reality we must now face is that the father figures that we worship, empower, and pretend to elect all too often turn out to be government officials embroiled in scandals, priests who molest innocent children, gurus who exploit their followers, or swindlers out to make a buck. With the plunge in George W. Bush's approval ratings, the father figure's dangerous shortcomings are revealed to all who care to look, stripping the role of its numinosity and power. This psychological patricide brings about a slaughter of his outmoded beliefs and values, requiring the child to find its own values and wisdom.

The roads that have led us to this point, laid down with the best of intentions, are now leading us astray. With the mother long gone, and the father falling from grace, we have no choice but to give up our passive powerlessness and step into our true authority. As individuals, we are being asked to stand up, speak out, and co-create a reality that has never before existed. We are, as Jean Houston has said, "people of the parentheses" (1), living in a time between eras, where we are no longer innocent children who take what they need without worrying about where it comes from, yet still not adults with the requisite knowledge and maturity to run an entire planet effectively.

Saving four billion years of evolution from the possibility of extinction is not a task for children. This is a task for a species on the verge of godlike powers of both creation and destruction, equally capable of either. For either the problems that we face in our world today will bring us to our cultural maturity, or else they will end the experiment here. Today's problems are the evolutionary drivers—the contractions of the birth process—that will spawn an awakening so massive that history has no precedent. For the planet itself is our teacher and initiator, taking us through a rite of passage from adolescence to adulthood, and from an organizing principle based on the *love of power* to one based on the *power of love*. This rite will challenge every facet of life, both individually and collectively, asking each of us to undergo the task of self-reflection, individuation, and the spiritual growth necessary for maturity.

Cultural Adolescence

One need only turn on the televised news to see adolescent behavior raging through all ages, races, creeds, and genders. Creative but disrespectful, powerful but reckless, narcissistically obsessed with our looks, insisting on immediate gratification of our whims, and bursting with libido, we are sorely lacking in social and environmental conscience. Like teenagers thoughtlessly cleaning out the refrigerator while entertaining their friends, human populations are insatiably consuming the once-vast cupboards of oceans and forests in the attempt to satisfy gargantuan appetites. And why not? Hasn't Mother Nature always kept the cupboards well stocked in the past, free to her children, just for the asking?

As adolescent children face the abrupt halt of their biological growth, they must take their prodigious life force and learn to grow in a new dimension. At best, this dimension is spiritual, growing toward deeper understanding of themselves and their world. But if this passage is blocked or distorted, adolescents act out recklessly, often harming themselves and others. Without understanding the longer view of life, they can destroy essentials before they learn their true value. In the case of adolescent suicide, this essential destruction can even be their own life.

To become adults, adolescents who have previously been nurtured, cared for, and educated by elders must learn to provide for themselves and others, in turn. They must learn about the meaning of life, the structure and order of the world, and their purpose within it. Yet they are also compelled—by the unique life force within them—to question and change that structure as they grow

into it. It is a tumultuous time, as any parent knows, and there are days when
we may look at our teenagers with exasperation and wonder if they will *ever*
grow up. Yet we have no choice but to move forward as best we can, holding a
container for their process.

Just as adolescence marks the end of physical growth, our human population
has grown to its adult size and can no longer continue to expand in the physical
dimension, producing more bodies at an exponential rate. We have reached (if
not surpassed) the carrying capacity of our biosphere. World population has
more than doubled in the last half-century, climbing from 2.5 billion in 1950
(Brown, Gardner, and Hallwell 17) to more than 6.5 billion in 2007 (U.S. Census
Bureau). Just for perspective, this means there has been more population growth
in the last half-century than in the four million years since the earliest humans
walked on their hind legs (Brown, Gardner, and Hallwell 17)! If not checked,
this number could double again in the next fifty years. From the depletion of
topsoil and underground aquifers used to grow our food, to the diminishing
oil reserves that bring our groceries to the table; from the disappearing forests
and the creatures who live there, to the greenhouse gases that are raising global
temperatures; from urban smog, to waste disposal; from the billions who live
in poverty, to the epidemic diseases that threaten life—every facet of human
and nonhuman society is impacted by our unchecked population growth. What
Thomas Malthus predicted back in 1798 is now a reality:

> I say, that the power of population is indefinitely greater than the power in the
> earth to produce subsistence for man. Population, when unchecked, increases
> in a geometrical ratio. Subsistence increases only in an arithmetical ratio. A
> slight acquaintance with numbers will show the immensity of the first power
> in comparison of the second.

It is not only population growth that must be curbed but the way that we
view progress and success. Since the time of the Industrial Revolution, progress
has been measured by growth. The success of a company is usually defined
by its expansion, not its social contribution. Growth is measured in terms of
more products, bigger markets, larger infrastructure, and ultimately greater
profits. Whether that means building more housing developments, expanding
roads and highways, infiltrating indigenous cultures with Western products and
lifestyles, or simply crafting a way to make more with less—our "industrial
growth society" must place its value on something other than growth before we
exhaust our life support systems. We are quickly discovering that growth-based
futures do not lead to a sustainable future.

Yet, typical of adolescence, growth has been the driving force of our biology
since its earliest beginnings. Prehistoric nomads focused on images pertaining
to birth. The Bible tells us to go forth and multiply. From the farmer's apple

tree to the corporate sales charts, growth symbolizes success. In the earlier eras of our collective childhood, this was entirely appropriate. That's what healthy children do—they grow from birth to adolescence. Yet this is a force that has its own momentum. Like the infamous ship *Titanic*, it's not easy to turn such a colossal system around—even when we see the iceberg up ahead. In order to survive, we must harness that creative urge to multiply, and we must point the evolutionary arrow in a new direction. Such potential has never occurred before in our evolutionary history. It signals an extraordinary need for responsibility and a driving imperative to wake up. For us as a collective, it signals the passage from adolescence to adulthood.

But even more, it calls for an awakening of the heart. For the values of the heart are the integrating elements of individuation, the key to finding depth, authenticity, and meaning. The *puer* society that is consuming our world with its rampant consumption and delusions of grandeur needs to find its sacred ground in the Earth, acknowledge its denied Shadow, and balance the archetypal energies of Masculine and Feminine. This is unlikely to occur without entering deeply into a profound healing process.

Culture on the Couch

Our society, though full of wonders and achievements, is ill, and that illness is spreading beyond the human world to the entire web of life. The defense strategies of our collective childhood now work against us. The power to dominate nature and each other has created a separation that has grown into a dangerous dissociation. In *Civilization in Transition*, Jung said, "The sickness of dissociation in our world is at the same time a process of recovery, or rather, the climax of a period of pregnancy which heralds the throes of birth" (*CW* 10: para. 293). Rather than our original birth as helpless infants in the Garden of Eden, this birth could instead be the birth of our young adulthood. But first we need to understand and heal our collective wounds.

It's time to put the culture on the couch.

What if Western Civilization were a client that came in for analysis? What would be the healing process, and what jewels would we discover ? What are the dreams that must be examined, and what must be integrated to move from a predominantly *puer* society typified by inflation, rebelliousness, violence, denial, and self-indulgence into a cultural maturity that is not only sustainable and sane but joyous and creative? How do we move from a society based on obedient children who merely do what they are told in order to become good citizens, to a society of awakened individuals, not only awake to their own depth and creative potential but awake to a vision of what we can become collectively? How do we co-create a future that enables us not only to survive but to thrive, and not just a future we can live with but one we can love? What will move us from our adolescent love of power to the young adult realization of the power of love?

Though we cannot imagine a couch large enough for a whole culture, varied and diverse as it is, we can still examine the problems of the collective psyche through a therapist's eyes. Arguably, Western Civilization has the greatest leverage to lead our world into death or rebirth; I will limit my discussion to its collective values that shape our dreams, behaviors, beliefs—and consequently our world. Granted, these values are most pronounced in America, but since the United States was originally shaped by European values that reflect the development of Western Civilization in general, I will refer to this client simply as "W. C."

The Case of Western Civilization, Spring 2007

Initial Observations

If we were writing a case study on this client, we would begin by stating that W. C. appears to be a high-functioning, adolescent, white male. This is not to say that men are to blame for our culture's condition, or that only men are influential, but that the feminine aspect of this client's psyche is still largely repressed. Most often, W. C. appears dressed in male clothing (tailored suits and muted colors), expressing predominantly male goals. His conversation focuses on issues of power and wealth, with monetary cost cited as the chief factor informing his decisions. He lives largely in his rational and logical mind, relying on scientific evidence more than personal experience, and he favors thinking and sensation more than intuition and feeling. (We might note, however, that many of his decisions and behavior appear to be quite irrational.) In his fantasy life, he has a preoccupation with women's bodies and breasts—typical contents of an adolescent boy's interests—and these images are pasted on the surfaces of magazines and billboards everywhere, much like the pin-ups in a boy's bedroom.

The most influential parts of W. C.'s complex consciousness occur between patriarchal figureheads who still hold great power in his psyche. Hence, I will refer to this client as "He," though we would do well to remember that everyone contains both masculine and feminine elements, and we certainly do not want to perpetuate this division by falling into the trap of thinking our client is solely male. I would note that the feminine aspect of this client does show signs of awakening yet is still poorly integrated into the client's psyche. "She" remains largely unrecognized, appearing mostly as idealized images in dreams and fantasies, the content of which we will explore further on. And while I describe W. C. as predominantly white, we must remember that other cultural influences exist as well, but these are largely subsumed by the client's need to conform to the values of the white, ruling class that appears to hold the privilege he so desires to keep.

W. C.'s tendencies reflect behavior typical of mid- to late-adolescence. He is undergoing a surging physical growth spurt, accompanied by voracious consumption. (Oil seems to be the adolescent growth hormone that is fueling this growth, but we know this hormone won't last forever.) He uses resources wastefully with little regard for the future. Like most teenagers, he is obsessed with image and popularity, and he is narcissistically absorbed with how he looks. He recklessly seeks danger, experiments with drugs of all kinds, and is tormented by the simultaneous lure and taboo of his libido. Upon observation of his self-destructive activities, we suspect that W. C. harbors suicidal tendencies with the means to carry them out. Needless to say, the thought of this adolescent possessing nuclear weapons while driving the home planet under the influence is of grave concern.

Yet W. C. has been quite successful thus far in life. He has been privileged to receive the best of education and has had most of his wants granted—more so than any of his contemporaries. Even at his still-young age, he is a world leader with discoveries and accomplishments under his belt that suggest genius. He exhibits (even flaunts) immense power and clearly has the capability to achieve anything that captures his interest. With such a promising start, what might he accomplish in his adulthood?

Presenting Problems

W. C.'s presenting problems are many. He lives in a rapidly deteriorating environment that, despite his power, he feels helpless to address. Instead he resorts to denial of its seriousness, allowing the deterioration to continue. His financial affairs are unstable, with an increasingly expensive lifestyle that is taking him deeply into debt. His health is of concern, with increasing chronic problems that his highly sophisticated understanding of medicine cannot address. (Due to a health care crisis, many parts of him are ineligible for treatment.) He has difficulty getting along with those of differing cultures, and he frequently resorts to violence and warfare, both offensive and defensive, to deal with conflict.

Not surprisingly, W. C. shows paranoid tendencies. He is obsessed with the threat of terrorism and the existence of weapons of mass destruction, even though he himself harbors enough weapons to wipe out the entire world. His paranoia is delusional to the point of imagining that terrorists might blow up airplanes with the toothpaste or shampoo found in carry-on luggage, and he has enlisted a good part of the population into enabling this delusion. He believes there is an "axis of evil" located in various places on the other side of the world, where the cultures are conveniently different enough to absorb that projection.

Jung said of such a split: "Ignorance of one's other side creates great insecurity. One does not really know who one is; one feels inferior somewhere and yet does not know where the inferiority lies" (*CW* 10: para. 425).

His inflated savior complex shows co-dependent tendencies by his desire to "fix" others, while ignoring many of the problems in himself and his relationships. In fact, he is so insecure within himself that he has created an entire department to make him feel more secure. His delusions of grandeur are reflected by the fact that he thinks he knows the one true, right, and only way, while he shows pointed denial and avoidant tendencies in regard to his more pressing problems. Meanwhile, he distracts himself with cheap entertainment, such as mindless television and Internet pornography. He frequently hurries from one task to another, eats a lot of junk food, and is in poor physical condition.

These converging elements of his life are rapidly approaching crisis. Is it possible that this breakdown will bring about a breakthrough?

Client History

W. C.'s profile makes sense when viewed in light of his history. We notice that in both personal and public affairs, he never mentions his mother, and in fact, he has no recollection of ever having had a mother. He speaks often of his "founding fathers," without even questioning his belief that there was never a mother influence. So normal is this state that he denies having come from a broken home and is unaware of the gross imbalance between masculine and feminine archetypes in his waking consciousness. His sense of the divine is generally referred to as "He" and "Him," and he refers to himself as "man," though this may be changing. Research into his birth records revealed that his mother was an ancient primordial goddess, equated with the living Earth, but this is a fact that he is not ready to embrace fully. We hope that a reunion can be arranged before She expires.

Understandably, he holds great love for his powerful father who was known to all yet remained distant throughout his life. His father worked hard to feed the ever-expanding family and instilled in W. C. a solid work ethic. While there was very little direct contact between them, this distant father was W. C.'s only role model. Without a feminine influence for balance, he tried to copy his father's behavior. As a result he is preoccupied with conquest, yet he feels separated from almost everything around him. In the absence of a mother *or* father in the home, older brothers enforced strict laws that kept the household in order, to which his obedience was expected. If he failed to meet that expectation, he was severely punished. Most of his middle childhood was spent in institutions that became his main social environment.

Exploring W. C.'s relationship to his brothers, we discover that from as far back as he can remember—for the last five thousand years, really—the brothers were constantly fighting with each other, and these fights were horrendously violent. As the fighting escalated over the millennia, more and more of W. C.'s energy went into creating defenses, forcing others to do the same. By necessity, he trained himself as a soldier at a very young age, learning to fight and defend himself. As he grew older, he created ever larger armies of men to assist him in his defense, at times engaging in full-scale warfare in which many of his brothers died and many more were wounded and traumatized. As a result of this repeated devastation, W. C. believed that militarization was the only way to survive, so he put increasing amounts of his resources into it.

As expected, his body is rigidly armored, especially around the heart, and his movements seem mechanical. Millennia of trauma have numbed his feelings to the point that he is no longer connected with his inner world, and in fact, he devalues the whole realm of feelings and emotion as an exhibition of weakness. Out of touch with his deeper self, he is obedient to authority figures, from whom he longs for recognition, reflecting his longing for connection with his distant and authoritarian father. We suspect that his early experiences of repeated domination of his personal will led to his obsessive love of power.

What of his sisters? W. C. claims that he never knew his sisters very well. So different were their worlds that once he even suggested they came from a different planet! While at battle, he was completely separated from his sisters, often for years at a time, living entirely in the world of men. Any feelings of longing to be home with his family were seen by the other soldiers as weak or effeminate, and he was summarily humiliated. Understandably, he learned to put such feelings aside (along with any fears for his life). In peacetime, he scarcely noticed his sisters, except as they served his needs. Lately, he is finding himself fascinated by them and of course attracted to them sexually—quite normal for an adolescent. However, his idealized image of maidenly perfection is often disappointing in reality. Furthermore, the strength of this idealization is driving his sisters to ever more extreme attempts to fit that illusion, including plastic surgery, anorexic dieting, and a huge proportion of income spent on beauty products—all attempts to maintain the appearance of youth so as to fulfill his fantasy. The reflection of these projections indicates how young W. C.'s anima seems to be. With his poorly developed relational skills, most of his attempts to form lasting relationships with the opposite sex have been short-lived and superficial. Furthermore, many of his sisters seem angry much of the time, and their anger frightens him, echoing into his unacknowledged mother wound. It is not surprising that he sometimes experiences gay relationships as more satisfying—and certainly more familiar.

Diagnosis

W. C. exhibits the qualities of the *puer aeternus,* the eternal youth, living the fantasy of a carefree life. He believes that he can take whatever he wants from wherever he finds it, without having to consider the consequences. He lives in the realm of ideas and images, at a loss for how to relate deeply and authentically with others. He is dissociated from his body as his innate ground of being. He suffers from addiction and consumption as a way to fill his emptiness, through the compulsive use of drugs, merchandise, food, entertainment, and sexual fantasy. He is paranoid and delusional, with an avoidant personality syndrome, evident in the denial of his environmental problems and his refusal to deal with increasing debt. He is dissociated and depressed—in fact, according to the *Diagnostic and Statistic Manual of Mental Disorders* it seems that W. C.'s diagnoses fit most everything in the book—almost as if it were written for him!

Prognosis

Despite such a multilayered diagnosis, the prognosis for this client would be hopeful, *provided he receives treatment early and often.* W. C. is very intelligent, highly talented, and extremely high-functioning, with an enormous amount of untapped resources. He is still young enough to be open to new ideas, though his strong father complex makes him quite critical of anything new before it can be adequately developed or implemented.

The issue of greatest concern seems to be the race between his self-destructive tendencies and his still-unrealized future. I would suggest that this client be watched closely while in the critical phase of the healing process and that all materials that could be used for suicide be summarily removed.

Dreams

The movies and television programs that are daily broadcast through our collective media represent the contents of W. C.'s dreams. More often than not, they are quite violent, indicating immense battles within the client's psyche. The archetypes that repeatedly appear in these dramas represent the underdeveloped portions of the collective psyche and, when understood, can help these unconscious elements come to the light of awareness. We believe this understanding could greatly further the maturing process.

One of these recurring themes is a drama that falls under the heading of "cops and robbers." We can see here a perpetual conflict between the parental forces of law and order and a childish rebellion that initially thwarts but eventually succumbs to authority. These elements are quite polarized: the robber seldom has any redeeming value and is portrayed as a purely shadow character—one who takes what he wants out of sheer greed without regard to others. It is only through external forces that the robber is brought to justice. These forces win by sheer might: the cops employ a whole department to solve one crime; they race to the scene of the crime with dozens of vehicles, completely surrounding the criminal with armed personnel, rendering him helpless. Clearly this parental force holds tremendous power in the client's psyche, as indicated by how much energy is amassed to deal with a single criminal's activity.

What we rarely see is any maturation in the outlaw figure. He seldom realizes his effect on others, never goes back to school or develops more functional methods to obtain his needs, nor do we see him helping his fellow criminals wake up to any kind of moral conscience. This lack of character evolution necessitates the victory of the police in the end as a necessary balance. Yet the cops show no love for the criminal—they are not benevolent parents who teach wisdom and values—and why should they be, with W. C.'s history being mostly devoid of such parents? Thus, these conflicts continue, unresolved, and the dreams recur. As it is in the dreams, so it becomes in the streets and ghettos.

Another theme in W. C.'s dreams is the romantic infatuation with the feminine, which is most often frustrated by circumstance. The women who play these romantic roles are usually young and beautiful, with emaciated maidenly bodies and demure behavior that supports—or is even rescued—by the man's power. Thus, the feminine is kept in a *puella* state from which she seldom matures. These dreams tend to stay in the initial "attraction" phase of a relationship and seldom come to sexual fulfillment. In the cases where the man and woman do come together in the end, one seldom sees how their relationship plays out through its difficulties, almost as if the client "wakes up" from the dream at exactly this point.

The exception to this lack of sexual culmination is found in the class of dreams called pornography, where contact between the masculine and feminine is superficial and impersonal. Here the masculine element clearly dominates: he reaches climax *on* the woman, and she rarely has a climax at all. And here, more than ever, the female appears in an idealized physical form and makes no emotional demands or criticisms of her partner. It is, indeed, a dream.

Other dreams, appearing more often of late, feature repeated near-misses with explosive devices. In these dramas, the superhero protagonist is nearly destroyed, as he flies through glass doors of buildings while entire urban complexes explode and collapse all around him. These fiery explosions indicate a great deal of repressed anger toward the institutional structures that form the backdrop of his home life, combined with an obvious desire to escape them. You'd think their collapse would bring him back, once again, to his neglected ground, yet he never seems quite able to discover that ground, erecting the structures again and again, as fast as they fall. Not knowing the ground of his mother, he understandably recreates what he knows, even though its influence is deadening to his soul. Jung pointed out that when an inner situation remains unconscious, it occurs in our external world as fate (*CW* 9: para. 126). We note that these dreams were prevalent even before this scenario occurred in reality, through the collapse of the World Trade Center in September 2001, as well as other terrorist bombings. The continuation of these dreams is of grave concern to the function of these ego structures that, for better or worse, do currently support much of the client's psyche. Unless he learns to find a deeper ground of his being, this kind of destruction could prove to be quite devastating to his ability to function in his day to day life.

Treatment

There is need for considerable healing to turn this client into a healthy and thriving adult. We suggest a multivalent strategy that simultaneously addresses mind, body, and spirit, with a deep exploration of the client's history and a supportive opportunity to grieve what has been lost. From this grief of truly experiencing the denied wounds, compassion and maturity may begin to develop.

W. C. needs a deeper exploration of his primal roots, so that he can understand and truly feel the wounds of having lived most of his life in separation from his true Mother. Frequent excursions into the wilderness to experience her natural state could help to restore that lost connection, but he must begin this quickly before these places are destroyed. Deeper contact with the Mother will, we hope, reduce his compensatory behaviors of greed and consumption, as we see that his philosophical rejection of matter (*Mater*) has produced the shadow side of materialism and greed that is bringing about her demise. Contact with her ground of being will give him a direct appreciation for his original home environment, and such contact will also increase his desire to defend it. He can witness firsthand the way natural systems live in harmony, and we hope that he can apply these principles to his social environment. Reclamation of this connection with the Mother can bring him into contact with his sacred ground, offsetting the Flying Boy aspect of the *puer*, who prefers to stay high and free.

Perhaps the connection with his true Mother and her exquisite beauty will allow his anima to mature, as well. His projections of the idealized feminine maiden would need to be withdrawn and replaced by a development of his own *anima* or inner feminine. But, as Emma Jung has warned us, "When a man discovers his anima and has come to terms with it, he has to take up something which previously seemed inferior to him" (23). His judgment of such things as softness, yielding, kindness, and receptivity must change if he is to develop these important aspects of his own wholeness.

His lust after the "perfect body" can be redirected to a deeper regard for his own body, with more attention to fitness and health. Since rites of passage into adulthood, by nature, involve events that occur beyond logic, developing connection with his emotional and intuitive voices can instill inner guidance to help him navigate the challenges of his initiation process. Learning compassion and gentleness will make it easier for him to approach the confrontation with his shadow, which we believe must comprise a major part of his healing work.

Jung pointed out that the anonymity of living in a conformist culture intensifies the action of the shadow side. As evidenced in the endless conflict within W. C.'s dreams, there is a great deal of shadow material that needs to be faced and integrated. Millennia of trauma and domination have created a deep well of hostility and insecurity, both of which are patently denied. As a result, the majority of the client's psychic and financial resources are directed toward bolstering his insecurity, with an inflated sense of power and the illusion of being the "do-gooder" or savior of other nations. This highly defensive strategy periodically seeks an aggressive outlet, starting wars or provocations that allow the client to display and exercise his power and intimidation.

In point of fact, W. C.'s military strategy has contributed to the deaths of countless innocent civilians who experience this shadow side all too brutally. In addition, W. C. has manufactured dangerous weapons and sold them for profit to cultures that then use them against each other, perpetrating upon others the same denied trauma for generations to come. These defenses are wasting precious resources that are clearly needed for restoration and healing, to say nothing of the tragedy of countless lives lost. Though W. C. thinks himself to be very powerful, he would need help to understand the extent of his submission to others' authority and to find and develop his own, internal authority.

Understanding this shadow involves recognizing its healthy roots, which lie in the noble cause of saving home and family from potential destruction, as well as the need to express one's anger and individuality. If this can be redirected to the planetary situations of global warming and resource depletion, this primal urge to survive has an outlet that is based on restoration rather than destruction. Then the many parts of the client's psyche may be united—not against a common enemy he can kill but against a threat that requires massive cooperation among all parts of the Self to be overcome: in short, an awakening of wholeness. Global warming can be seen as the *rubedo*, or heating up of the alchemical process of planetary transformation, following the *nigredo* of facing his shadow.

W. C.'s father represents an incomplete archetype with a strong split between light and shadow. The extensive persecutions during the Christian era (from approximately 400 CE to the Renaissance) greatly increased this split, with its central savior archetype in the father's only acknowledged son and with brutal murder and torture directed toward any heresies in accepted doctrine. Over the many generations of this thousand-year period, this produced a compulsive need to be "good," for fear of retribution in this life or the next, perpetuating the light/shadow split. Though these persecutions no longer occur, the complex is buried deeply in the psyche and keeps many aspects of W. C. locked in fear of God's retribution, thus perpetuating the split.

Denial of the shadow material has its compensation in the frequent portrayal of images of the rich and famous, happily sipping their drinks by the pool while talking about their latest acquisition or stock option—almost as if they were the norm, or majority, of society. In actuality, this image represents a very small percentage of the population. Beneath the veil of public awareness, the plights of two billion people without access to safe drinking water, or the tens of millions who are homeless refugees, or the millions of Americans without health insurance, or those who work menial jobs at poverty-level wages, reveal shadow aspects of the larger Self that still remain largely unconscious. Thus, the narcissism is perpetuated: lack of contact with the true Self, and thus lack of the development of compassion for its dispossessed parts, requires a constant affirmation of the inflated image, complete with the compulsive striving to attain it. Yet this attainment produces not satisfaction but a need for more inflation, resulting in an addiction to consumption as a mark of achievement. True satisfaction would instead be found in the deepening process of the soul's individuation through healing and awakening.

Such a need for healing may announce itself in a thirsting for water, which reflects a thirst for contact with the soul, for the feminine, and for the depths from which new life can spring. (Are tsunamis and floods the return of the watery elements of emotion?) Conversely, an increasing problem with home-lessness represents dissociation from the Earth as our collective home. Health care crises are symbolic of dissociation from the body. Reclaiming the more feminine values that earth and water represent makes it possible to temper the fires of power and the more masculine intellect associated with the element air. Thus feminine and masculine may be balanced in the basic quaternity of the ancient Greek elements: earth, water, fire, and air.

It is not only that the feminine needs to be integrated, but a new realiza-tion of the masculine is needed, as well. W. C. must heal his relationship with his brothers, through increased opportunities to experience closeness and intimacy, authentic communication, and heartfelt feelings, something that his stated values seem to abhor. This can occur through men's groups and seminars that illuminate men's issues, much as his sisters developed their feminism in "consciousness raising groups" during the sixties. This would help him find a sacred sense of the masculine within and greatly improve his self-esteem.

In addition, seminars that teach effective communication skills and conflict resolution would help offset the need for violence. Techniques from Marshall Rosenberg's *Nonviolent Communication* are highly recommended. Conflict resolution studies that are now offered in many colleges, as well as the formation of thousands of peace groups worldwide, show great promise in this area.

W. C. would need numerous structures to support his growth: twelve-step programs for his addiction to consumption, yoga and meditation instruction for his spiritual growth. These transcendent practices leading toward internal peace could go a long way toward the creation of external peace. We would need to help him to find the spirit of his true Self, to clarify his values, and to communicate these values to others effectively without force or domination. He would need to find supportive communities to help him on his journey—others of like mind who were healing their own wounds and creating a path to the future.

We recommend an entire team of healers, comprised of both genders who would offer different skills and perspectives: from depth psychologists to physical trainers, from yoga teachers to breathworkers, meditation instructors to sustainable business coaches. Because of the extent of the mother wound, there is a strong need for a female therapist, despite the likelihood of negative transference toward her, though both genders are necessary on the healing team.

Unfortunately, there are some crises—global warming, in particular—that seem inevitable at this point. We regard these crises as initiatory challenges that lead to W. C.'s rite of passage into adulthood. This rite results in fundamental changes in beliefs and values that we see as essential for the world's future survival. We only hope to undertake as much depth work as soon as possible, to support the client in this process.

Progress Notes

Early application of these treatments shows that W. C. is slowly opening his heart. He is beginning to reach out to others with compassion, insight, and wisdom. Even if he is not yet successful in halting the violence, he is beginning to express a deep longing for peace and stability, something we consider to be a good sign of progress. His internal feminine is finding a stronger voice; he also is beginning to open to a realization of other races and cultures as viable voices within him. That these archetypes are working their way into mass consciousness is especially evident in the fact that both a white woman and a black man are candidates for president in the next election. Regardless of whether or not they win, we see this as a true sign of progress, so much so that

W. C. is no longer self-referent as entirely male but recognizes a larger body of awareness that includes many selves, both male and female, as an emerging and highly complex "we."

When focused on a common purpose, the numerous conflicting voices inside this client are beginning to experience greater harmony and agreement. W. C. is beginning to acknowledge the gravity of environmental problems and is learning to ask for help in solving them. Beliefs and values are changing to reflect a more sustainable, compassionate, and conscious society. A new sense of hope and possibility are rippling through the collective.

As W. C. continues this journey of healing, the newly strengthened collective self will eventually be ready to lead others along a similar path. Those with sustained traumatic stress might learn by example to heal their own wounds. Cultures that resort to violence might notice that there is another way. Examples of how to take better care of our home and environment would become inspirational models for others.

Concluding Remarks for the Healing Team

As therapists, we know this journey well. We have seen it many times as we have guided our clients along the healing path, bearing witness to the miraculous awakening process that turns suffering into joy. Our task now is for all of us to apply our healing skills to the culture itself, both for ourselves and each other. For humanity has come a long way through a tortuous history, and the wounds are many. But those wounds, once brought to resolution, bring us up to date with our past, so that we can cleanly and clearly create a glorious future.

If we are to reach planetary adulthood, we must heal our wounds, both individually and collectively. We must reclaim the ancient Mother and restore her relationship to the archetypal Father. We must face our collective shadow of domination and greed. We must find structures that support our spiritual natures, with disciplines to strengthen mind and body, and—most of all—to deepen our soul. We must learn to live authentically, with fully embodied lives and mythically inspired visions.

As individuals enter their own healing process, they open new possibilities for action. As we apply these healing principles to our collective existence, the culture itself begins to heal. No one can do it alone, and the good news is that no one has to. The one and the many work together as a complex field of mutual influence and co-evolution.

The possibilities that await us are unknown, but remember that we contain within us great genius and are guided by a profound archetype of wholeness—the thrust of the evolution toward greater realization and consciousness. What we are now is a mere shadow—in every sense of the word—of what we

can become. A glorious banquet awaits us on the other side of this transformation. But the doors to this banquet will open only when we have the ability to
walk through consciously, peacefully, and with a maturity that is worthy of
parenting the future.

What lies ahead is beyond our imagining, nothing less than the dawning
of the next age of civilization, the young adulthood that takes the reins from
the decaying patterns of the past and hitches them to an evolving vision of the
future. For in the healing crisis of adolescent transformation, we are all being
called to awaken to our adult potential.

The world is in our hands. The journey toward wholeness is now thrust
upon us as a collective. We can all be a part of this process. In fact, that's the
only way it will happen.

Works Cited

Brown, Lester, Gary Gardner, and Brian Halwell. *Beyond Malthus: Sixteen Dimensions of the
    Population Problem*. Worldwatch Paper 143. New York: Norton, 1999.

Campbell, Joseph, in conversation with Bill Moyers. *The Power of Myth*. New York:
    Doubleday, 1988.

Goode, Erica. "The Heavy Cost of Chronic Stress." *New York Times* 17 December 2002: F1.

Houston, Jean. *Jump Time: Shaping Your Future in a World of Radical Change*. New York:
    Tarcher & Putnam, 2000.

Jung, C. G. *The Collected Works of C. G. Jung*. 20 vols. Trans. R. F. C. Hull. Ed. H. Read,
    Michael Fordham, and Gerhard Adler. Princeton: Princeton UP, 1953–1989.

Jung, Emma. *Animus and Anima: Two Essays by Emma Jung*. 1955. Rpt. Dallas: Spring,
    1981.

Malthus, Thomas. *An Essay on the Principle of Population, as it Affects the Future Improvement
    of Society with Remarks on the Speculations of Mr. Godwin, M. Condorcet, and Other
    Writers*. London: Johnston, 1798.

U. S. Census Bureau. *U. S. and World Population Clocks—POPClocks*. April 1, 2007 <http://
    www.census.gov/main/www/popclock.html>.

World Health Organization. Signposts 2004. Trends datasets/Population and Health/Life
    Expectancy. CD-ROM. Worldwatch Institute, 2004.

Puer and Hellmouth

Buffy the Vampire Slayer and American Myth

SUSAN ROWLAND

The medieval carnivals . . . were abolished relatively early. . . . Our solution, however, has served to throw the gates of hell wide open.

—C. G. Jung, *Collected Works* 12

We live in a terrible split. . . . The danger lies in splitting the duplex into only senex or only puer. We had one-sided puer in the sixties, and now that chaotic style of destruction is giving way to a programmed style of senex destruction.

—James Hillman, *Inter Views*

The descent into hell has precisely the purpose of restoring the imagination. . . . It is not that "my life is hell," but rather that "hell (hell's imagination function) is my life."

—David Miller, *Hells and Holy Ghosts: A Theopoetics of Christian Belief*

Introduction

Buffy the Vampire Slayer, a series that was popular on both sides of the Atlantic, follows the adventures of a teenage girl hero. Accompanied by her friends and adult "Watcher," Giles, Buffy wages war on the undead. Two factors ensured *Buffy* cult TV status: the "cool," witty, and self-referential irony of the scripts, and the makers' willingness to engage with the fans through the Internet. Drawing upon religious motifs (orthodox, heretical, and pagan), occult beliefs, ghost stories, and literary and national history, *Buffy* reworks traditional narratives into the relentless modernity of suburban America, represented by the fictional town of Sunnydale. Unfortunately situated over a hellmouth, Sunnydale also stands for the tremendous repression needed to seal up the dark side of the American dream. *Buffy*'s multiple intertextual echoes are an attempt to explore the psychic cost of that denial.

To that end, *Buffy* deconstructs myths, particularly the Christian savior myth that bedevils America, as one would expect an ironic and *critical* TV show to do. Yet I wish to go further to argue that *Buffy*, the cult phenomenon, also reconstructs myth. In *Buffy*, TV has found a form in which irony and "cool" are building blocks of a new cultural myth of puer and senex. *Buffy the Vampire Slayer* invokes the deep collective psyche by intertextual irony: surprising as it sounds, "teenspeak" and a tissue of quotations enable us to save the world (a lot!).

The Gods of TV

Writing in the 1980s, James Hillman warned of a dangerous oscillation in America between the poles of senex and puer, between a heavy-handed devotion to order, tradition, history, and power, and heady youthful, light, and spiritual excesses. Today, senex and puer thrive on TV in all their unconscious constellation of each other. So, is Western culture, and in particular the dominant American culture, doomed to drift repeatedly between these archetypal extremes?

In this chapter I am going to look at *Buffy the Vampire Slayer* as an example of popular culture with a positive ensouled mission.[1] Not only does it deconstruct the established order, but it also aims to reconstruct psychologically—to offer a new myth. For, I argue, all the knowingness, irony, and self-referentiality typical of *Buffy* attempts a dialogue between senex and puer, both in the content of the stories and, more crucially, between show and audience. Moreover, the particular style of *Buffy* represents an aspect of TV able to be self-conscious about engaging with the deep psyche of its audience. To be precise, the irony, knowingness, and "cool" at multiple levels of dialogue, characterization, and plot, is not a barrier to deep engagement; it is rather a *means* to reach into the collective psyche. Irony, knowingness, and "cool" are the methods by which puer and senex are articulated within the show; they draw in the viewers to its erotically charged hinterland. By making conscious (through irony and so forth) senex and puer, *Buffy* starts to do something dynamic and potentially healing for American cultural myth: it starts to move these archetypal beings away from static stand off into a narrative of meaningful connectedness. Where at one level irony, "teenspeak," and so forth debunk traditional forms, at another they construct a new, more plural myth by forging a new relationship of senex and puer. No longer can they pose as exclusive alternatives.

First of all, we need to look a bit more closely at puer, senex, and TV. Senex is a figure of time, history, order, tradition, the abstract, and the regulated. As a heavy and depressive personality, senex is easily seen in opposition to puer in its immature lightness of being. Puer summons to psychic life immediacy, experiment, the overthrow of traditions and laws. It is characterized by idealism, charm, and in a deeper sense it invokes the spirit (Hillman, *Blue Fire* 227).

So puer and senex belong together, are essentially two parts of a psychic whole. The narrative of a human life could be understood as a dialogue between them (which is not to exclude other archetypal divinities):

> History is the senex shadow of the puer, giving him substance. Through our individual histories, puer merges with senex, the eternal comes back into time, the falcon returns to the falconer's arm. (Hillman, *Blue Fire* 223)

Consequently, an imbalance of senex-puer on a collective level leads either to a darkly paranoid oppressive state or to an irresponsible carelessness uprooting the national psyche. Arguably, it is the dissociation of senex and puer that troubles American self-identity, American myth today. For while terrorist outrages prove dangerously potent in darkening the mechanisms of state in the (understandable) desire for order and security, TV also is liable to split off senex and puer.

Keith Polette has pointed out how far TV fulfills senex obsessions:

> TV fulfills the fantasy of omnipresence, an all-pervasive position that was once reserved for the "senex god of our culture." (Polette 95)

Slotting into monotheism's senex structure, TV is the father god's material incarnation. The creature of money and power, TV permits no real dissent to the status quo and demands a monolithic version of truth, as Polette shows. TV thereby ignores the essential polysemy of the psyche (Polette 97). Moreover, its images embody truly demonic power in their ability to possess, rather than engage with, the viewer's psyche. TV reduces culture from archetype to stereotype: it drives viewers into the most childish, undifferentiated, base version of puer without its spiritual energies (Polette 107–12).

Polette's argument is powerful and convincing. TV as a phenomenon does indeed instate a particularly baleful version of senex-puer stasis. Senex here is the psychic imposition of the rule of money and power in the name of order, tradition, and stability. Puer is conscripted as the means of reinforcing control by keeping the psyche childish and unindividuated.

However, I would like to argue that *Buffy the Vampire Slayer* represents an attempt, one that may not altogether succeed, to weave together senex and puer in order to address the most oppressively senex variety of teleological myth, the myth of American heroic destiny. For here is a show that is conscious of the demonic powers of TV. Indeed, its aim, I would suggest, is to convert the demonic into the daimonic, to trans-form TV from psychic external coercion to something that brings the interior life of the viewer into that productive exchange that Jung called individuation.[2] To be precise, *Buffy*'s wholehearted embrace of puer as stereotype, the childish in popular culture, is in the interests of invoking puer as archetype, the divine child of spiritual rebirth. By bringing to cultural awareness both the gods of the medium and the myths that they sponsor in structuring the historic mission of the United States, *Buffy* enables both senex and puer to change. Whether they change enough is another matter. *Buffy* was designed to unite with the inner life of its audience; the show was made to be loved (Whedon, "Buffy Wraps"). So here is popular culture that aims to add a loving relationship to its demonic senex grip on the viewing psyche. *Buffy* tries to offer a new puer-senex myth out of its critical scrutiny of existing modes of power.

The rest of this chapter will focus on heroes and endings. In a show given to repeated apocalypses, how does its urge to individuate senex and puer (power, love, and its youthful audience) manage to survive its own ending? After all, one of the darkest aspects of Christian monotheism's senex qualities is its historic embrace of apocalypse. The Bible ends with the apocalyptic Book of Revelation. Twentieth-century materialism, in which monotheism descended into matter, money, and scientific *singleness* of vision, faithfully replicated apocalyptic myth in producing its own world's end in weapons of mass destruction. Can Buffy, who rose from the dead and "saved the world, a lot" avoid ending in a rein-forcement of the myth of apocalyptic violence? Can the dialogue of senex and puer in *Buffy the Vampire Slayer* succeed in offering a myth of healing without incarnating an-other's annihilation?

Senex and Puer in *Buffy the Vampire Slayer*

Buffy and Giles

In the narrative frame of the seven seasons of *Buffy the Vampire Slayer*, the most obvious senex-puer pairing is Giles, Buffy's middle-aged British "Watcher," and Buffy, the young hero herself. Buffy stands for youth. She begins as a high school teen, goes to college, drops out, and takes a low-paid job on the death of her mother. As vampire slayer, she fulfills many of the iconic roles of the puer. (I will consider the matter of her gender later.) The puer

> archetype tends to merge in one: the Hero, the Divine Child, the figures
> of Eros, the King's Son, the Son of the Great mother, the Psychopompos,
> Mercury-Hermes, Trickster, and the Messiah. (Hillman, *Blue Fire* 227)

Mild-mannered librarian Giles makes an attractive senex figure. As Buffy's "Watcher" sent by the "Council" based in England, he certainly stands for history, tradition, and order. Indeed it is his Britishness that is key to both his identification with senex as *history* and the narrative and political structures that enable him to individuate beyond restriction to that one archetypal form. For, politically, Giles's and Buffy's relationship renegotiates British imperialism as it becomes British weakness in the face of the strengthening American Messiah-hero.

Crucial to the previous sentence is the word *relationship*. Giles is an echo of the British colonization of America. So his "Council" is quickly revealed as senex faded into senility. Out of touch with the (archetypal) realities of living on the hellmouth, Buffy's revolution rejects the Council as the authority of the "old" country. For Giles, it then becomes personal commitment to Buffy that out-weighs his original role. When the Council places Buffy in danger by ordaining that she defeat a vampire without using her special powers, Giles breaks the rules to help her and is sacked. Yet Giles's "change of heart" is not a change of nature. While he stays with Buffy, he is a source of learning, tradition, and history—yet now in the service of the puer hero rather than confining her by rules and regulation. In the final episode of all (ending Season Seven), Giles describes Buffy's plan for defeating the evil of The First as flying in the face of all history, tradition, and as "bloody brilliant!" Senex does not so much renounce history and tradition as allow the structuring of an-other, a newness in relation to the old. It suggests a new configuration of senex and puer for a new age.

So I would suggest that the progress of Giles as senex-in-relationship is a clue to the story of Buffy herself. The problem with puer, despite (his) spiritual effervescence, is that puer does not grow up. Human individuation requires that puer no longer be the sole archetypal image of being. Buffy becomes progressively sadder throughout the seven seasons because her calling as puer hero will not allow her to live normally. It is brought more and more home to the audience that the warrior hero is too intimate with death for life to prosper. Doomed to die young, killing as her calling, extracted from death twice for more of the same, Buffy's closest relationship is to death itself with the hellmouth her direct route *under*. Heroic destiny means a stunted life with all the senex potential for living a personal history repressed into the unconscious as blinding depression. Narratively, Buffy's embrace of death is enacted in her love affairs with vampires, emphasized as impossible relationships. Buffy Summers is the American hero as American depression: a California teen who likes the mall (the consumer both formed by and fueling material culture) and whose other reality is the requirement to kill again and again in the belief that it (military action) will avert apocalypse. Can Buffy/America ever escape this story?

Senex and Puer in Fans and *Buffy the Vampire Slayer*

Unlike the typical senex-puer articulation between viewers and TV, *Buffy* consciously promotes something dynamic and ensouled. Whereas senex TV works to install a stereotypical version of puer in the audience by psychically numbing childish content, *Buffy* deliberately sets up a senex-puer negotiation as a *relationship* with the audience. At times the show is the puer that reaches out to the senex in the audience by taking seriously their sense of history, their *personal* history *within* popular culture. The pop culture references—most obviously the core group's calling themselves the "Scoobies"—are a liminal discourse of senex and puer. For they weave time, history, and pastness into the story while simultaneously making them "playful." So the self-conscious historicizing of *Buffy* within the history of television provides possibilities for maturation. Childhood as the route to maturity, rather than away from it, is narratively explored in Willow's "big bad" conclusion to Season Six. Determined to destroy the world to end her own pain, Willow is stopped only by Xander's standing in her way. He presents himself as the one who has loved her from childhood, explicitly as an icon of her personal history that she has to kill or integrate. Yet *Buffy* the show can be senex reaching to the childish in puer audience, as well. Indeed, the texture of *Buffy*'s interface with wider culture is making conscious the hope that puer and senex can embrace.

For example, Buffy's long-doomed romance with Angel is also a structure for the fans' impossible desire to unite with the show, as explored by Elizabeth Krimmer and Shilpa Raval. *Buffy the Vampire Slayer* is ageless, seductively beautiful, and it preys upon the psychic energy of the viewers. Or, conversely, the fans take the place of the vampires in haunting the fringes of the show, on Internet chatrooms or fan conventions. For the Eros of *Buffy* is an excess of the script of death and desire (Krimmer and Raval 162). If all modernity's vampires seem to have read too much Freud, *Buffy*'s regular, weekly vampires make the rehearsing of sex and death routine, while Buffy's relationships with Angel and Spike push the equation of desire and death beyond the ability of psychoanalytic discourses to account for it. This is both playfully puer in going beyond the limits of understanding the human psyche written into *any* psychological theory, and it engages senex, as Buffy, Angel, and even Spike, come up against historic destinies and duties that keep them apart. So, if the narrative of Buffy and her dead lovers enacts a senex-puer negotiation, both at the levels of play versus historic destiny, and as discursive understanding and beyond it, these elements feed into (feed on?) the audience's playful/historical union with the show. Pop culture references and "cool" language put the audience "inside" the show; impossible desire keeps them out. This inside/outside ambivalence is a core ingredient of the show's puer-senex myth; *Buffy* becomes liminal to the collective psyche of the fans.

Of course, *Buffy* has further ways of luring the fans into the interior. During the run of the show a vast amount of fan fiction appeared on the Internet. Some of it was deliberately referenced on the show, even, arguably, to the extent of molding major story lines. For example, slash fiction romantically pairs the most unlikely characters. While Spike and Buffy were mortal enemies, fans found a way to unite them offscreen. This alternative *Buffy* penetrated the screen in the "knowing" episode when an enchantment caused Buffy and Spike to believe that they were about to get married. However, *Buffy* never remains mere play for the childish element of puer. The episode anticipates, seeds, provides a vital psyche-logic for Spike's later infatuation.

A more in-depth, darker attempt to integrate the fans is the rise of the nerds, Warren, Jonathan, and Andrew, from teenage misfits to Buffy's true enemies. Throughout the seasons of *Buffy*, the nerds' chronic inability to grow up and take responsibility becomes progressively more dangerous, culminating in Warren's murder of Tara and his subsequent killing by Willow. And the nerds' main distinguishing feature is their fandom of teen TV and teen popular culture at large. These males have substituted a language of pop culture references for authentic feeling. Therefore Warren, Andrew, and Jonathan are a perfect demonstration of the emptying infantilizing function of senex TV. Except that they are on it—as objects of criticism.

In the episode "Storyteller," Andrew enacts the fantasy of fans everywhere in both "directing" an episode (with camcorder) and placing himself at the center of a heroic *Buffy* story. Crucially, the viewer is given the nerd's-eye view, as we are shown Andrew's limited understanding of the Scoobies and their true heroism. As Sue Turnbull explores, Andrew invokes styles of high and low culture TV. He is a fan who has crossed (impossible) boundaries to the interior of the show. Andrew presents himself as director, author, and evil genius antihero. This is fan in demon form, showing the demonic power of TV to distort reality and corrupt the psyche. So he is structured as a dark puer using pop culture to blot out his own history (senex) of murder. It is only when Buffy makes Andrew face his own death that he can start to accept responsibility for killing Jonathan. "Storyteller" ends with Andrew no longer telling stories, for his are only twisted quotations from pop culture. Instead he admits that he cannot know the end of the story he is in. He renounces the fantasy of being able to control his own life by *uniting with the shows* on TV, such as *Buffy the Vampire Slayer*.

By connecting with his own history, Andrew's brush with death gives him the basis for making his own story from the perspective of actually living it.

Does his education out of his stereotypical "heroic" teleology offer anything to Buffy, increasingly trapped in the slayer story?

The Feminine Puer

So far, I have argued that a TV series about demons enlists fans in a reciprocal relationship that makes even more potent the liminal boundary between screen and viewing psyche. That liminal space is a domain of psychic meaning: its harnessing of imaginative desire is the shaping energy forming the new puer-senex myth. Moreover, *Buffy* enters the psyche *responsibly* by demanding and structuring self-conscious engagement. The fans' demonic, vampiric *presence* is alternate to the predatory nature of the show. Both types of demons (fans and show) are regularly extinguished by laughter or are invited to individuate into a subtle re-alignment of senex and puer. For, just as senex can be vampiric as predatory power in the name of order and time, so puer is demonic as Andrew, when only capable of feeding on TV, as a denial of human feeling and responsibility.

At this point, *Buffy* could be placed in the wider context of American religious culture. For, as Gregory Erickson shows, American evangelical Christianity draws upon a growing belief in the reality of demons (116). If *Buffy* is educating the viewer by consciously renegotiating boundaries between real and unreal, then is it addressing or simply replicating a cultural explosion of the "other" or super-natural into collective experience? I want to argue that by gendering the puer as feminine, *Buffy* allows a critical edge to its intervention into contemporary senex and puer that *directly challenges* the invocation to the demonic in contemporary religion. The *Buffy* myth is daimonic in ways that counter the demonic myth of evangelical Christianity.

Buffy Summers is described by her creator, Joss Whedon, as a female hero, not a heroine (Whedon, "Television with a Bite"). Further, he points out that the very idea was considered aberrant by the (senex) powers of TV corporations. So, as I have been suggesting, Buffy is puer—not puella. She has the qualities of the puer hero in female form, giving *Buffy* a clear relationship to feminist attempts to challenge traditional gender norms (regulated by senex *as* regulation). After all, Buffy cuts down to size the first High School Principal, the evil Mayor, the CIA-like government body, the Initiative, and finally a demonic, gynophobic preacher in Caleb.

At the same time, Buffy is prepared to make relationships with "the other," notably vampires, and sees her mission as protective, not aggrandizing. Buffy is no imperialist after new territory. She patrols the same old graveyard for years. No wonder she gets depressed! Effectively, Buffy's feminine difference from traditional patriarchal religious images enables the show to operate by distinguishing the daimonic from the demonic. In the first place, as feminist icon she is used to explore, and eventually herself consciously explores, the notion of leadership and heroism. In all seasons of the show, the stories grow out of a dialogical relationship between the unique role of the one chosen hero and the necessity of the group. While the latter variety of collective heroism is often preferred by feminism, the show suggests how even collective hero groups depend upon a productive tension with a single vision. *Buffy* ends Season Seven by trying to escape that dialogical exchange, as I shall show later.

Similarly, the feminine puer provides an oppositional position from which the show interrogates traditional senex patriarchal power such as the Mayor, the government, and so forth. A third way of peeling back what is congealed as power in culture from the shaping psychic energy itself (demonic from daimonic) is the use of Buffy's gender as a distancing (but not complete detaching) from traditional monotheism. True, she is a puer Messiah with many Christ-like features, in particular a habit of resurrection, but *Buffy* cannot be simply co-opted into Christian conventions.

The show preserves a resistance to collapsing into American Christianity by methods including gender, "cool" language, and narrative excess. Here Buffy's self-conscious entanglement in her culture's femininity (from clothes to sexuality), the ironic detachment of "cool" speak, and the *repeatability* of Buffy's heroic deaths and resurrections, means that the show cites Christianity rather than embraces it. Yet this citation is not a postmodern emptying of meaning. Rather it is an attempt simultaneously to uncover and create the puer spiritual heart in the frozen senex framework of American religion. Where evangelicals evoke the heavy tradition of witchcraft and the demonic (as in the witches of Salem), *Buffy*'s demonic is *played with* by its "distancing" and re-citing that is a re-*siting*. *Buffy* enables the demonic in both senex and puer to be redeemed into their healing roles as daimonic energy.

In a culture in which orthodox religion has become entangled with economic power, a feminine puer as California teenage consumer is liminal because she is both the creature of materialist culture and its victim—one who has learned to fight back. Her character echoes C. G. Jung's treatment of the feminine that oscillates between describing it as abject inferiority to masculine consciousness and power, and acknowledging it as radical, sublime, unknowable, and transforming (Rowland 54). So, on the one hand, Buffy is a teenager very happy to conform and consume: the willing accomplice of American popular capitalism. On the other hand, Buffy's powers to disrupt and embrace "the other" overturn what is dead senex in the so-called real world. Moreover, she achieves the disruption of social conventions without replacing it with a form of ordering liable itself to become deadening senex without puer. If Buffy's repeated requirement to save the world is a little dispiriting in its continuous necessity, then at least she maintains the sublime in her repeated standing for the *unknowable, unfeasible plan to stop the unstoppable this time.*

Buffy as feminine puer has taken on the American religious and political myth of the Messiah and has, first of all, exposed the high price it exacts in depression and violence. Can she re-form the myth to make it a dialogue between inner being and social participation? Can the American Messiah discourse be healed by envisioning it as daimonic rather than demonic?

Myth, Creation, and Apocalypse

One structuring of gender and myth particularly germane to the show's struggle with American destiny is creation myth. In fact, Buffy and Willow come more and more to embody the painful intersection of the two great creation myths of Western modernity. These myths are badly aligned and require a better relationship if fractured modern consciousness is to be restored. For example, Buffy's Messiah tendencies place her in relation to monotheistic stories of sky father gods. Sky father creation myths, of which Judaeo-Christianity is just one, describe the world as made by a separate divinity that remains "above" and apart from "his" creation. Matter, earth, and body are seen as inert products of the divine mind and are figured as feminine inferiority to a patriarchal transcendent god. Therefore, consciousness is predicated upon separation, distinction, objectivity, and rationality.

By contrast, earth mother creation myths regard the earth herself as sacred and generative. All creation flows from the divine mother and dies back into her embrace. Theologies, matter, body, and sexuality are part of the divine for earth mother. Consciousness is dependent upon relationship rather than separation. Unsurprisingly, the human psyche needs both sky father and earth mother modes of consciousness if it is to be healthy. Unfortunately, Western modernity itself is constructed from a long overvaluing of sky father consciousness with its attendant repression of unconsciousness, body, and the feminine. Indeed, sky father myth *is* that repression narratively enacted. While the psyche requires discrimination and rational thinking, it also needs to value the *embrace* of the other and to know the unconscious as a source of being.

In this context of great, overarching structures of consciousness, senex and puer appear again as aspects of the two myths. With senex as the archetypal figure closest to the sky father, puer is the divine child of the earth mother, Hillman tells us. His description of puer here could serve as a neat summary of the career of Buffy:

Whether as her hero-lover or hero-slayer, the puer impulse is reinforced by this entanglement with the Great Mother archetype, leading to those spiritual exaggerations we call neurotic. (Hillman, *Blue Fire* 228)

Buffy's story is largely one of puer who traces the lineage of senex when she embarks upon Messiah narratives. Her earth mother qualities are another image for the way *Buffy* the show is at an angle to, and critiques, American Christianity (heavily senexed). *Buffy*'s potent qualities of Eros, feeling, and engagement within the stories and with the fans are a way of digging up the buried script of the earth mother in modern culture. And this return of the undead (m-other), regarded as demonic from the perspective of patriarchal Christianity, is reconfigured by the show as daimonic, a necessary part of the loving exchanges of consciousness in the psyche.

The stories of Buffy and Willow point the way, which is to eschew exclusive identification with puer (earth mother) or senex (sky father). Individuation into moral and mental health demands a dialogue of both. So puer Buffy in Seasons Six and Seven is forced into more of a senex position. Firstly, she is *forcibly* resurrected *out of the embrace of the earth* and into a Christian Messiah form closer to sky father separation. In turn, this move leads to a painful dis-connection from family and friends. Buffy does not individuate puer and senex easily. Finding herself in a parental (senex) role for her sister Dawn after the death of their mother, Buffy suffers senex negatively in the form of depression. It is not until the very end of Season Seven that she finds a way to embody puer in the senex. For such a union is to reconcile her historic destiny of separateness (the chosen one, and so forth), with the only means of fulfilling it, which is also to be puer as connected, loving, playful, and spiritual.

Similarly, Willow has an almost fatal fall into one exclusive archetypal image when her magic connects her to all reality in the manner of the earth mother. Such is the overwhelming nature of Willow's bond that it figures as addiction: she acquires energy without the ability to control it, without the conscious discrimination of sky father senex. Therefore, at a point of maximum power, or archetypal inflation when the ego is subsumed, Willow cannot bear the revelation of human pain. Fortunately, her human history can still reach her. Xander is an unlikely representative of senex discrimination, but he manages to fuse senex and puer by reaching out to Willow with a history of love.

Hillman states that puer has a tendency to spiritual excess. Attempting to destroy the world probably qualifies as excess! After rehabilitation with senex Giles in senex England, Willow returns to *Buffy* uneasily overidentifying with senex separateness and order. She is tormented by her *history* of violence to the extent of being afraid to *reconnect* to her spiritual power. New love and reinvigorated friendships enable her to trust connecting again, in time for her earth mother magic to help Buffy to save the world (again).

The seasons of *Buffy the Vampire Slayer* are stories of apocalypse averted. This reflects both the senex myth of TV, in which *Buffy* the show could never be sure that it would be recommissioned, and Christianity/secular modernity's underlying apocalyptic structure: the Christian apocalyptic narrative of revelation converted into a culture of world-destroying weaponry. So, how do *Buffy* and Buffy cope with the "real" end? An end, after all, is built into the very nature of a TV show; it is, if you like, a *first* principle. Season Seven's apocalyptic enemy, The First, that which produces evil, proves terrifying indeed with its refrain in the early episodes: "from beneath you it devours." To defeat The First, it is necessary to use the greatest weapon of all—the slayer myth itself.

Ending *Buffy the Vampire Slayer*

Like *Buffy the Vampire Slayer*, the work of C. G. Jung is devoted to converting myth from an external coercive form to which the psyche is made subject, to providing a method (a technology of the soul) by which a human life is narratively structured in dialogue with the collective. Such is the shift that ends *Buffy*, when a slayer story that locks Buffy and ultimate evil into an annihilating embrace is rewritten to liberate healing psychic energies. For Jung's answer to modernity's myth of apocalypse was a new creation myth, or, more precisely, his own deconstruction of the two fundamental creation myths. The living out of apocalypse by repressing the other, individually and collectively, can be replaced by a myth of self-creation, which is creation by the self.

Here Jung's idea of the self needs a little elaboration. The self stands for the psyche as whole, as bordered by the unknowable so knowing no bounds, and, also for the archetypal goal of principle toward which psychic development tends. Fascinatingly, therefore, the self is a psychological notion that draws upon both earth mother (wholeness, connectedness), and sky father (a goal, a direction, a teleology). In order to avoid apocalypse, the repressed darkened other must be brought into relationship. The self is Jung's term for the creative powers of the psyche that work beyond and behind the more limited vision of the ego toward wholeness of being. For Buffy, it means nothing less than restructuring her entire relationship to those she protects and those she kills. For these are the elements of the "self" that may enable the slayer myth to change.

So, Buffy faces The First in Season Seven needing something more than her apocalyptic narrative of slaying to prevent annihilation. This time, not only is she not strong enough alone (a repeated motif in developing a more social concept of heroism), but she is also not strong enough with her core group.

Nor even with the extra potential slayers who might one day replace her is the enlarged gang strong enough.

It is easy to see a critique of America here. An insufficiently individuated puer-senex state (Buffy) faces its own slayer myth (aggression in the name of greater security) and finds it is becoming impotent to deal with a multifaceted enemy. Loyal traditional allies and even new inexperienced allies cannot make up the numbers. Such a slayer myth is teleological in being oriented to the future: killing and slaying is justified in order to prevent the coming apocalypse. Buffy/America is trapped in a Messiah complex that "she" cannot fulfill. For, as Season Seven makes all too apparent, Buffy/America's second coming will enact the apocalypse rather than avert it—unless the slayer script be rewritten. In "Bring on the Night" Buffy says: "If they want an apocalypse, we'll give them one."

Interestingly, *Buffy the Vampire Slayer* has been here before with Dawn in Season Five. Dawn's apocalyptic destiny was so momentous to the preservation of the world that Buffy was presented with a stark choice: the best protection from the evil that could be unleashed through Dawn was to kill Dawn. For only Dawn's blood could seal the portal, the hole in reality through which destructive chaos would engulf everything. Buffy refused to choose between saving Dawn and saving humanity. Instead, she sacrificed herself. Luckily, her blood, as sister to Dawn, was sufficient to prevent apocalypse again.

What is also apparent in this narrative re-solution is that refusing Dawn's myth also changes Buffy's. The mission of the vampire slayer, the chosen one, and so forth, is to kill all supernatural threats to humanity. Surely, sticking closely to the teleological script, Buffy should have killed Dawn (who only *looked* human), and then she would have been still around to carry on slaying. So, it is possible to escape a teleological myth, or heroic destiny, by recognizing and refusing to accept the destructiveness embedded in such narratives. Or more precisely, where Dawn and Buffy are successively presented with a myth as an external imperative—"you are the key to the portal," "you are the one slayer," and so forth—by sacrifice, which also entails a sacrifice of certainty, it is possible to reshape the myth you are in. Buffy does not give up teleological myth by dying to save Dawn. She merely moves out of a totalizing myth where she has no autonomous role (no *choice* at all that would save Dawn *and* the world) to a myth of self-sacrifice that heals as she surrenders herself. Buffy becomes a player in her own myth, which does not mean that she controls it. After all, Buffy as puer dies into the Great Mother, but her friends find this intolerable and so resurrect her into Messiah-senex torment.

The death of Buffy at the end of Season Five shows myth to be inescapable but not necessarily totalizing. Myth can be a structure for autonomous action as a mode of participation with the "other" as others, in society. The philosopher

James South argues that the end of *Buffy the Vampire Slayer* in Season Seven represents an attempt to do away with teleological myth altogether. He uses Plato's metaphor of the cave to show how a dialectical understanding of good and evil comes about. A good/evil dialectic is a key ingredient of a teleology because the structuring of good and evil as antitheses is an engine of forward thinking. Plato's cave metaphor attempts to explain why humans behave badly. Because of our desire-induced fantasies, we are like cave dwellers looking at shadows on a wall. Only the few (philosophers) are able to glimpse the sunlight of truth outside. Such a metaphor sets up a relationship between good and evil that means that they depend upon each other (South 18). South argues that Buffy cannot defeat The First in Season Seven because as the *origin* of evil, "he" is hardwired into the slayer story: the evil bedrock upon which teleological heroism is constructed. The First is the evil origin of the evil she needs to sustain the myth of the slayer. All that Buffy endures in Season Seven contributes to her realization that she can and must change the slayer myth. And the achievement of that realization, making it *real,* is to forge a relationship within herself between senex and puer: puer child-lover and senex-Messiah must unite within Buffy and unite her also to her "others" who also change their relation to the slayer myth. So, for example, Giles the senex can let go of tradition for once, and Willow learns earth mother connectedness without being swamped by the dark.

Buffy escapes the cave of her slayer myth by giving up her status as "the One." All the potential slayers are endowed with their powers through Willow's realization of her connective energies. I do not, however, agree that this renunciation by Buffy is a complete escape from teleological myth. Rather, it is a conversion of teleology into psychology. For *Buffy the Vampire Slayer* demonstrates the huge psychological price paid for, and by, "the chosen one/nation." At the end of the show the earth is populated by slayers. So, no single woman is in the position of *having* to avert the apocalypse every week. One hellmouth is destroyed. Yet, as Giles helpfully points out, there is supposed to be another one in Cleveland. Fortunately, it no longer has to be Buffy who closes it. She has a real choice at last.

Instead of the oppressive demand of the myth on a single individual, the ending of *Buffy* offers autonomy and moral responsibility. Buffy really can choose what to do, and the fate of the world does not automatically hang upon it. Teleology is not now world-heroic destiny, but rather it is psychic and moral on-going development, or what Jung called individuation. Buffy is connected to a world of slayers (puer earth mother), yet she can function as autonomous with her own history (senex sky father). *Buffy the Vampire Slayer* has at last given to the world what Jung called his "personal myth" of puer-senex individuation (*Memories* 195, 224).

Buffy the Vampire Slayer ends with its long-suffering hero's tentative smile. Before this pleasing final shot, we see what she is smiling at: a huge, dusty crater where Sunnydale once was. While the ending of *Buffy* is easily read as a political metaphor in which a destructive teleological myth is replaced by an empowering collective vision, the ecological resonance needs digging up from the (undead) earth. *Buffy* ends with a group of friends gazing upon a desert crater and wondering how to live. The structuring of relations with the other (unconsciousness, other people, the supernatural), via apocalyptic myth sponsored by senex sky father separation, results in terrible wounds in mother earth. Buffy may have given up over-identification with senex as apocalyptic myth in favor of psyche as self-creation (earth mother and sky father together), but the legacy of modernity's senex repression of feminized nature remains.

As usual, the show spins its stories by extending and collapsing metaphors. For that is how the image-ination works. Buffy really is in a desert; she really does reseal the mouth of hell, yet also, for us, the viewers drawn into the liminal psyche of TV, it is our desert and our hell. As Hillman says: "Images and metaphors present themselves always as living psychic subjects with which I am obliged to be in relation" (Hillman, *Blue Fire* 48). By populating the psyche's hinterland, Buffy and her companions invite the senex and puer of Western modernity to stop living on the hellmouth and start living with it.

Notes

1. I would like to thank Dr. Terrie Waddell of La Trobe University for discussing *Buffy* and TV with me.
2. I am grateful to the artist Rachael Steel for describing C. G. Jung as aiming to distinguish the daimonic from the demonic.

Works Cited

Erickson, Gregory. "'Sometimes You Need a Story': American Christianity, Vampires, and Buffy." Wilcox and Lavery 108–19.

Hillman, James. *Inter Views: Conversations Between James Hillman and Laura Pozzo on Therapy, Biography, Love, Soul, Dreams, Work, Imagination and the State of the Culture.* New York: Harper & Row, 1983.

———. *The Essential James Hillman: A Blue Fire.* Intro. and ed. by Thomas Moore. Great Britain: Routledge, 1990.

Jung, C. G. *Psychology and Alchemy*, CW12. London: Routledge, 1968.

———. *Memories, Dreams, Reflections.* Ed. Aniela Jaffe. Trans. Richard Winston and Clara Winston. Great Britain: Routledge, 1963.

Krimmer, Elizabeth, and Shilpa Raval. "'Digging the Undead': Death and Desire in Buffy." Wilcox and Lavery 153–63.

Miller, David. *Hells and Holy Ghosts: A Theopoetics of Christian Belief*. New Orleans: Spring, 2004.

Polette, Keith. "Airing (Erring) the Soul: An Archetypal View of Television." *Post-Jungian Criticism: Theory and Practice*. Ed. James S. Baumlin, Tita French Baumlin, and George H. Jensen. New York: SUNY P, 2004. 93–116.

Rowland, Susan. *Jung as a Writer*. London and New York: Routledge, 2005.

South, James. "On the Philosophical Consistency of Season 7." *Slayage: The Online Journal of Buffy Studies* (13/14) http://www.slayage.tv/Numbers/slayage13_14html.

Turnbull, Sue. "Not just Another Buffy Paper: Towards an Aesthetics of Television." *Lounge Critic: the Couch Theorist's Companion*. Ed. Annabel Rattigan and Terrie Waddell. Melbourne: Australian Centre of the Moving Image, 2004. 3–15.

Whedon, Joss, creator. *Buffy the Vampire Slayer*. 20th Century Fox Television et al. TV Series 1997–2003.

———. "Buffy the Vampire Slayer: Television with a Bite." *Buffy the Vampire Slayer*. Season Six DVD, Disc 6. 20th Century Fox Television et al., 2004.

———. "Buffy Wraps." *Buffy the Vampire Slayer*. Season Seven DVD, Disc 6. 20th Century Fox Television et al., 2004.

Wilcox, Rhonda V., and David Lavery, ed. *Fighting the Forces: What's at Stake in Buffy the Vampire Slayer*. New York and Oxford: Rowman and Littlefield, 2002.

Puer in Nature

The Monster and the Grizzly Man

RINDA WEST

In its response to the natural world, Western culture continues to suffer from its dualist orientation. Whether you ascribe the origins of the estrangement between humans and nature to Christianity, agriculture, Descartes, the Industrial Revolution, or simply to the way things are, it seems nearly impossible to move beyond the habit of regarding nature as either a resource to be exploited or a source of transcendent meaning. By far the more common attitude in the West is the former, utilitarian notion of nature. It is the modern expression of an older, more fearful stance that grew from the human perception that nature is dangerous. Survival required the "conquest" of nature: predators, droughts, floods, vermin, storms, bacteria, sewage, pollution, even global warming, have all threatened a fragile civilization. As humans developed industry, the martial language shifted slowly into a rhetoric of use: people harnessed, mined, fabricated, drilled, dammed, and bioengineered their way to the world we all know, where most people in developed countries have virtually no encounter with nature that isn't mediated. In the process, I believe, the Western psyche constructed itself with a wary regard for its own "nature." As the industrial processes of the last three centuries have controlled some of nature's self-regulating wildness, the psychology of utilitarian capitalism has dedicated itself to the control of psyche, in an effort to render people fit workers in a modern economy. More recently, we have developed technologies and desires that lead people to sculpt even their bodies in service of a persona-driven mass culture. In this way we hope to be able to render the puer perpetual, finally to conquer aging. One consequence of this callous disregard for nature and human nature is a kind of pervasive cynicism, bred, in part, by the very technology that we are told will somehow rescue us from nature's depletion or her revenge.

The complement to this is a romantic idealization of nature, which receives political expression in the movements to preserve wilderness and to protect endangered species. Its most extreme proponents are often represented as tree-huggers who value darter snails and spotted owls more than people. We owe the

Endangered Species Act, the Wilderness Protection Act, and the preservation of significant tracts of wild land to the understanding fostered by modern Emersons and Thoreaus, but their spiritual energy can easily be balked by the resistance of the political order, goading them into a puer flight from political engagement.

While it might be tempting to assume that the users have a senex problem and the dreamers are all puers, in the context of a youth-centered culture these characteristic responses to the natural world devolve into a couple of interesting inflections of the *puer aeternus*: the slacker and the purist. Slacker culture spins a utilitarian approach to nature into cynicism, inaction, and gratuitous or vicarious violence, while the purists invert the traditional Western dualism and shun humans, whom they blame for all the suffering of the natural world. They prefer trees to people and, at the extreme, isolate themselves from human company in the name of protecting nature. They often perform important roles within an environmental strategy, calling attention to the destruction of forests or the vulnerability of wild creatures. The young people who perch in ancient redwoods strike a classically puer pose in their altitude and attitude. However, the personal cost to them may be high, to put it mildly. Slackers, by contrast, adopt a protective cynicism that is the deflated inverse of the purists' romantic view of nature. In this chapter I will look at Werner Herzog's 2005 film *Grizzly Man* as an amplification of the romantic puer in nature. Then I will turn to several versions of the slacker, looking briefly at two other iterations of the slacker puer—Richard Linklater's 1991 film *Slacker* and the *Beavis and Butthead* cartoon series—and focusing on John Gardner's 1971 rewriting of *Beowulf*, from the point of view of the monster. *Grendel* articulates the consciousness of the negative puer, and as such it is an extended study in what it feels like to inhabit that psyche.

Grizzly Man documents the experiences of Timothy Treadwell, who styled himself an amateur expert on grizzlies in Alaska. For thirteen seasons he lived among the bears, camping in their habitat, interacting with them, and, as he puts it, protecting them. In 2003, he was killed and eaten by a grizzly, along with his companion and assistant, Amie Huguenard. For the last five seasons Treadwell took documentary footage of the bears and of himself. Herzog weaves Treadwell's own footage in with interviews of people he knew, or who knew his work, in a study of a man apparently more comfortable with bears and foxes than with people. The scenery is stunning, the footage of the bears astonishing. The film is a visual banquet, but it's also very disturbing.

Treadwell's presence in the film reads like the amplification of the *puer aeternus* that James Hillman describes: "In him we see a mercurial range of these 'personalities': narcissistic, inspired, effeminate, phallic, inquisitive, inventive, pensive, passive, fiery, and capricious" (50). Treadwell tries on personae on camera: he is nature photographer, sports announcer, children's television performer, conspirator. Herzog includes several instances of Treadwell's repeating shots of himself talking as he fine tunes not simply the message but also the self he presents. His believes himself the protector of the bears, a kind warrior. "I am now proving myself as being able to hold my ground and therefore earning their respect," he says early in the film, as he films a bear "just feet away," and the breathy voice strives to be both instructive and cool. "That was a challenge, and you have to remain cool in the challenge, in the moment. If you don't, you're dead." Beneath the persona, however, there's a sense of a man uncomfortable in the human social world, happier with children than with adults, troubled by his history of failed relationships, and constructing himself for himself. "I run so wild, so free, like a child with these animals," he remarks, but in practically the same moment, "How alone you are." This switch from the first to the second person suggests part of the split in his experience.

Herzog distinguishes Treadwell's response to the bears from the responses of others he interviews. The pilot who took Treadwell into the bush describes the bear that killed him as "a mean-looking dirty rat of a bear," and comments that Treadwell was acting like he was "playing with people in bear outfits." Larry van Daele, a bear biologist, talks about "harvesting" bears, since hunting is a part of the local economy. While Treadwell understood that bears are predators—and he also knew the predatory qualities of humans—he put himself in the way of danger, almost as though he were in love with death. Danger satisfied the longing to be a warrior, but the curious juxtaposition of his assertions of danger and his boyish love of the bears is more suggestive of a child playing a violent video game than it is of an adult facing a real threat. David Denby calls him "an American saint and fool—a man who understands everything about nature except death" (101).

Herzog constructs a brief biography of Treadwell, touching on his childhood, his difficulties with alcohol and drugs, his serial relationships with women. Treadwell tells the camera how he negotiated with the bears to give up drinking. "It was a miracle, and the miracle was the animals," he says. Thereafter he reflects that if there is a God, "God would be very, very pleased with me" because of how much he loves, indeed adores, the bears, and because he takes his videos to people *"for no charge."* His voice is italic on this last phrase, suggesting Marie-Louise von Franz's remark that the puer has difficulty finding an appropriate job. For Treadwell, it would seem, accepting money for his work would contaminate it.

At the same time, Treadwell is strategic: "Hidden down below in those trees somewhere is my camp. I must stay incognito. I must hide from the authorities. I must hide from people who would harm me. I must now even hide from people who seek me out because I have made some sort of, um, I don't want to say celebrity." Herzog includes several takes of this shot, of Treadwell standing on a ridge overlooking what he calls the Grizzly Sanctuary, talking about his need for stealth in relation to humans. Mixed with the hide-and-seek quality of this scene, in which he clearly takes pleasure, is a hint of adult strategizing: the presence of other humans would, in truth, disturb the bears, and Treadwell has set himself out to protect them. In this he expresses the mercurial qualities of the puer—trickster and guardian at the same time. Even his romance with death has a strategic dimension, as he considers how much his death would call attention to his work.

Throughout, Treadwell maintains a sense of wonder and playfulness, clearly besotted with the bears. He is parental toward them, coaching them, scolding them for being naughty, and then repeating, "I love you, I love you," in the tones one uses with a four-year-old child. His approach to them reminds me of Mr. Rogers, the television persona of Fred Rogers, who charmed generations of preschoolers with imaginative puppets. In addition to his bears, Treadwell shares his domestic space with foxes, who are charming and playful. In one episode, he is speaking with a fox, who is evidently named Timmy (Treadwell's own name for himself from time to time) and he says, in a childish voice, "Timmy is the boss of all foxes and all bears. Thanks for being my friend." I found this quite disturbing: it suggests that in Treadwell's identification with the animals he has gone beyond blurred boundaries. However, he also knows that the bears are not puppets. Many times in the film Treadwell also reflects on the danger to which he exposes himself, and he seems fascinated by the possibility of being eaten. One of Treadwell's friends whom Herzog interviews, Marnie Gaede, says that Treadwell "wanted to mutate into a wild animal." It's almost as though he was courting the possibility that being metabolized by a bear might mean becoming a bear, himself.

A mixture of spirit and immersion in matter, Treadwell expresses many of the contradictions of the puer archetype. He speaks to the bears in a high pitched, "Hi! how are you?" then scolds them in a gruff voice, "Don't you do that," which segues back into the high pitched "I love you! I love you! I love you!" He has named the bears such childish names as Mr. Chocolate, Aunt Melissa, The Grinch, Downy, Tabitha, and Mickey, and the foxes he calls Timmy, Spirit, and Ghost. His footage of the bears and foxes is stunning: a huge bear scratching his back on a tree, foxes sniffing his fingers and racing across fields, bears galloping in what appears to be a high-spirited game.

Throughout Herzog's film, Treadwell insists on the danger of his project. He underlines the need to appear powerful to the bears, saying, "If I show weakness, I will be killed." Late in the film we see him saying that his "is the most dangerous living in the history of the world." The danger was clearly tonic to him, and he enjoyed the thrill of knowing he could be killed by the very bears he was sworn to protect. Time after time he says, "I love these bears. I would die for these bears," and "I will die for them but I will not die at their claws and jaws. I will fight. I will be strong. I will be one of them. I will be master." Treadwell calls himself a "Soul of a kind warrior" and a samurai; more than one commentator refers to him as Prince Valiant.

Treadwell spent a great deal of time in the Alaskan wilderness alone, but even when he had company, he wanted to appear to be alone. Herzog notes that Amie never appears full-face in Treadwell's videos. This, too, suggests that Treadwell liked the romance of the lone warrior, the knight on a crusade. His inflation that he was living in the most dangerous place on earth, that it would kill anyone else, but that he had managed to survive, his self-image as Prince Valiant, his effeminacy—all contribute to the sense that he is not of the earth. However, he is very much of the earth, embraced by wilderness, intimate with seven hundred-pound wild creatures, with foxes as his household companions.

Hillman says, "Puer figures often have a special relationship with the Great Mother, who is in love with them as carriers of the spirit; incest with them inspires her—and them—to ecstatic excess and destruction" (52). Wilderness—wild nature, including wild bears—functions for Treadwell as the Great Mother: it rescued him from alcohol, it gives meaning to his life; indeed, he believes the bears gave him his life. The Alaskan wilderness where Treadwell worked felt boundless, simple, and harsh. Disappearing into the wilderness was a way to escape the contamination of human society and live amid perfection. Treadwell says again and again of his love for the bears, "I would die for these animals. I would die for these animals." This Christ-like affirmation gives the film its acute poignancy.

Near the end of the film, we see Treadwell speaking to the camera about his role as a protector of the bears. It's at the end of his field season, and he's taking his leave of the place for another year. He begins with a humble self-presentation as a man who simply wants to ensure that poachers and polluters don't destroy the bears or their habitat. But his talk devolves into an obscene rant against the government and, in particular, the Park Service. Rant gives way to rage: "I beat you. I beat you. I'm the champion!" he declares to the Park Service. "Animals rule!" He declares he is "fighting civilization itself." As the mask of mock humility shreds and the inflated victor emerges, we wonder how strategic each is.

Because, of course, in some ways Treadwell is right. Civilization as we know it *is* the enemy of wild nature. The Park Service is underfunded and its mission inadequate to protect the habitat necessary to top predators like the grizzly. His films brought some attention to the bears, but more to Timothy Treadwell, whom Michael Atkinson accuses of "TV-poisoned narcissism," but the dangers besetting wilderness globally are real and unrelenting. Exactly how Treadwell was "protecting" the bears is unclear; he may have believed that media attention was what would save them.

Treadwell also understood the value of wild places to humans. Speaking of his alcoholism, he says:

> It was killing me until I discovered this land of bears and realized that they were in such great danger that they needed a caretaker, they needed someone to look after them, but not a drunk person. So I promised the bears that if I looked over them would they please help me be a better person. They became so inspirational, and living with the foxes too, that I did, I gave up the drinking. It was a miracle . . . and the miracle was animals.

I believe we need to take this seriously: the wild place and the wild animals were a miracle to him, transformative. They freed the puer spirit from its chemical highs and gave it direction and purpose.

Marnie Gaede tells Herzog that Treadwell believed that death might be the best option for him, since his death would lead people to look seriously at his work. Herzog laces *Grizzly Man* with footage of Treadwell's speaking of danger, fear, and the potential that a bear might kill him. He was right that his death brought his work to the public; it certainly shaped Herzog's film, which circles around the death in ever-decreasing orbit. While Herzog includes some stunning footage of the Alaskan wild, he is primarily interested in understanding Treadwell, so, ironically perhaps, the film does not do as much as it could have to further Treadwell's work. Also ironic is the hatred Treadwell expressed for the "people world," which was nonetheless the audience for all his self-construction.

Writing in *The New Yorker*, David Denby concludes his review of *Grizzly Man* with these thoughts:

> As Herzog frames it, the entire movie is a very dark joke. Yet there's an element in the comedy which Herzog may not have intended: the contrast between the self-dramatizing American, with his naïve egotism and optimism, and the hyper-cultivated European, who brings his own burden of despair to nature. Whereas the tormented Treadwell longs for harmony and doesn't seem to understand that death is at the center of any ecological balance, Herzog sees *nothing* but death. (101)

Denby frames the dialogue between Treadwell and Herzog as the puer-senex conversation, won by the senex, who survives.

Of course the same conversation—between spirit and matter, human and nature—applies to Treadwell's relations with the bears. It is not a simple dialogue. If Treadwell felt contaminated by civilization, he wished not to fly above it but rather to transform himself into its opposite. He believed the animals represented "perfection," and he was troubled by what he saw as his past failures. To enter the world of the bear is to escape mind, language, and complication. But the way he spoke to the bears—as children—suggests that what he really wanted was to return to childhood, to the "perfection" of a child's sense of wonder and protection. He wanted to be father and child, man and bear, spirit and flesh.

In this, Treadwell misunderstood the bears. They are not children. They are not human. Herzog interviews Sven Haakenson, a curator at the Alutiiq Museum, and a member of the Alutiiq tribe. "He tried to be a bear," Haakenson remarks. "You don't invade their territory. For him to act like a bear . . . [was an] act of disrespecting the bear and what the bear represents. . . . When you habituate bears to humans they think all humans are safe. . . . Treadwell crossed a boundary we have lived with for 7000 years." Other people Herzog interviewed also spoke of Treadwell's attempt to transgress a boundary, and this liminality is part of what fascinates the viewer. There is something sacred in that boundary. This transgression is not a case of puer and senex; if anything, it is more a kind of incest with the Great Mother.

But, for the native people, it is also a matter of respect, as Haakenson says. To invade the bears' territory is to try to make them into some version of a human, and that is a violation. In the traditions of many native people, projection onto nature is both unnecessary and rude. It's no more acceptable to project playfulness on a bear than it is to project savagery onto a human. Because their worldview incorporates both humans and nonhuman life not in a hierarchy but rather in a web, there is no need to "rescue" nature. We are all in this together. Each creature, including each human, has a role to play, and to confuse or neglect those roles is to fall into disorder, which threatens everyone.

Timothy Treadwell has many fellows: Ed Abbey, whose *Monkeywrench Gang* inspired a generation of environmental activists, never let on that his family were with him in the Arches over the many seasons that he distilled into the single summer of *Desert Solitaire*. Julia Butterfly Hill treesat in a thousand-year-old redwood (named Luna) for 738 days. Steve Irwin died in the course of his work; like Treadwell, a media gem, Irwin also promoted conservation and environmental causes. The puer energy that inspires all of these, and countless other idealistic lovers of nature, cannot be dismissed. The movement to preserve our habitat needs this energy, just as we also need the strategic intelligence of many people who immerse themselves in the daily soil of meetings, lawsuits, water quality testing, restoration, and scientific data gathering. Nature needs both puer and senex, and at this point, it's not at all clear how we are going to get ourselves out of the mess we've created. As James Hillman has written, "The ego today is a 'mind at the end of its tether.' All it can do is leave itself open to the possibility of grace and to a renewal which might then take place in its absence" (66).

Beavis and Butthead and Slacker Culture

At the opposite end of the spectrum from Treadwell's romantic puer posture is another stance in contemporary culture, the slacker. The term *slacker*, originally used pejoratively in relation to draft evaders in World Wars I and II, took on a new connotation following Richard Linklater's 1991 film, *Slacker*. Perhaps its most universal application refers to a taste for idleness in preference to paid employment. Wikipedia, the cooperative and organic Internet compendium of knowledge, says this about slackers:

> Apart from meaning lazy, *slacker* may also be used to insinuate habitual procrastination and a disorganized, slovenly lifestyle. Proponents of *slacker theory* assert that managing to survive by doing things at the last possible moment improves intellect as a compensatory way to cope, fashioning a wily yet lazy person. Similarly, a disorganized lifestyle may be superior to an organized one from the pragmatic perspective that a slacker will adapt to disorderliness by improving skills at memorization and at effortlessly rummaging, whereas actively organizing would require serious effort. Hence, the epithet *slacker*, while often used in the pejorative, is growingly signifying a complimentary, cerebral quality of an unconventional person.

Whoever wrote this definition appears pretty sympathetic to slackers.

Linklater's film represents a collection of young people in a series of episodes, none of which is connected to the others. Each, then, appears to be an iteration of the slacker persona. One runs over his mother, killing her. In the next episode, a gaggle of young people in a café speak of "intensity without mastery," the "obsessiveness of the utterly passive," the "immense effort required not to be creative." One character indulges a cynical rant about the space program and aliens, another about G. H. W. Bush; a third rails about a gunman on the highway and then tries to sell what she claims is a jar full of Madonna's pap smear. Character after character rants on something; no one listens. These randomly assembled short episodes share not only a quality of drifting, unfocused energy, lacking connection, engagement, or direction. They also share significant dissociation from nature.

In form and to a degree in content, the film appears to have been a source for *Beavis and Butthead*, cartoon teenagers created by Mike Judge. The show aired on MTV from 1993–97. Will you think worse of me if I confess that I never watched *Beavis and Butthead* when they were on TV? But when I told some friends about this paper, they assured me that I needed to see these two, and they were right. Beavis and Butthead are roughly drawn teen boys whose adventures in subverting authority enact the frustrated, depressed, libidinous, hopeless energy of the negative puer, the slacker. Their suburban habitat lacks any spaces that are not domesticated. In many ways *Beavis and Butthead* reflects a culture in which children have little or no contact with wild nature and very little unstructured play time. Like many young people today, they suffer from what the writer Richard Louv calls "nature deficit disorder." Their suburban world is so constructed that they have no opportunity to develop any imagination; only television provides that. They also live in a no-place. There is nothing distinctive about their habitat; as a result they live everywhere and nowhere. (The recent success of television shows identified with a city, such as the *CSI* series, suggests that Americans may be hungry for place-specificity.)

Their solipsism, desire to be cool, longing for easy money, and anarchic energy locate Beavis and Butthead (B&B henceforth) as puers; the bankruptcy of the authority figures determines the negative inflection of their puer energy. Their appeal to viewers came in large part from their skewering of the absurdities of the adult world; given that there are no alternatives to these authorities, Beavis and Butthead are destined for provisional lives. Louv has described how growing up without contact with nature contributes to childhood ADHD and obesity and interferes with both creativity and childhood functioning. While Beavis and Butthead are not obese, they certainly exhibit symptoms of ADHD and chronic cynicism. The rich imagination of Timothy Treadwell has been replaced by the fantasies of consumer culture, and Treadwell's puer energy has become impulse without control and a longing for something for nothing. B&B snicker constantly. They don't laugh, they snicker. Everything sounds like a double entendre to them, and of course the writers make it so. They are tricksters led around by their penises, and they are stupid and destructive. But they're also very funny.

Authority figures—teachers, police officers, the principal—on *B&B* are uniformly bankrupt, ineffectual, hypocritical, and pompous: all spew hot air. They are stupid, patronizing, mean, boring. Teachers (especially Mr. Buzzcut, the ex-marine) hate B&B. Mr. Anderson, who hires them to do his yard work and is too dense to realize he's hiring the same two boys in every episode, goes off to drink beer while B&B inhale paint thinner or break into his garage to get his backhoe. "Back when I was your age, I'd spend fourteen hours a day pruning trees and still have time to cut the lawn," Mr. Anderson tells them and then goes off to the bar while they figure that if he wants some of the branches cut, it would be even better to just cut down the whole tree. High on paint thinner, they paint his barn, his grass, his dog, while they crow enthusiastically, "Breakin' the law!" Viewing their massive destruction, they pronounce, "Cool!"

As in *Slacker*, episodes of *Beavis and Butthead* are short. Each tells a small story organized around B&B's anarchic energy, their subversion of the bankrupt authorities, and their general lustiness. Like the classic puer, they begin all sorts of projects, but all of them are attempts to get rich quick by collecting reward money for capturing escaped serial killers or getting themselves included in rich people's wills. Their attempts at gainful work end in chaos: they bulldoze the concrete into the hole excavated for Mr. Anderson's swimming pool; they put his dog in the dryer; and when the dog appears intoxicated afterwards, they jump in themselves. Their obliviousness to the damage they cause is very funny, and it's hard not to agree with their assessment of the authorities.

When it's not B&B themselves causing the laughs, the writers insert absurdities in the form of TV programs they're watching: *Asbestos in Obstetrics* plays at one point, and at another there's an advertisement for a correspondence school for judges. In one episode, a malfunction in the electrical grid causes a blackout. B&B take over the job of directing traffic, which leads to huge crashes and urban chaos. When someone asks them "What happened?" they respond, "Our TV broke." In another episode they encounter a fortune teller. Informed that a fortune teller "tells your future," they reply, "What's that?"

The world of *Beavis and Butthead* is divorced entirely from nature, and it has no credible authorities. How can they develop meaningful interior lives if they have no opportunity to experience the Other in nature? How can Beavis and Butthead grow up if they have no models? The puer energy that James Hillman admires needs a significant senex. There is none in the world of Beavis and Butthead. By way of a contrast, Homer Simpson may be a naive, lazy, and gullible doofus, living in a world full of shysters who promise free riches, but episodes of *The Simpsons* end by reaffirming the values of family and commitment.

Slacker culture expresses the rootlessness and placelessness of contemporary life, which, coupled with a media-inflamed desire for material goods, is a breeder of puers. John Gardner's 1971 novel *Grendel* gives us a more developed look at another facet of the psychological configuration.

Grendel: The Puer as Monster

If the nature-romantic is one iteration of the puer in our time, the cynic is another. *Grendel,* which retells the Beowulf story from the point of view of the monster, casts Grendel as himself a force of nature. Gardner has taken the Other and made him the subject of the story, rendering all the activities that give life meaning absurd. Like a teenager looking at his stupid parents' phony world, Grendel is unconstrained by filaments of affection, loyalty, or conviction, free to devour and terrify at will. When occasionally he discovers some sympathy with humans, he suffers pangs of conscience, but they are always short-lived. He can see through authority, through heroism, romantic love, art, and religion. They are all a sham. If all the structures of life are corrupt, there's no reason not to please yourself. Of course it's lonely. Treadwell was lonely, too. But if the Grizzly Man thought people are destructive, Grendel thinks they are delicious.

Before there were highways and factories, antibiotics, and plasma TVs, nature *was* scary. In *Beowulf*, the great poem of Anglo-Saxon England, we see how premodern Western European people embodied their fear of the unknown and the undesirable, both in nature and in themselves. John Gardner's *Grendel* revisits the myth, this time from the point of view of the monster. In it we see how overdeveloped reason and a language that has lost any connection with the world produce a puer who is also a monster. At the same time, Gardner's prose makes him charming, a winsome outsider who calls to mind the puer Marie-Louise von Franz describes as "very agreeable to talk with" (4), especially if you are the reader and not a member of Hrothgar's court.

In the original *Beowulf*, Grendel operates as a stand-in for instinctual nature. He makes his "joyless home in the fen-slopes" (37). The narrative describes him as "a rover of the borders, one who held the moors, fen and fastness" (28). Grendel's home is "the mere of the water-monsters . . . [where] the water was boiling with blood" (38). Grendel is identified with "the secret land, the wolf-slopes, the windy headlands, the dangerous fen-paths where the mountain stream goes down under the darkness of the hills, the flood under the earth" (44). In this welter of images the coincidence of darkness, water, and fear repeats. The *Beowulf* poet is believed to have written the poem in the eighth century about events that probably took place in the fifth. For an audience of island people, of course, the sea held many terrors, as the number and variety of sea monsters in legends testify. But inland waters—fens, swamps, bogs, lakes—also inspired terror, menace, or at least distrust. Insects breed there, and slimy things. Ordinary language reflects our dis-ease in many ways: we feel swamped; we get bogged down; we suffer cold feet.

The power of the story of Beowulf is undeniable; the world it creates is almost tangible. At its heart is a mystery, embodied in the monsters Grendel and his mother. They are introduced in this passage:

> The grim spirit was called Grendel, known as a rover of the borders, one who held the moors, fen and fastness. Unhappy creature, he lived for a time in the home of the monsters' race, after God had condemned them as kin of Cain. The Eternal Lord avenged the murder in which he slew Abel. Cain had no pleasure in that feud, but He banished him far from mankind, the

Ruler, for that misdeed. From him sprang all bad breeds, trolls and elves and monsters—likewise the giants who for a long time strove with God: He paid them their reward for that. (28)

This interesting passage suggests the doubleness of Grendel: he feels painful human feelings of exclusion for a crime that he did not commit, but he is also an agent of evil, the offspring of God's vengeance. He is human—descended from Cain—but deformed, morally monstrous. In every way, Grendel's associations with darkness, rage, gluttony, and death—as well as his location in the dark, cold, wet, and frightening "wasteland" (44)—contrast with the light, music, hospitality, and treasure associated with civilization and Heorot. Inside are wine, women (and the comforts of home), and song; outside are darkness, fens, moors, and monsters.

In *Beowulf*, the hero conquers the monster; nature and instinct have to be controlled for civilization and consciousness to develop. Beowulf is no puer but a proper hero who acts for his culture to bring order and safety in a frightening world. By the time Gardner wrote *Grendel*, however, consciousness itself had become a problem, a rationalism so consuming that it had become monstrous. With Grendel as the central character, Beowulf appears only in the final scenes. Like his namesake, this Grendel is an outsider, an exile. He is, moreover, a puer, frustrated by language and nature from ever entering a world he longs for, and Emil Antonucci's illustrations sketch him in suggestive doodles: hominid, fanged, furry.

At the same time, Gardner's Grendel is a monster with which I can identify, at least more than I can identify with Timothy Treadwell. Grendel is clothed in language, conscious through language, slippery with language, coy, deceitful, plaintive, posturing, and categorical by turns. I don't know what to believe about him. And he knows that, speaks to me directly, charms me, enjoys my discomfort. The whole narrative exists to construct a self for Grendel; in that, it resembles *Grizzly Man*, and indeed it's like the story I tell myself about myself to which I am the primary, if not the only, audience. Sometimes I believe myself; sometimes I snort at my posturing. But Grendel, unlike me, lives in radical isolation; he has no one to talk to, no peer; everything except his mother is Other, and he quickly arrives at a solipsism that scorns a universe that ignores him.

Grendel is an elaborate, extended enactment of a blocked puer energy that grows from the mechanistic view of the universe, that denies people are connected to one another, to other species, to the planet. All he can see is

the cold mechanics of the stars. Space hurls outward, falconswift, mounting like an irreversible injustice, a final disease. The cold night air is reality at last:

indifferent to me as a stone face carved on a high cliff wall to show that the world is abandoned. So childhood too feels good at first, before one happens to notice the terrible sameness, age after age. (9)

Chaos is his element, and he watches the world of the humans who struggle to create order and make meaning. As the puer who prefers the possibilities of chaos to the safety of order, Grendel's antagonist is King Hrothgar, with whom he has engaged, as he tells us on the first page, in a twelve-year-long "idiotic war" (5). The lights and music of Heorot draw him, but he remains an outsider, not by choice but by nature. What he cannot join he scorns. What he cannot believe he ridicules. His mechanistic vision of the universe disables hope and meaning. Grendel is reason cut off from soul, and as such, he's monstrous.

This condition in many ways makes Grendel a character who would be at home in a postmodern world that only laughs at the earnestness of someone like Treadwell. Culture seems to Grendel a tempting lie: courage, beauty, virtue, even politics all shams. Grendel is too smart to be drawn in; he aches too much to be content outside. In this he resembles all of us some of the time. Mostly I live my daily life in Heorot with Hrothgar; I achieve some community, cherish some values, make some meaning in my life. There's some menace outside my shelter, but I go on. (I'm street smart.) I do so with some irony, of course, but it's usually not disabling. Hope mostly trumps despair. How could I live, if I really knew what we really do know—about terrifying wars in distant places where real people are maimed, tortured, imprisoned, and killed, about children burned and beaten by their parents, about the deep poverty of people on the other side of my city, about the devastation of rainforests by oil companies, about the catastrophe that threatens our planet from global warming? There's a sense in which we're all caught between Hrothgar and Grendel: we live as though it mattered what we do, as though story and courage and beauty could hold off the night. But we suspect, somewhere, in the back of our minds, that it doesn't. In a cosmic sense, we're all dust. We watch ourselves getting and spending, and we snicker.

Like his forebear, Grendel lives in a mere, in an underground hall beneath a lake inhabited by firesnakes. I am not, however, to identify him with the beasts or with simple instinct; that much he makes clear right at the beginning:

Do not think my brains are squeezed shut, like the ram's, by the roots of horns. Flanks atremble, eyes like stones, he stares at as much of the world as he can see and feels it surging in him, filling his chest as the melting snow fills dried-out creekbeds, ticking his gross, lopsided balls and charging his brains with the same unrest that made him suffer last year at this time, and the year before, and the year before that. (He's forgotten them all.) . . . "Why can't these creatures discover a little dignity?" I ask the sky. The sky says nothing, predictably. I make a face, uplift a defiant middle finger, and give an obscene little kick. The sky ignores me, forever unimpressed. Him too I hate, the same as I hate these brainless budding trees, these brattling birds. (6)

No, Grendel is not to be confused with a force of nature; or does he protest too much? He invites response; his tone of supercilious amusement outlines him and sets him apart from the riot of the rest of indiscriminate nature.

But in the passage that precedes this, Grendel has pitched a hissy just because an old ram wouldn't leave when he asks him to: "I stamp. I hammer the ground with my fists. I hurl a skull-size stone at him. He will not budge. I shake my two hairy fists at the sky and I let out a howl so unspeakable that the water at my feet turns sudden ice and even I myself am left uneasy" (5). Both these passages represent the quality of painful isolation that characterizes Grendel throughout. Like Treadwell he is lonely, in part because he is painfully self-conscious. He surprises and scares himself. He gives in to impulses and then rushes to distance himself from them, and his view of nature is as bleakly ironic as his estimate of himself. He talks to himself, acts out his story, inflates and deflates himself. He is alone.

Von Franz describes the puer as suffering from too great a dependency on the mother. Early in the novel, Grendel tells us that "of all the creatures I knew, in those days, only my mother really looked at me. Stared at me as if to consume me, like a troll. She loved me, in some mysterious sense. I understood without her speaking it. I was her creation. We were one thing" (17). Grendel later recounts a childhood experience of separation from his mother that formed his lonely view of the world: he stepped by mistake into a cleft in a tree and got his foot wedged there. Unable to free himself, he wailed for his mother, who didn't come. Everything ignored him: the whole universe was "an infuriating clutter of not-my-mother" (19). Even the bull that tried to gore him, tearing up his knee, acted merely on instinct, not by choice.

Trapped in matter, Grendel thinks,

I understood that the world was nothing: a mechanical chaos of casual, brute enmity on which we stupidly impose our hopes and fears. I understood that, finally and absolutely, I alone exist. All the rest, I saw, is merely what pushes me, or what I push against, blindly—as blindly as all that is not myself pushes back. I create the whole universe, blink by blink.—An ugly god pitifully dying in a tree! (21–22)

I-I-I. Solipsism is the thesis of Grendel's existence, where, "The world resists me and I resist the world. That's all there is. The mountains are what I define them as" (28). In rhythmic, dense, metaphorical language, he decries his isolation by language: "Talking, talking, spinning a spell, pale skin of words that closes me in like a coffin" (15). This is the outsider's view of himself, the exile's; like adolescents everywhere, Grendel feels superior to the adult world and longs for it, as well. It is a familiar posture in postmodern literature, the multiple self, socially constructed, self-conscious through and in language, skeptical that there is anything outside the text.

Indeed, Gardner constructed Grendel as an expression of the nihilism of Sartre's *Being and Nothingness*, an example of "the rational soul gone perverse" (Silesky 164). This rationalism is the thinking outcome of the split from nature and the necessity to control it. To be imprisoned in language, in culture, is to be separate from, most often, "above," the rest of nature, which remains stubbornly Other. Timothy Treadwell felt that he had to reject civilization in order to embrace the bears. If "I-I-I" is Grendel's theme, his was "Thou-thou-thou," in a passionate, desperate effort to lose his human mind and become "pure." These seem to me to be two sides of the coin of a dualist divorce from the world.

Anthony Stevens argues that, when parents withdraw their projections from the child prematurely, "the result can be the development of *anxious attachment* and the start of a quest for parental substitutes, the child remaining stuck meanwhile in adolescent psychology" (118). Grendel's isolation, in this view, expresses his entrapment in the puer, as surely as his being stuck in the tree. Grendel watches Hrothgar, the old King, and the clumsy but also familiar crowd at Heorot, where three characters, each representing a different possibility for meaning, tempt him to give up his lonely superiority. The first and most potent is the Shaper, the poet whose songs and stories remake the world. The others are Unferth, the hero, and Wealtheow, the beautiful queen of Hrothgar.

In a flashback early in the narrative, Grendel remembers listening as the blind Shaper recounts the history of the Scyldings, a history of savagery ("no wolf was so vicious to other wolves" [32]) that Grendel—and indeed the thanes assembled in the hall—had personally witnessed. In the poet's song Grendel discovers the power of art: "The man had changed the world, had torn up the past by its thick, gnarled roots and had transmuted it, and they, who knew the truth, remembered it his way—and so did I" (43). Such is the power of this language that the poet can take lies and make them feel true, can take scraps of old stories and the victors' word about midnight raids and make them glorious.

Before he hears the bard, Grendel describes how Hrothgar's thanes "hacked down trees in widening rings around their central halls and blistered the land with peasant huts and pigpen fences till the forest looked like an old dog dying of mange" (40). As he returns from his evening outside the hall, entranced by the scop, he revises his earlier description: "The moors their axes had stripped of trees glowed silver in the moonlight, and the yellow lights of peasant huts were like scattered jewels on the ravendark cloak of a king. I was so filled with sorrow and tenderness I could hardly have found it in my heart to snatch a pig!" (44)

The Shaper inspires Hrothgar to build Heorot, "a glorious meadhall whose light would shine to the ends of the ragged world" (47). Grendel watches, divided in his mind: "I knew very well that all he said was ridiculous, not light for their darkness but flattery, illusion, a vortex pulling them from sunlight to heat, a kind of midsummer burgeoning, waltz to the sickle. Yet I was swept up" (48). Grendel tries embracing the poet's path, but he can't do it. All he feels in himself is "eternal posturing" (49), a divided mind performing for itself, aware of its own self-deceit. You can almost hear the envious academic in Grendel's voice, watching the accumulation of power and wealth by the inhabitants of the corrupt world of profit. Indeed, Gardner remarked that when he began *Grendel*, "'I started out thinking I was going to do a sort of tirade against the intellectual stuff you get in the universities—this locked in, systematic thought. But then in order to make him an interesting character, I had to become more and more sympathetic'" (qtd. in Silesky 166).

Grendel understands that his posturing is a form of shaping, constructing a world out of words, yet he senses that the poet is "moved by something beyond his power, and the words stitched together out of ancient songs, the scenes interwoven out of dreary tales, made a vision without seams, an image of himself yet not-himself beyond the need of any shaggy old gold-friend's pay: the projected possible" (49). What the poet here seems to understand escapes poor Grendel: he can be himself yet not-himself. He can open himself to a power beyond the caviling ego. For Grendel the not-himself part, the assent to transformation just feels phony. Still, it's powerful. Like Treadwell—who wished to renounce his human form in order to become a bear, whose innocence seemed to mock the monstrous temptations of consciousness—Grendel would like to believe, even if it means he has to believe that he is one of "the dark side . . . the terrible race God cursed"(51).

The Shaper tortures Grendel in his isolation with phantasms of meaning and community, but the dragon puts an end to that. After hearing the Shaper, Grendel feels a "presence," cold and dark, that lurks behind his rejection of the Shaper's stories. Revolted by his mother's wordless need ("She whimpered, scratched at the nipple I had not sucked in years. She was pitiful, foul, her smile a jagged white tear in the firelight: waste" [55]), Grendel leaves the cave and falls "like a stone through earth and sea, toward the dragon" (56). This fall, the complement to puer's flight, leads Grendel to the philosophy that will inflect his monstrousness and define him thenceforward as a cynic, slacker, and negative puer. One critic, Norma L. Hutman, remarks that "the monster represents some older form of ourselves, that lone, chaos-proclaiming, violent alien to society from which our fraternal, ordered, ethical selves have sprung"

(25). For those who have left behind the puer energy of rebellion and rejection of the social order, both Treadwell and Grendel are useful reminders of the potentials both for violence and for immersion that still stir in even the most orderly heart.

Clearly juxtaposed in the text with the Shaper, the dragon expresses a cosmic indifference born of omniscience. After dazzling Grendel with philosophy, he settles down to describe the world as "'A swirl in the stream of time. A temporary gathering of bits, a few random dust specks, so to speak—pure metaphor, you understand—then by chance a vast floating cloud of dustspecks, an expanding universe'" (70). That's all it is. Brute, mechanical, mindless, meaningless, it is a universe without God, without purpose, one where foolish humans "'rush across chasms on spiderwebs, and sometimes they make it, and that, they think, settles that! I could tell you a thousand tiresome stories of their absurdity'" (64). To Grendel's protests that one can at least be ethical, the dragon wonders why? Why not frighten people? He calls Grendel "'the brute existent by which [people] learn to define themselves. The exile, captivity, death they shrink from—the blunt facts of their mortality, their abandonment—that's what you make them recognize, embrace! You *are* mankind, or man's condition: inseparable as the mountain-climber and the mountain. If you withdraw, you'll instantly be replaced. Brute existents, you know, are a dime a dozen'" (73). The dragon's negative senex energy confirms Grendel's cynicism. In a meaningless universe, one might as well hoard gold. The dragon's worldview, moreover, leaves Grendel with a charm: weapons cannot wound him. No steel, no words can pierce that cynicism.

Two other forces tempt Grendel: heroism and love. Treadwell, too, had to joust with these: he wished to be the hero of bears, tilting against the U.S. Park Service, and he ruminated over his failures with women, proclaiming rather vigorously his heterosexuality. While Treadwell seemed to take these postures seriously, Grendel characteristically mocks. Unferth is the thane who would be hero; his grand words and grander gesture send Grendel into fits of laughter. "'For many months, unsightly monster, you've murdered men as you pleased in Hrothgar's hall,'" Unferth declares. "'Prepare to fall, foul thing! This one red hour makes your reputation or mine!'" (83) Grendel, "wickedly smiling," replies: "'I've never seen a live hero before. I thought they were only in poetry. Ah, ah, it must be a terrible burden, though, being a hero—glory reaper, harvester of monsters! Everybody always watching you, weighing you, seeing if you're still heroic'" (84). Shortly Grendel is pelting Unferth with apples, reducing the hero to a crying boy. Overpowered and undermined, Unferth is unmanned.

Grendel refuses to perform when the antagonist Unferth needs to be a hero. Instead, he enacts an indifferent universe for Unferth who dribbles off into what sounds like a sophomore lit-crit essay: "'Except in the life of a hero, the whole world's meaningless. The hero sees values beyond what's possible. That's the *nature* of a hero. It kills him, of course, ultimately. But it makes the whole struggle of humanity worthwhile'" (89). Reduced to rhetoric like this, heroism itself seems to have been put on the discount rack. Grendel gets the last laugh by carrying Unferth, unharmed, back to Hrothgar's meadhall. From now on the two are ironic mirrors of each other, each immune—Grendel by the dragon's charm and Unferth by Grendel's mocking refusal to kill him. "So much for heroism," Grendel concludes (90). We hear no more of Grendel, Ruiner of Meadhalls, Wrecker of Kings. However, in deconstructing heroism, he knocks out his own illusions, too.

If heroism attracts him only momentarily, love and beauty have a greater magnetism. Like the Shaper, Wealtheow exerts a charm on Grendel. Given to Hrothgar by her brother to cement a truce, she draws Grendel in with her gracious self-sacrifice. Almost immediately, however, he looks at his mother, who

> would gladly have given her life to end my suffering—horrible, humpbacked, carp-toothed creature, eyes on fire with useless, mindless love. Who could miss the grim parallel? So the lady below would give, had given, her life for those she loved. So would any simpering, eyelash-batting female in her court, given the proper setup, the minimal conditions. The smell of the dragon lay around me like sulphurous smoke. (102)

As an outsider, Grendel sees what humans deny about themselves; he is not exactly their shadow, but he sees their shadows—the tawdry facts the Shaper transforms, the commonality of self-sacrifice in which Wealtheow takes her place.

Like the adolescent slacker, he sees the adult world as bankrupt, the authorities as pretenders. To him, only shadow is real. Everything else—love, art, heroism—is self-deception. In a sense, the whole novel is an extended meditation on what it feels like to be Grendel. Since Grendel's is the only mind I encounter in the novel, and since he sees both himself and the others so clearly, at least in the sense that he pierces surfaces as easily as he bites off heads, I find myself caught up, sympathetic. In lots of ways, Grendel mirrors postmodern consciousness.

First, of course, there's the mechanical universe. Modern science has taught us to see ourselves as inhabitants of a universe too large to imagine and composed of particles too small for thought. From such a point of view, my hopes, my fantasies, my imaginations, my longings seem absurd, incommensurate with what I know of deep time, the big bang, and entropy. In virtually the same moment I feel a longing for meaning and I laugh at myself for falling into that old bag. Then there's language. I recognize how language both shapes and encloses me, structuring my perceptions, my preferences, my experience of myself. Grendel feels himself "talking, talking, spinning a spell, pale skin of words that closes me in like a coffin" (15). Even—especially—at emotional moments he cannot take himself seriously because he watches himself posturing, playing his feeling to himself. Grendel's egocentrism is an extreme form of the belief that there is nothing I can know apart from the language with which I know it.

If this is what it feels like to be Grendel, what is the Grendel-force? The dragon called him a "brute existent." He defines himself in opposition to the civilization that excludes him; his enemies define themselves through him. "I am hardly blind to the absurdity," Grendel says; "Form is function. What will we call the Hrothgar-Wrecker when Hrothgar has been wrecked?" (91) he asks himself and proceeds into a self-dramatizing monologue that includes three little songs expressing the entwined relationship:

> Pity poor Hrothgar
> Grendel's foe!
> Pity poor Grendel,
> O,O,O!

> Grendel is crazy
> O,O,O!
> Thinks old Hrothgar
> Makes it snow!

> Pity poor Grengar,
> Hrothdel's foe!
> Down goes the whirlpool:
> Eek! No, no! (92)

Grendel and Hrothgar, shadow and substance, puer and senex, but which is which? When Grendel plays at being the Shaper, he mis-shapes everything, blurring boundaries with his slithery words. Grendel has "made" Hrothgar, the king defined by his trials.

Thus, stories are defined by their endings. Werner Herzog's film would most likely not have reached much of an audience had Timothy Treadwell not died, and Herzog has to make that death the ratifying fact about Treadwell. However, because *Grendel* is fiction, Gardner can fashion a force to oppose Grendel's deadly ironies: the regenerative power of nature. In the deepest dark of winter, all possibilities of meaning exhausted, when "the days are an arrow in a dead man's chest" (125), and "the trees are dead and only the deepest religion can break through time and believe they'll revive" (125), Grendel senses that "Something is coming, strange as spring" (126).

"Something," of course, is Beowulf. He comes as a force, as an intuition, as a mystery—as spring. Beowulf is "big as a mountain, moving with his forest" (153). The terms in which Grendel describes him are drawn from nature:

> He had a strange face that, little by little, grew unsettling to me: it was a face, or so it seemed for an instant, from a dream I had almost forgotten. The eyes slanted downward, never blinking, unfeeling as a snake's. He had no more beard than a fish. He smiled as he spoke, but it was as if the gentle voice, the childlike yet faintly ironic smile were holding something back, some magician-power that could blast stone cliffs to ashes as lightning blasts trees. (154)

A snake, a fish, lightning. Hardly warm and fuzzy—hardly human. But Grendel recognizes Beowulf as "an outsider not only among the Danes but everywhere" (154). Snakes, fish, and lightning are not unfamiliar to Grendel, who navigates the firesnakes, lives beneath the fish. Beowulf has "grotesquely muscled shoulders—stooped, naked despite the cold, sleek as the belly of a shark and as rippled with power as the shoulders of a horse . . . as if the body of the stranger were a ruse, a disguise for something infinitely more terrible" (155).

This piling on of animal metaphors suggests that Beowulf, not Grendel, acts as a natural force. Indeed, that seems to be how Grendel understands him, as a man of a single mind. At Heorot, Beowulf narrates his famous victory over the sea monsters in terms both simple and unself-conscious; Grendel reflects: "He believed every word he said. I understood at last the look in his eyes. He was insane" (162). He specifies that insanity in the next breath: "The madman's single-mindedness would be useful in a monster fight" (163).

It is right that the hero should be single-minded. Grendel's woe has all along been his split, his cynicism. Infected with the dragon's vision of cosmic entropy, drawn against his will to the humans' simpler bulwarks against despair, Grendel could only kill what he could not share. In his solipsism he believed himself alone in the universe, everything else defined only as not-Grendel (or "not-my-mama"). He could name absurdity but not transcend it. He could identify his instincts but took no pleasure from them. He pierced through the fragile skins of art and love and action. If they couldn't withstand his cynicism, they had no worth for him. Either the dragon was wrong or the humans were, and the dragon wasn't wrong.

Self-conscious, self-mocking even in his final battle, Grendel stalks Heorot one last time; he could have chosen not to go. Beowulf's grip closes "like a dragon's jaws" on his arm and Grendel sees them "grotesquely shaking hands—dear long-lost brother, kinsman-thane" (168–69). Just as Grendel's isolation has led him to a kind of madness, Beowulf's heroism is also beyond the norm of sanity. In Beowulf, Grendel has met his match.

As they battle, Grendel sings what the *Beowulf* poet calls his "terrible song, song without triumph" (37): "*A meaningless swirl in the stream of time, a temporary gathering of bits, a few random specks, a cloud . . .*" (Gardner 170). Over and over he repeats these words, his defense against communion. Beowulf responds:

> *As you see it it is, while the seeing lasts, dark nightmare-history, time-as-coffin; but where the water was rigid there will be fish, and men will survive on their flesh till spring. It's coming, my brother. Believe it or not. Though you murder the world, turn plains to stone, transmogrify life into I and it, strong searching roots will crack your cave and rain will cleanse it: The world will burn green, sperm build again. My promise. Time is the mind, the hand that makes (fingers on harpstrings, hero-swords, the acts, the eyes of queens). By that I kill you. . . . Grendel, Grendel! You make the world by whispers, second by second. Are you blind to that? Whether you make it a grave or a garden of roses is not the point. Feel the wall: is it not hard? He smashes me against it, breaks open my forehead. Hard, yes! Observe the hardness, write it down in careful runes. Now sing of walls! Sing!* (170–71)

If everything is meaningless, Grendel is free to "murder the world, turn plains to stone." His indifference to life is like that of the mechanistic worldview that has justified despoiling the planet; it leads Grendel to inflate his own power.

However, Beowulf shifts the focus. He does not deny the prison of time, and he acknowledges the seduction of language, but his lyric philosophy insists on the power of renewal, nature's power, the reality of the world, the connection that Grendel would deny with his "I and it." "I understand him all right, make no mistake," Grendel says, "Understand his lunatic theory of matter and mind, the chilly intellect, the hot imagination, blocks and builder, reality as stress" (172). But, dying, he clings to his viewpoint: "It was an accident . . . blind, mindless, mechanical" (173).

Still, he feels something close to ecstasy as he approaches death: "I look down, down, into bottomless blackness, feeling the dark power moving in me like an ocean current, some monster inside me, deep sea wonder, dread night monarch astir in his cave, moving me slowly to my voluntary tumble into death" (173). The "dark power" moving him to death may be the dragon, but it may also be an encounter with a reality beyond his ego, both "wonder" and "dread night monarch." In any case, his tumble into death is voluntary: an action, rather than a refusal to act, as he refused to kill Unferth, the Shaper, or the Queen. For once, Grendel seems almost to choose.

Gardner closes the novel with a nicely ambiguous farewell from Grendel: "'Poor Grendel's had an accident,' I whisper. '*So may you all*'" (174). A curse or a benediction? Or a prophecy?

Beowulf comes to Grendel as a menace, but he comes into the narrative as a possibility, a hope. Gardner allies him with nature; what he wields against Grendel is the promise of spring, of renewal, for "the world will burn green, sperm build again." But throughout the novel, the dragon has called Grendel a force of nature, a "brute existent," and he has been invulnerable and overpowering. So what is Gardner about here? Which one is the force of nature—Grendel or Beowulf?

One of the ways Beowulf is different from the Scyldings is that he does not fear Grendel. In that respect, he establishes a non-dualist relationship with Grendel-as-nature. If Grendel's nihilism has allowed him to see past the surfaces of human values, the humans involved heretofore in the story have regarded Grendel as monstrous and terrifying. The first time he exposes himself to Hrothgar's court, before he has killed anyone, Grendel has just heard the Shaper tell the story of Cain and Abel. "And I, Grendel, was the dark side . . . the terrible race God cursed" (51), he thinks, but nonetheless he is so moved ("Oh what a conversion!") that he staggers toward the hall, groaning, "'Mercy! Peace!" (51). The humans rush from the hall to attack him, and he understands that they could kill him—would kill him if he gave them a chance. He goes on to terrorize them, but only after they have cast him out (in both mythic and specific terms).

Grendel is, in that respect, the vengeance of nature, its refusal to be conquered, its pain at being disfigured; Grendel is Katrina. When Beowulf comes into this narrative he is a synthetic force, the promise of a new way of being in the world that does not obliterate either the senex or the puer, either human culture or nature, but in his synthesis transcends them. Gardner can't say much about such a way of being, but I think the novel offers some glimmers.

The Beowulf story is ancient, close to myth. "Myth," Jung writes, "is not fiction: it consists of facts that are continually repeated and can be observed over and over again. It is something that happens to man, and men have mythical fates just as much as the Greek heroes do" (96). The patterned and repetitive nature of myths suggests their source in the nature of humans. They are, to use the language of chaos theory, "strange attractors," that "[combine] pattern with unpredictability, confinement with orbits that never repeat themselves" (Hayles 9). Jung talks of myths as riverbeds through which psychic energy flows. If it is the nature of oaks to grow tall and spread their branches, it is the nature of humans to act out mythic patterns.

If Jung is correct that people have mythical fates, then you and I may both have Grendels that make nightly raids on us. We may even have an inner Timmy Treadwell. We probably need to go at it with our Grendels—and our

Timmys—over and over again. But at least our Grendel-nature is familiar, our Timmy-selves vestiges of a romantic adolescence. What will our new Beowulf look like? What new myths do we need in order to grow a new consciousness? James Hillman claims that "archetype provides the basis for uniting . . . fact and meaning" (33) and that "myth is the language of ambivalence" (65). In the eighth century, the *Beowulf* story encouraged the development of senex consciousness and an orderly society; in the twentieth, it questioned the exaggeration of that consciousness into the Saturnine dragon-logic of absurdity. The *Beowulf* we need now will need to hold mind and nature in tension, privileging neither but moving beyond dualism. It is a heroic challenge.

Theodore Roszak, in *The Voice of the Earth: An Exploration of Ecopsychology*, argues:

> The modern industrial societies have been reared on a vision of nature that teaches people they are a mere accident in a galactic wilderness: "strangers and afraid" in a world they never made. What stance in life can they then take but one of fear, anxiety, even hostility toward the natural world? . . . The picture of the cosmos we carry in our minds can dictate a range of existential conditions. We may live sunk in bleak, defensive despair or we may find ourselves gracefully at home in the world. In addition to *what* we know, there is *how* we know, the spirit in which we address the world. (40)

Perhaps the Beowulf consciousness John Gardner implies in *Grendel* can help us "find ourselves gracefully at home in the world." I believe that it's a consciousness that loves, trusts, and inhabits nature, including the swampy places, the scary spots, the shadows; it's a consciousness that understands humans to be part of nature, not above it or separate, but truly members of a community. This consciousness embraces myth and includes but transcends both reason and instinct. It is a kind of negotiation between Timothy Treadwell and Grendel. Ultimately, becoming conscious is an ethical issue. When we stop projecting our "monstrous" nature onto Others or the land, then we can choose to extend love and community to include those humans who had been banished and, beyond the human, to embrace in community the animals, plants, soils, and waters with whom we must live in mutual dependency.

Works Cited

Atkinson, Michael. "Claws and Effect: Bad news bears: Obsession meets feral reality in Werner Herzog's frontier disaster doc." *Village Voice* 9 August 2005. http://www.village voice.com/film/0532,atkinson1,66670,20.html.

Beowulf. Trans. E. Talbot Donaldson. *The Norton Anthology of English Literature*. 6th Ed. Vol. 1. New York: Norton, 1993. 27–68.

Denby, David. "Loners: 'Broken Flowers' and 'Grizzly Man.'" *The New Yorker* combined issue 8 August 2005 and 15 August 2005: 100–01.

Gardner, John. *Grendel*. 1971. New York: Vintage Books, 1989.

Grizzly Man. Dir. Werner Herzog. Lions Gate Films, 2005.

Hayles, N. Katherine, ed. *Chaos and Order*. Chicago: U Chicago P, 1991.

Hillman, James. *Senex & Puer*. Putnam, CT: Spring, 2005.

Hutman, Norma. "Even Mothers Have Monsters: A Study of *Beowulf* and John Gardner's *Grendel*." *Mosaic* 9.1 (1975): 19-31.

Judge, Mike, creator. *Beavis and Butthead*. Music Television (MTV) Animation, 1993–97.

Jung, C. G. *Answer to Job*. New York: Meridian, 1960.

Linklater, Richard. *Slacker*. Detour Filmproduction, 1991.

Louv, Richard. *Last Child in the Woods: Saving our Children from Nature Deficit Disorder*. Chapel Hill: Algonquin, 2005.

Roszak, Theodore. *The Voice of the Earth: An Exploration of Ecopsychology*. New York: Touchstone, 1992.

Silesky, Barry. *John Gardner: Literary Outlaw*. Chapel Hill: Algonquin, 2004.

"Slacker." *Wikipedia*. 30 November 2006 http://en.wikipedia.org/wiki/Slacker.

Stevens, Anthony. *On Jung*. London: Penguin, 1990.

von Franz, Marie-Louise. *Puer Aeternus*. Santa Monica: Sigo, 1970.

Grounding Icarus

Puer Aeternus *and the Suicidal Urge*

DUSTIN EATON

> . . . what was normal for a child is improper in an adult.
>
> —C. G. Jung, *Collected Works 8*

A man sits in the kitchen of his sprawling Seattle home and addresses a letter: "To Boddah" (Cross 339). Using a fine-tipped red marker, the man writes about the mysterious, chronic pain in his stomach, the loss of enthusiasm he feels toward his work, and his frustrated urge to lead a passionate, authentic life free of compromise. He calls himself a "sad little sensitive, unappreciative, Pisces, Jesus man!" and reminds those he leaves behind that "its better to burn out than to fade away." In one sentence, the man claims that he simply "loves people too much," while in another that he has become "hateful towards all humans in general." In an aside to his wife and infant daughter, the man apologizes for the act he is about to commit and writes the words "I love you" in letters twice as big as the rest. He begs his family not to follow him and promises them that when they need him, he will be "at their alter." The man signs the letter with three simple words: "Peace, Love," and "Empathy" (Cross 339).

Removing a hidden panel from his bedroom closet, the man pulls out a Remington shotgun and a case of shells. Retreating to his greenhouse, he sits on the cold tile floor where, removing the letter from his coat pocket, he stabs it through with the red marker and lets it dangle from a bag of potting soil. After a final drag on his cigarette and a final sip from a can of root beer, the man injects himself with a double dose of heroin, places the shotgun in his mouth, and pulls the trigger (Cross 341).

So ends the life of Kurt Cobain, the twenty-seven-year-old poet, singer, husband, and father whose searing music almost restored the lost vitality of a generation. More than a decade later, it is hard to overestimate the effect the music of Kurt's band, Nirvana—like The Beatles thirty years earlier—has had on the word's popular culture. By the late 1980s, the American musical landscape had been reduced from the soaring jazz improvisations of John Coltrane, the take-no-prisoners funk of Motown, and the hide-your-daughters rhythm and blues of Elvis Presley, to a scene saturated with corporate hair-metal and elevator Muzak. In response—as much out of collective instinct as conscious rebellion—a small group of nattily clad Seattle artists, poets, and musicians created a new sound: Grunge, named for the ubiquitous anti-fashion of its earliest proponents. A sound characterized by punk chord progressions, thick bass riffs, and a throbbing, ritualized drumbeat, the underground movement broke onto the American airwaves with Nirvana's 1991 single "Smells Like Teen Spirit." Becoming the anthem of the newly come of age, newly disenfranchised "Generation X," "Smells Like Teen Spirit," Nirvana, and its lead singer/song-writer Kurt Cobain became overnight sensations.

Over the next three years Cobain, like the doomed Icarus, would soar to the heights of artistic expression and fame, only to fall into the yearning abyss of depression, drug addiction, and suicide. What makes Cobain's fate archetypal, even inevitable, is his continuous identification with the *puer aeternus*, the eternal boy: a psychological complex wherein an adult male comes to identify himself with his own preadolescent ego, as well as with the archetype of the divine child. Such men live out the seemingly autonomous archetypal pattern of behavior of the *puer aeternus*, which includes a fascination with the trappings of childhood, issues of emotional dependency, and the overwhelming requirement never to be "pinned down" by inauthentic work or relationships. If the autonomy of an archetype is nothing more than the fate that befalls an individual blessed or cursed enough to be wholly possessed by one, then a *puer aeternus*—a man wholly possessed by the archetype of the divine child—must die, either psychologically, in which case the death is followed by a rebirth, or physically, in which case the act is dreadfully permanent.

When we consider the case history of a suicide, the unique "soul history" of the individual must be honored, while at the same time the historic biography can be used as a lens through which to view a collective phenomenon. What it means to *be* the individual Kurt Cobain, and what were the private reasons he chose to take his own life, will forever remain a mystery, but we may, by considering his biography and public life, come closer to understanding the archetypal pattern of the *puer aeternus* and its complex relationship to suicide.

James Hillman writes:

> One needs to read the biography of artists, because biographies show what they did with their traumas; they show what can be done . . . by the imagination with hatred, with resentment, with bitterness, with feelings of being useless and inferior and worthless. (*We've Had* 30)

The *puer aeternus* is a complex made up of two opposing urges—the urge to create, and the urge to destroy. While Kurt Cobain, like many *pueri*, channeled his "feelings of being useless and inferior" into his artwork and music, he also projected the fire of his resentment and bitterness into the destruction of his own body. Like all true *pueri*, Cobain's entire life can thus be understood as one long tug-of-war between the poles of empathy and apathy—one long denial of the inferiority of the ego to the Self—one long suicidal crisis. In this chapter, I will present the life of Kurt Cobain as a paradigmatic representation of the phenomenon of puer-flightiness. I will show how biographical features, as well as archetypal urges, when combined with an inability to find the proper venue in which to express their unique voice, all add up to an unbearable situation in which *pueri* too often find themselves.

Going Up

From an archetypal perspective, the divine or eternal child is that kernel of innocence and purity that resides within us, unsullied by the tempests of time, the ambiguity of personal relationships, and the wounding nature of our world. This imaginal child represents our own greatest potential and the promise of our brightest future. The image of the divine child that comes to us in myth, dreams, and reveries is not the child of experience, nor does it represent the ideal childhood I would liked to have had. The divine child is not "me" at four years old, nor is it the "me" I wish I could have been.

C. G. Jung writes:

> [T]he mythological idea of the child is emphatically not a copy of the empirical child but a symbol clearly recognizable as such: it is a wonder-child, a divine child, begotten, born, and brought up in quite extraordinary circumstances, and not—this is the point—a human child. (*CW* 9.1: 274n)

The image of the archetypal child is a symbolic representation of the binary relationship between life and death, as well as a choice between either growth or stasis. The potential danger of inflation arises when an image of the eternal child is produced within "the deepest archetypal level of our being" (Sullwold 19), and the conscious ego begins to identify itself with this "wonder-child" of our imagination. By unconsciously identifying with the divine child itself instead of the future it represents, the adult *puer aeternus* finds himself exhibiting particularly childish modes of thoughts and behavior. He is "vulnerable to the least failure and craves admiration and adulation. . . . The child in the adult is tormented by feelings of envy and rage, inner despair, isolation and depression" (Abrams 118). This identification with the divine child "may lead to a superficially entrancing but basically immature child-man who is incapable of commitment or generativity, a flighty Little Prince with unrealistic hopes and inappropriate dreams" (Hopcke 108). If a metaphorical death experience is a prerequisite for maturity, then the puer's difficult task is the demise not of the man but of the archetypal boy that tempts him to fly.

"I guess you could say I've a call."—Sylvia Plath

For most, "[t]he soul goes through many death experiences, yet physically life goes on" (Hillman, *Suicide and the Soul* 68); however, for those wholly identified with the divine child, the "organic death through actual suicide may be the only mode through which the death experience is possible" (Hillman, *Suicide and the Soul* 83). Men and women of every social class and psychological type commit suicide for a variety of reasons, but it is with the puer type—the adult man who is gripped so firmly by "the romantic attitude of the adolescent" (von Franz 8)—that suicide too often becomes the final desperate (or destined) act of self-destruction.

Jolande Jacobi reminds us that "to abandon's one infantile fixations and adapt oneself to responsible adulthood is a severe trial" (18). To die to his sense of childhood omnipotence and to accept the strictures of adulthood—a trial every human must naturally endure—is made all the more severe for the *puer aeternus*, due to his infantile attitude of entitlement. This attitude, called narcissism in psychological terminology, is in philosophical and religious discourse known as *hubris*.

In the thirteenth chapter of *The Poetics*, Aristotle describes the ideal protagonist of Greek tragedy as one whose moral character is to be found between the two extremes of vice and virtue—neither a seething villain nor a faultless hero: "One whose misfortune is brought about not by vice or depravity, but by some *hamartia*" (2325). A term taken from the sport of archery, the word *hamartia* was used by Homer to denote a spear that had missed its mark; it has been defined by literary critics as a fatal or tragic character flaw. St. Paul uses the word in his epistles when speaking of a deliberate act that contravenes the revealed law of God. But Aristotle's *hamartia* is not sin in the Pauline sense; it is not the protagonist's moral transgression but his mistaken choice that affects his earthly well-being, not his eternal soul. Neither is *hamartia* a dysfunction in the psychological sense until it is *hubris*, or narcissistic pride.

Frederick Copleston defines the man with an inflated, hubristic ego complex as a man who "goes too far, who endeavors to be and to have more than Fate destines him" (Copleston 19), while Edward Edinger writes that "*[h]ybris* is the human arrogance that appropriates to man what belongs to the gods" (Edinger 31). To rephrase the argument in psychological terms, *hubris* (or *hybris*) is the human arrogance that appropriates to the ego what belongs to the Self. The ego, especially the child's still largely unconscious sense of identity, is in as subordinate a position to the Self as the boy Icarus is to Helios, the immortal sun. A man who identifies himself with the archetype of the divine child and its unconquerable promise of future success and development becomes wholly defined by an attitude that is antithetical to adult reality.

The hubristic attitude in the puer manifests itself as a flight from some otherwise healthy relationship, whether it is to his work, partner, sobriety, or existence itself. The puer's hubris is a pride that maintains that his own childhood suffering is somehow more traumatic, or more meaningful than anyone else's, and thus his mission to save himself and the world takes on cosmic significance far greater than a fully functioning ego-Self relationship would permit. The result of the unavoidable breakdown of this elaborately constructed fantasy world is a melting of the ego's fragile waxen wings and a sudden, deadly deflation, for as Jung writes: "*the experience of the self is always a defeat for the ego*" (CW 14: 778; italics added). This sudden *katabasis*, or fall from on high, is the only possible outcome when such a pathologically inflated ego-orientation develops.

Second Interlude

Born to Don and Wendy Cobain in February 1967, Kurt was the typical American adolescent. A gifted artist from his elementary school days, Kurt would spend his time developing elaborate fantasies of becoming a musician or painter, obsessing over his favorite television programs, and playfully annoying his younger sister. Athletically talented, Kurt cheerfully joined the local Little League and would later become a member of his high school's wrestling team. In his interviews after becoming world famous as the lead singer of Nirvana, he would often belittle his small Washington hometown and his lower-class upbringing, yet even in his suicide note, he admitted that he had felt normal and happy (sometimes blissfully so) until he turned seven. It was at this time that the cracks in his parents' marriage began to show, and the looming shadow of divorce first descended on the Cobain household.

Kurt's father, Don, supported his family by working as a mechanic at a local garage, while Wendy tended to the daily duties of child rearing. Kurt's mother, herself a product of a lower-middle-class environment, resented her husband's low-paying job and was never one to keep her strong opinions to herself. Although neither of Kurt's parents was ever physically abusive, both had the tendency to become emotionally distant and bitingly sarcastic toward each other and their children (Cross 16). At the same time that Kurt was becoming comfortable and popular at school, the animosity between his parents became oppressive, so much so that Kurt "began to retreat to the closet in his room," to avoid the sound of their constant bickering (Cross 16). Not long after Kurt's ninth birthday, his mother casually "informed Don she wanted a divorce" (Cross

20). The news, long expected by the adult members of the extended family, hit Kurt like a bombshell.

After the lengthy divorce proceedings were finalized, Kurt's mother was granted custody of her two children. Don had been the family's primary breadwinner, and Wendy was quickly overwhelmed by the double responsibility of raising two children and working full time. To avoid the growing tension between mother and son, Kurt began to spend long weekends with his maternal grandparents who, though kind enough, knew little about raising such a precocious, intelligent child. It would not be long before Don Cobain was granted full custody of Kurt, while his sister remained in the custody of her mother. The family thus split in two, Kurt would forever feel as though each of his parents had alternately abandoned him. As a relative later observed, Kurt believed that his parents' divorce "was his fault, and he shouldered much of the blame. . . . [H]e saw everything he trusted in—his security, family and his own maintenance—unravel in front of his eyes" (Cross 21).

He had already been a hyperactive child before the divorce, and his parents and teachers soon suspected that Kurt's "endless energy might have a larger medical root" (Cross 19). The decision to put Kurt on Ritalin was not made lightly; each member of his family voiced an opinion, but the final decision fell to Kurt's mother, Wendy, who, like so many parents before and after her, reluctantly began administering Ritalin to her son. From this time onward, Kurt's dependency on drugs would be constant and all-consuming, ultimately leading to more than a dozen accidental overdoses, one genuine drug-related suicide attempt, and an injection of a lethal dose of heroin into his arm only moments before he shot himself with his Remington shotgun. Kurt's wife Courtney Love later told interviewers that she and her husband often discussed their use of Ritalin as children, linking this initial reliance on pharmaceuticals to their subsequent propensity to addiction. Courtney once asked rhetorically: "When you're a kid and you get this drug that makes you feel that feeling, where else are you going to turn when you're an adult?" (Cross 20).

However, Charles L. Cross suggests that "[h]eroin became, in many ways, the hobby [Kurt] had never had as a child: He methodically organized his 'works' box the way a small boy might shuffle his baseball card collection" (Cross 226). In any event, whatever the specific origin of Cobain's adult drug addiction, the links between his childhood trauma and adult behavior are clear: Edward Edinger writes that, "[i]n cases where the child experiences a severe degree of rejection by parents, the ego-Self axis is damaged and the child is then predisposed in later life to states of alienation which can reach unbearable proportions" (Edinger 54). For Kurt, the two primary childhood traumas, the ones he returns to again and again in his journals and lyrics, are the divorce of his parents and their decision to put him on Ritalin. No other events "had more of an effect on the shaping of his personality" (Cross 21). Whether or not the events were as extreme as Kurt later remembered them, both decisions were understood as personal rejections by his parents, and they would ultimately lead him to an overwhelming identification with the archetype of the divine child—the development of a pathological puer complex.

A female friend of Kurt Cobain's once remarked that he "made women want to nurture and protect him. He was a paradox in that way, because he also could be brutally and intensely strong; yet at the same time he could appear fragile and delicate" (Cross 199). At 5'7" and sometimes weighing as little as 120 pounds, the rock star could nonetheless be "extremely intimidating" (Azerrad 353). His "piercing blue eyes, his moodiness, the question of whether he was high or not, his fame and especially his almost palpable charisma" (Azerrad 353) made fans and friends alike feel that Cobain was simply unapproachable. Yet, by patiently removing the mask of his constructed persona, one could encounter "a kind, sweet man who listened sincerely, who was capable of dispensing thoughtful advice and comfort" (Azerrad 353).

Cobain was a lifetime serial monogamist who always treated his women like an erotic extension of his mother, depending on them for his emotional, sexual, and financial needs. Exhibiting a typical puer habit, Kurt would throw himself completely into a relationship, declaring several times that he had found his soul-mate, the only woman who could make him truly and eternally happy, only to find that the perfect woman of his dreams was as fragile and flawed as he was. Yet, "rather than lose someone he cared for he would withdraw first, usually by creating some mock conflict as a way of lessening the abandonment he felt was inevitable" (Cross 67).

His dread of baggage and all things burdensome makes perfect sense when one considers the primary metaphor used to describe the puer—that of the eternal *flying* boy. The puer must pack lightly, for he is ready to travel at a moment's notice, to uproot his stakes and "light out for the territories." Punching the clock for an honest paycheck, eating the same breakfast cereal while staring at the same familiar faces, day in and day out—things that the non-puer is able to endure without complaint and even come to relish—is for the puer-identified man a death sentence. For a *puer aeternus* the most intolerable sin is stasis; thus, no matter what the cost, he demands the freedom to fly at will, to sever emotional ties at random, or like a caged bird he will ossify and eventually find no other recourse but the final solution of a literal suicide.

Indeed, throughout his short life, references to suicide found their way into Cobain's journals, into his personal conversations, and especially into his lyrics. Along with heroin, suicide quickly became the twin refrains in the music of Nirvana: "Virtually every interview Kurt did in 1993 had some reference to suicide" (Cross 285). However, it was actually not long after the divorce of

Kurt Cobain's parents, a time described by his grandmother as "Kurt's year in purgatory" (Cross 33), that the young man began to contemplate taking his own life. Years before he even owned a guitar, Kurt announced to his friend John Fields: "I'm going to be a superstar musician, kill myself, and go out in a flame of glory" (Cross 33). After an abortive first attempt at sexual intimacy, Kurt records in his journal:

> I couldn't handle the ridicule so on Saturday night I got high & drunk & walked down to the train tracks & layed down & waited for the 11:00 train & I put 2 big pieces of cement on my chest & legs & the train came closer & closer. And it went on the next track beside me instead of over me. (Cross 27)

This account may be a slightly apocryphal version of events, but the story does reveal how casual Kurt had become with regard to taking his own life. Kurt's childish flippancy toward suicide would cause several friends to remark that he "was not long for this world" (Azerrad 351) and that "fame or no fame, Kurt was doomed" (Azerrad 354).

A few years later, after Kurt unceremoniously dropped out of high school, a friend asked Kurt where he expected to be when he was thirty; Kurt's answer had by this point become typical: "I'm never going to make it to thirty. You know what life is like after thirty—I don't want that" (Cross 76). The friend who provoked this response said in hindsight that Kurt was "the shape of suicide. He looked like suicide, he walked like suicide, and he talked [like] suicide" (Cross 76).

At one point, Cobain considered naming Nirvana's third studio album *I Hate Myself and I Want to Die*, an only partly tongue-in-check mantra that he repeatedly scrawled in his journals. The album would instead be titled *In Utero*. That the change of title reflected the similar oscillations in the psychological state of the singer is obvious. Tragically, what Cobain hoped he could successfully midwife with the release of *In Utero* (namely a musical career based on his poetic artistry, and not on his attractive looks or hard rock mystique) would come to be overshadowed by a string of personal and professional controversies that plagued the last months of his life.

Living as a *puer aeternus* leads to what H. G. Baynes describes as "the provisional life," that is, "the strange attitude and feeling that one is not yet in real life" (qtd. in von Franz 8). The puer finds that his current job is not quite the right one, and that his current relationships, with men or women, are less than what they could be—less than pure. Always with his eyes on the horizon, the puer stumbles from one relationship to another, while never giving himself wholly to any emotional or economic venture. Like a young child, the puer needs to be taken care of completely and will unfailingly seduce his friends, family, and co-workers out of their time, energy, and love. In this way the puer's life is "reduced to an all-too-familiar pattern of intimacy, conflict and banishment, followed by isolation" (Cross 71). Eventually, if the *puer aeternus* takes literally, instead of metaphorically, the natural urge to transform his present condition into something entirely different, he leaves his life altogether.

"This is my substitute for pistol and ball."—Herman Melville, *Moby-Dick*

What draws a man toward such a fate, and what, if anything can save him? Marie-Louise von Franz, relating the words of her mentor, offers this tantalizing, yet ambiguous clue:

> Jung spoke of one cure—work—and having said that he hesitated for a minute and thought, "Is it really as simple as all that? Is that just the one cure? Can I put it that way?" (von Franz 10)

In former times, a young man was expected to follow in his father's occupational footsteps, or at least to engage in a business deemed suitable and thus meaningful by his extended family. In tribal cultures the pattern is similar, with the variety of career choices severely limited by geography and technology. For most young men, the choice of profession was simply a natural extension of their familial responsibilities as a son or brother, and deviation from a tribal or familial mandate was unthinkable. In the book of Genesis, immediately following the consumption of the forbidden fruit, the Lord God curses the tempting serpent, the beguiled Eve, and the hapless Adam, saying:

> Cursed be the ground because of you;
> By toil you shall eat of it
> All the day of your life:
> Thorns and thistles shall it sprout for you.
> But your food shall be the grasses of the field;
> By the sweat of your brow
> Shall you get bread to eat,
> Until you return to the ground—
> For from it you were taken. (Gen. 3:17–19)

The traditional interpretation of this passage articulates the typical puer attitude toward physical labor: that it is *nothing* but a curse. The verse reminds the reader of the golden age, when our food, once readily available in abundance, now comes to us only by painful, repetitive *work*, "the one disagreeable word which no *puer aeternus* likes to hear" (von Franz 10). However, the last two lines of the passage are ambiguous: "Until you return to the ground—For from it you were taken" does not necessarily imply a physical death. It could suggest that only by becoming intimate with the ground of our own being, with our own personal history and limitations, will we fulfill some primal need left unsated by the childlike, disembodied existence of the Garden of Eden.

The flight from work is itself an expression of the suicidal urge, since work is the prerequisite for the primary necessities of life—food, clothing, shelter, community—and thus for life itself. When a man remains identified with the child archetype he forgets *The Work*—the literal physical and psychological labor needed to bring his creative urges to fruition. As a result, his mind, goals, and perhaps even his environment become as disorganized as a child's play-room. For the sake of independence he disregards the advice of his mentors; spontaneity is replaced by the temper tantrum, and his healthy "beginner's mind" remains locked in the narcissistic patterns of a child. Of course, it is not as simple as telling a puer to work and expecting him to find a career that will save him from the yawning abyss he soars above, forever searching for his permanent perch. An absolutely mind-numbing job will simply exacerbate his feelings of cagedness and will accelerate his usual pattern of inflation and alienation. Also fraught with danger is the type of seemingly exciting and desir-able career Cobain chose (or was he chosen by it?). The life of the intensely popular poet has, since the time of Orpheus, been known to leave many young men wishing they had simply gone into the family business. The pressure to produce art, even popular "low-brow" art, is enormous, especially in this time of mass media, overstimulation, and slick production values passing for genuine artistic achievement. Pop art with mass appeal may in fact exacerbate the puer's problems, rather than providing an outlet for the expression of his most artistic and personally violent urges. This is the reason that, as Marie-Louise von Franz has succinctly framed the problem, it does no good "just preaching to people that they should work, for they simply get angry and walk off" (von Franz 10). Icarus cannot be grounded and remain Dedalus's son—a puer without his dangerous charisma, regardless of the *hubris* behind it, also loses something vital and positive. Nevertheless, since literal suicide is no one's ideal end, a grown-up Icarus must be imagined.

The Transcendent Function

"Work" for Jung did not necessarily mean physical labor, though as his construction of the tower at Bollingen shows, he was not adverse to that type of activity. Jung saw the "universal question" to be: "How does one come to terms in practice with the unconscious?" (*CW* 8, *Function* n). One of his answers, and one that holds much applicability for the plight of the *puer aeternus*, was that an individual needs to cultivate the transcendent function, defined as that which "arises from the union of conscious and unconscious elements" (*CW* 8: para. 131). The transcendent function is the "third option" between two opposing propositions, which in the case of the puer may be the choice between literal suicide and remaining trapped in his current life situation. Without the transcendent function, the conscious and unconscious contents of the psyche will remain eternally at odds with each other. Rather than developing a one-sided psychological attitude that favors either the conscious or unconscious, the *puer aeternus* will instead find himself dangerously fluctuating between the two sides of his psyche. One moment he will find himself lost in an especially absorbing reverie, while the next he is assaulted by the harshness of a reality that he has hitherto ignored. This confusing and dangerous state will persist until an *enantiodromia*, or a reversal in the flow of psychic energy, is effected—until the "third option" of the transcendent function presents itself—and the puer is able to land his feet safely on the ground.

After detailing many possible ways of creating a bridge between the conscious and unconscious—such as dreams, Freudian slips, free associations, and spontaneous fantasies—Jung hit upon the art of active imagination as the *via regia* to the transcendent function. Jung recommends that a person "makes himself as conscious as possible of the mood he is in, sinking himself in it without reserve and noting down on paper all the fantasies and other associations that come up" (*CW* 8: para. 167). The key to Jung's technique is the "noting down on paper," which separates active imagination from mere daydreaming. However, once the mood, fantasy, or association has been followed and noted, it is not to be turned into a piece of art, nor is it to be interpreted to such an extent that the imaginer believes the image has been understood once and for all (*CW* 8: para. 172). The "goal" of active imagination is to redirect the psychological "energy that is in the wrong place" (*CW* 8: para. 167), thus effecting a transcendent function between the conscious and unconscious contents of the psyche.

In the case of Kurt Cobain, the process of lyric writing may be taken as an example of a failed process of active imagination. Many of Cobain's songs are full of dreamlike and even nightmarish imagery, but due to his drug use and puer personality, the nightmares leaked out of the pages of his notebook and into his daily life. Through the conscious composition of his lyrics, Cobain details his psyche's unconscious contents, which include a near-obsession with the female reproductive organs, as well as the themes of rape, homelessness, cancer, and the aforementioned addiction and suicide. Unfortunately, the expurgation of these primal images into his lyrics never served to produce any form of catharsis for Cobain. Instead of effecting an *enantiodromia*, Cobain continued to wallow in his world of perverse imagery long after he left the stage, the video shoot, or the recording session. Even before he was infamous for the imagery on his album covers and in his songs, Cobain would sit for hours in his hovel-like Seattle apartment making disturbing collages from images he found in old medical journals and porno magazines. He had a large collection of baby- and Barbie dolls from which he would amputate a head, a limb, or the stomach area, signifying the removal of the womb. Obviously, Cobain was trying to tell us something, trying to tell himself something, but the message was never wholly received. Perhaps a change of venue would have helped. Perhaps the waters of pop stardom were simply too shallow for such an obviously tortured and talented artist.

This phenomenon of the too-talented artist in the too-limiting venue has happened before. Men with enormous manic energy such as John Belushi and Chris Farley found the pressures of producing a commercially viable weekly television show stifling and, in the end, sought the reflection of their mania in brothels and bars. Jimi Hendrix, Janis Joplin, and Jim Morrison (all young, talented, and prematurely deceased) were saddled with musical projects that were simply too small to bear the weight of music that was inside them. And Sylvia Plath, the poet-laureate of all disaffected, suicidal youth, had a pact with death so strong that she would meet it every ten years until she got it right. The publication of her poetry, the awards, and the recognition were simply not enough to save her. The world of the academic poet—lunching at trendy restaurants, dining with the nouveaux riches—was not a venue that could satisfy the call to adventure that lurked inside Plath's thin frame. Perhaps Plath could have found satisfaction as a playwright instead of a poet. Perhaps Joplin could have been a Shamaness instead of a pop star. The point is: when a particularly talented individual becomes possessed by the traits of a puer or puella, it is a signal that waiting to be born is not only a new type of lifestyle for the individual but also a new art form, using as its vessel the mind and body of the fated artist. History shows that tragic consequences will result if the muses are ignored, and the artist continues to perform in the old way, or in the way he or she is told by managers, executives, spouses, or even the culture at large. Cobain's life and music has been lauded as representing something new, something never before heard. What is not acknowledged is that Kurt Cobain's artistry had flown far beyond the limits of popular rock music before he ever strapped on his first guitar. Imprisoning these performers in the venue of the please-them-all popular media was the drowning, and not the grounding, of the Icarus inside them. By drowning these puer-urges in the too-shallow waters of the wrong artistic venue, many successful artists find that their lives become sickeningly trivial. Undiscerning fans, instant riches, and sycophantic friends rob them of their rootedness, while the sudden onset of fame initiates a process of psychic inflation, which in the end leads to the most dangerous of all states for the puer aeternus: the hubristic state, where a man claims for himself what rightfully belongs to the gods alone.

The Famous Limping God

The opposite of *hubris* is humility, which, as Robert Bly reminds us, comes from the word *humus*: the stuff of the earth. Being humble is being grounded, being at home on the ground, close to the earth—to growing things—to humor, humiliation, and humanity. Being grounded in one's own being means acknowledging one's own personal instincts, walking one's own path and not another's, and knowing, without a doubt, that the life one leads is honest and authentic. When work is humble, authentic, and personal, we call this a *vocation*, a calling forth of something inherent in the individual.

In the Greek god Hephaistos we find a character who is able to overcome the *puer aeternus*'s relationship to literal suicide by shifting his psychic energy away from resentment and addictive revenge fantasies and into a productive *calling*. Hephaistos is able to shift his literal self-destructive urge toward a metaphorical understanding of the need to end one's own life and, like a butterfly, to emerge wholly transformed. For the puer, this shift in consciousness is one that takes a great deal of introspection, creativity, forgiveness, and courage—all traits exhibited by Hephaistos, "the famous limping god."

Hephaistos is the Greek god of fire, metallurgy, and smith work. A consummate artist, the god is said to have fashioned the elaborate armor of Achilles, the brass houses of the Olympians, and the two golden automata who assist him in his smithy far below the surface of an active volcano. This "god who works" beneath the fertile soil is praised in the Homeric Hymns as having freed men from their brutish life by introducing skillful labor. Known in Homer as "the renowned smith of the strong arms" (*Odyssey* 130) and "resourceful Hephaistos" (*Iliad* 427), and in Hesiod as "the famous limping god" (41), Hephaistos contains within his character a stirring paradox. Crippled in body, yet skillful in craft, the god of controlled fire transcends his traumatic past and physical limitations to become the prototypical artist and a patron of artisans, a mediator among the warring gods, and a living symbol of psychological interiority. Hephaistos is the only "crippled god," a seeming contradiction, through whose influence a transformative balance may be achieved in the man with a puer complex.

In Hesiod's *Theognis*, Zeus's wife, Hera, parthenogenetically gives birth to Hephaistos out of her resentment for Zeus's engendering of Athena (570). In *The Homeric Hymn to Hermes*, Hephaistos is born with shriveled feet and is flung by a disgusted Hera into the ocean, to be saved and brought up by the sea nymph Thetis. According to Pausanias, Hephaistos—out of revenge for Hera's ill treatment—constructs and delivers to his mother a beautifully wrought golden throne. While she sits on the throne, invisible fetters are lashed around Hera's white arms, binding her fast. All the gods implore Hephaistos to visit Olympus and free the Queen, but it is only when Dionysus, in whom Hephaistos "reposed the fullest trust," plies the limping god with intoxicating wine that he concedes to free his mother (Paus. 1.20.3, 3.17.3).

In *The Odyssey* (Book 8), Hephaistos's wife, Aphrodite, begins a love affair with his brother Ares. Unlucky Hephaistos is informed of the indiscretion by Helios, the sun, who sees all things; burning with anger, the cuckolded husband sets a trap for the two lovers. Hephaistos drapes the bed with golden chains and then feints a journey to Lemnos, whereupon Ares, believing the god in truth has left the scene, initiates his tryst with the love goddess. Immediately upon falling onto the bed, the two adulterers spring the trap and find themselves snared in unbreakable golden chains. Helios tells Hephaistos that his trap has successfully caught its prey, and the poor cuckolded god calls alls the gods together to witness the unbecoming scene. Hephaistos evokes both laughter and pity from his brothers: Hermes declares that for a night with Aphrodite he would endure chains three times as heavy, while prudish Poseidon—finding absolutely nothing amusing about the scene—convinces Hephaistos to free his captives. Hephaistos once again relents, and Aphrodite and Ares flee separately to the far sides of earth.

According to Murray Stein, the act of binding his mother, brother, and wife is an expression of Hephaistos's own suicidal urge:

> Caught in his own trap, Hephaistos would wither in the self-destructive heat of his resentment. A sort of anarchistic self-directed pyromania takes over in such cases, an attitude utterly devoid of creativity, rejoicing only in conflagration, even courting visions of pseudo-martyr death in the flames of its own kindling. . . . Only in Hephaistos, this anarchistic violence would be directed not outward . . . but inward against himself, against his own body and soul. . . . Dionysos comes, then, to save Hephaistos from himself, from suicide. (Stein 46–47)

Before these two episodes, Hephaistos is consumed with resentment against his wounding family, his deformity: the very facts of his existence. It is only after the loosening effects of Dionysus's wine—an injection of Zoë, of life in its most potent, authentic, and invigorating form—that a decisive shift takes place in Hephaistos's psychic orientation.

By releasing his relatives from their bindings, Hephaistos withdraws his misdirected identifications. Releasing Hera frees Hephaistos from his own traumatic history, from the wounded, narcissistic boy at the center of his psyche, and from the transpersonal archetype of the divine child. Releasing Aphrodite gives Hephaistos the permission to love himself, the man that he is, not the boy that he was and never will be again. Finally, by liberating Ares, Hephaistos acquires the power to confront, with warlike intensity, his own dysfunctions.

The binding and releasing of those who had wounded him, along with the choice to devote himself to the cultivation of his art, represent the ongoing process of psychic individuation. By choosing a profession in which he literally gets his hands dirty, by sweating and experiencing his body as an instrument that can bring forth great artistic inventions, Hephaistos is able to transform himself from a frightened, resentful puer into a healthy, soul-filled man.

In *Gods in Our Midst*, Christine Downing describes Hephaistos as an "effete yet reconciling, harmonizing god" (105). A "gentle, introverted intuitive artist," and "a peacemaking son" who makes beautiful objects to "compensate for his own ugliness," Hephaistos is even, according to Downing, a "male trying to become a woman" (107). However, Downing's interpretation of the myths surrounding Hephaistos subtly insults both the god and those men who find in Hephaistos not the effete mamma's boy, the cuckolded husband, and the sensitive artist, but an energetic firebrand of a man whose art, rather than compensating for his lameness, consciously complements and ultimately transcends it. True, Hephaistos becomes the god who engenders laughter in the all-too-serious Olympians. He becomes the peacemaker, who resolves conflict through calm words, patient actions, and a willingness to allow himself to become the source of great levity. But it is important to note, lest one assume that the gods are laughing *at* Hephaistos and not along with him, that "the god who works" never loses his temper in these brief moments of joviality. Imagine a scene in which the Olympians deigned to laugh at Zeus or Ares, at Hera or Athena. What would their reactions be? But calm, comedic Hephaistos has learned the hubris-puncturing power of his authentic calling and the healing sound of sympathetic laughter.

Coming Down

It is a psychological law that an adult male's immature attitudes must be sloughed aside for him to experience true adulthood. Not that childlike curiosity, creativity, and empathy need whither away completely; rather, these youthful qualities must mature, like a seed into a ripened fruit. The archetype of the divine child represents the dream of an untarnished relationship, of uncompromised artistic expression and unmitigated success. When a woman loves a puer deeply, it is never deeply enough. When fame or success does arrive, the sensitive puer knows that it is too fleeting to enjoy fully. The saddest aspect of the puer may be that "the actual culmination of [his] dreams deeply unnerves [him]" (Cross 195).

A rock journalist writing about a late Nirvana tour performance sums up the ultimate paradox confronting the *puer aeternus* when he says: "These guys are already rich and famous, but they still represent a pure distillation of what it's like to be unsatisfied in life" (Cross 205). The puer is constantly dissatisfied because he continues to look at the world through the eyes of a child and to imitate the behavior of a transpersonal archetype. Being thus identified, the fragile ego too often literalizes the suicidal urge—an urge which all humans share yet which for most men is manifested in the need to transform their lives and personalities inwardly, not to end it ultimately. The urge to quit a job, end a relationship, or take one's own life is really the manifestation of a psychological need to transform one's inner landscape, but the *puer aeternus*, like a child, only understands this need on the literal level.

Divorce and drug addiction, emotional dependency, and bouts of soul-crushing ennui—tribulations that so many men experience without resorting to the final solution of suicide—are for the *puer aeternus* an overpowering assault on his fragile, child-like ego. Even for a successful artist such as Kurt Cobain—a man of celebrated talent, financial security, and a small but devoted group of genuine friends and supporters—the suicidal urge, when taken literally, was simply too much to overcome. Cobain's suicide note proves that he was, until the end, being pulled in many directions at once, none of which was of his choosing. The ultimate irony is that a few months before Cobain's death, he had recorded his most critically acclaimed album with Nirvana, the haunting, live performance now known as *Nirvana: Unplugged in New York*. During this acoustic set, Cobain proved to everyone the depth of both his talent and his pain. During one cover song after another, Kurt's searing, gravel-strewn singing voice almost pleads with the audience for mercy, and for absolution. At last, during the final song of the set, Cobain launches into a vintage blues song called "Where Did You Sleep Last Night?" The piercing howl that is unleashed during the final moments of this song is the sound of Kurt Cobain giving up his spirit. It is the sound of Icarus crashing into the sea.

A month after the date of his suicide, Cobain was scheduled to begin work on a musical collaboration with R.E.M.'s Michael Stipe. This would have been a totally new type of project for Cobain, with a promise to lead him safely out of the by-now clichéd arena of Grunge rock, out of his addictions, and away from the image of the divine child that haunted him. Perhaps this untitled new venture would have been the project finally to spotlight Cobain as not just a rock star but a mature, creative artist, at last working within the best venue for his inimitable voice. We can hope, however, that through Cobain's example a new generation of *pueri* will find the strength not to kill their irreplaceable living selves but to ground their hubristic tendencies, to fly a middle course between metaphor and literalism, to find their authentic calling, and to transform their child-identified egos.

Works Cited

Abrams, Jeremiah, ed. and Intro. *Reclaiming the Inner Child*. Los Angeles: Tarcher, 1990.

Alvarez, A. *The Savage God*. New York: Random House, 1972.

Aristotle. *The Complete Works of Aristotle Vol II*. Ed. Jonathan Barnes. *Poetics*. Trans. I. Bywater. Bollingen Series 71.2. Princeton: Princeton UP, 1984.

Azerrad, Michael. *Come As You Are*. New York: Doubleday, 1994.

Copleston, Frederick. *A History of Philosophy*. New York: Doubleday, 1993.

Cross, Charles R. *Heavier Than Heaven*. New York: Hyperion, 2001.

Downing, Christine. *Gods in Our Midst*. New York: Crossroads, 1993.

Edinger, Edward F. *Ego and Archetype*. Boston: Shambhala, 1992.

Gad, Irene. "Hephaestus: Model of New Age Masculinity." *Quadrant* (Fall 1986): 27–48.

Grimal, Pierre. *The Dictionary of Classical Mythology*. Trans. A. R. Maxwell-Hyslop. Blackwell P, 1996.

Hesiod. *Theognis*. Trans. Dorothea Wender. Penguin, 1976.

Hillman, James. *Suicide and the Soul*. Dallas: Spring, 1990.

———, with Michael Ventura. *We've Had a Hundred Years of Psychotherapy and Things Are Getting Worse*. San Francisco: HarperCollins, 1993.

Homer. *The Homeric Hymns*. Trans. Michael Crudden. Oxford UP, 2001.

———. *The Iliad*. Trans. Richmond Latimore. Chicago: U. of Chicago P, 1951.

———. *The Odyssey*. Trans. Robert Fitzgerald. New York: Doubleday, 1963.

Hopcke, Robert. *A Guided Tour of the Collected Works of C. G. Jung*. Boston: Shambhala, 1999.

Jacobi, Jolande. *Complex, Archetype, Symbol*. Princeton: Princeton UP, 1974.

JPS Hebrew-English Tanakh. Philadelphia: Jewish Publication Society, 2003.

Jung, C. G. "The Psychology of the Child Archetype." Trans. R. F. C. Hull. *The Collected Works of C. G. Jung*. Vol. 9.1. Princeton: Princeton UP, 1990. 151–81.

Melville, Herman. *Moby-Dick*. New York. Random House, 2003.

Pope, Whitney. *Durkheim's Suicide*. Chicago: U of Chicago P, 1976.

Stein, Murray. "Hephaistos: A Pattern of Introversion." *Spring* (1973): 35–51.

Sullwold, Edith. "A Fresh Experiment: The Archetype of the Inner Child." New York: Abrams 17–24.

von Franz, Marie-Louise. *The Problem of the Puer Aeternus*. Toronto: Inner City Books. 2000.

The Puer as American Hero

SALLY PORTERFIELD

I want a hero: an uncommon want,
When every year and month sends forth a new one,
Till, after cloying the gazettes with cant,
The age discovers he is not the true one;
Of such as these I should not care to vaunt,
I'll therefore take our ancient friend, Don Juan.

—Lord Byron (George Gordon), *Don Juan*

Byron might have been describing contemporary American culture in these mocking but prescient lines expressing the universal urge that Carl Jung describes in its archetypal form. The hero is a mythological motif that, according to Jung, is "*a quasi-human* being who symbolizes the ideas, forms and forces that mould or grip the soul" (*CW* 5: 178). While "the image of the hero embodies man's most powerful aspirations and reveals the manner in which they are ideally realized" (Samuels 66), the "hero within" that each child longs to embody must be integrated or internalized in order for the individual to move on to the next critical stage of growth. Like Dickens's Pip, who vows to be the hero of his own life, so each individual must take up his or her burden and leave the world of myth for the real work of becoming a mature member of society.

A society, though, like an individual, can become stuck or fixated at a certain stage of development because of its inability to integrate a certain archetype, resulting in what Jung called a possession by that archetype. Have we, as a culture, become possessed by the archetype of the hero, thus keeping us in an artificial, provisional state of vicarious experience that characterizes the *puer aeternus*? Since we are speaking here of the public hero, the archetype's avatars, Byron's tongue-in-cheek choice creates an eerie resonance here in the Land of Oz, where the wizard remains securely hidden behind his curtain of faux reality created by the all-powerful mass media.

Individuality at Risk

Our society has fallen prey to a concentrated effort, by the commercial interests governing the media, to seduce us into becoming compliant consumers of everything from dog food to political opinion, and in so doing we have lost the independence that allows us to grow into the individuals we were meant to be through natural development, or what Jung refers to as the process of individuation. For Jung, individuation—or the drive to become most fully ourselves—is the meaning of existence for each individual. Anything less is a wasted opportunity to fulfill our highest potential in a lifelong quest for our own existential truth. The ubiquitous postmodern barrage of communication has thrown us back into a medieval anonymity in which the individual mind is subsumed by the collective.

In order to sell products, desire for those products must be created by appealing to our insecurities and our need for acceptance and community in a rapidly changing world. Television and film, our main sources of information, present impossibly glamorous images of life that make ordinary lives seem dreary in comparison. Bewildered by those differences, we look for models of behavior and success to guide us, but because of the split between reality and illusion the natural process of development becomes ever more difficult. Like young children who are unable to discriminate between the real and the imaginary, our society has become incapable of discerning truth from fantasy. Our heroes, who formerly had to earn that distinction, are now a commodity, designed to sell whatever product or belief is expedient to the seller.

This syndrome reaches far beyond the limits of commerce to influence every aspect of society—politics and religion being two of the most prominent areas that have become intertwined in recent years. The media machine, like the wizard behind his curtain, has managed to infiltrate every area of our life, thus presenting a challenge to each individual who cares about maintaining personal integrity of body, mind, and soul. To understand better the power of suggestion by the media, let us look to Jung for a clue as to how that power resonates within the archetypes of the collective unconscious.

Manufactured Mana

Jung's archetypes, despite their origin in the collective unconscious, are none-theless influenced by cultural context, assimilating contemporary standards that keep them fresh for each succeeding generation. Like the puer, "[t]he hero is a transitional being, a MANA PERSONALITY" (Samuels 66), which Jung describes as being "[a] dominant of the collective unconscious": this personality is more clever and more potent than ordinary people; whether it be a superman like Napoleon or a sage such as Lao-tzu, the mana personality, Jung claims, is what evolves into the hero in one or another of his incarnations (CW 7: 233). Historically, these mana personalities, or charismatic individuals, seem to have developed in all societies, in all circumstances, appearing as artists, generals, politicians, spiritual or intellectual leaders, saints, and sinners. Rare, but unmistakable in their effect on other people, they seem to spring, unbidden, from out of the same soil as the ordinary run of human beings. In other words, they have always been a natural phenomenon.

But now back to Oz and the wizard behind his curtain, from whence issue forth, in a bewildering stream, mana personalities to order, created by the mass media and presented to us as full-blown beings, accompanied, it would seem, by a suitably frenzied fan base, prepared to vouch for their extraordinary powers. Larger than life, they acquire, by virtue of the media, a sort of magic—or what Jung would call a false numinosity—whether they be entertainers, sports figures, politicians, or television evangelists. Manufactured mana is the new drug of choice for a society increasingly divorced from reality, the opiate of a nation dissociated from itself. How did we get here? Let us begin with a brief tour through late-twentieth-century history.

When that bubble burst in the '60s—with the Vietnam War, civil rights riots, a drug culture out of control, the assassinations of the Kennedys and Martin Luther King Jr.—we suddenly found ourselves jolted out of national complacency in a way that had never happened before. Our heroes were dead, and our sense of national pride and moral certainty was wounded, in some cases, fatally. Because of mass communications it was impossible to ignore what was happening. We as a nation were finally tossed out of the garden and forced to examine our assumptions about national virtue. Jung might suggest that we had finally been brought into realization of our national shadow.

So, like the groundhog, many of us dashed back into the burrow to see if we could ignore the cold or sleep it off. The '70s became a period of intense national narcissism, the so-called "Me Generation." Meanwhile, the effect of mass communications, especially TV, became increasingly pervasive. This decade of extreme self-absorption was fostered by a barrage of both print and electronic messages, urging us to improve ourselves—physically, spiritually, any way we could, in a sort of reversion to the personal, something that seemed more manageable than a world grown increasingly ambiguous. This period of national adolescence, with all its insecurities, was bolstered by the postwar Baby Boom, those born between 1946 and 1964—significantly, the year after John F. Kennedy was assassinated. A generation unto itself, the Boomers, encouraged by the media, became their own *in-crowd*, that bulwark of adolescent identity.

These cultural orphans became the protesters who worked for racial integration and against the Vietnam War—actually worked against the "establishment" that stood in favor of war and segregation. Eventually, though, as the Boomers grew older, that rebellious fire died down, quenched by the necessity of earning a living (many of them having become parents along the way). Then, in the wake of a low period in the country's history, along came Ronald Reagan, an old-fashioned father image that brought them back into the family fold, much like the young adult who finally realizes that his father might not have been wrong after all. It was Morning in America, and we were magically transported back to childhood, when father *did* know best and the work ethic equaled material success. Life became simple again. We were out of Vietnam; we thought the economy was better; minorities were on their way up the economic ladder; and the cultural shadow was dispelled by the benign sunshine of a supremely confident, optimistic father who gave us permission to love our country and, incidentally, ourselves again.

In *The New York Times* on June 20, 2004, Frank Rich mused on the recent phenomenon of Reagan's marathon funeral. Rich says that the one question that has still not been laid to rest is: "What in Heaven's name was going on?"

> Was this runaway marathon of mourning prompted by actual grief: A vast right-wing conspiracy? A vast reserve of displaced sorrow about the war in Iraq? Global warming? Whatever it was about, it was not always about Ronald Reagan. His average approval rating in office was lower than that of many modern presidents, including each George Bush. His death at 93, after a full life and a long terminal illness, was neither tragic nor shocking. (1)

The writer goes on to cite the media precedent of O. J. Simpson's car chase and numerous other examples of carefully constructed public sentiment for the insatiable beast the 24/7 news business has become. Rich ends his column with the suggestion that Reagan himself might find the whole thing funny, and he remarks that he can almost hear him saying, "There you go again" (1).

This is not to say that manufactured mana is a new thing, by any means. We only need look at the pomp and panoply of royalty, of the church, of the military, or of the medicine man in his mask, to see that construction of the appearance of power is probably as old as humankind. We have always needed our mojo, our good juju, in order to beat back the evil spirits that lurk just beyond our sight, hidden in the unconscious. But while the practice of manufacturing mana is not recent, it has become so common, so ubiquitous, that we have lost the ability to discriminate between real and false.

After the Reagan years and credit card prosperity, the nation found itself in the care of George Bush the First, another father figure of a different stripe. The first Gulf war was a terrifying but brief exercise that bolstered the fatherly presidency for awhile, but Bush lost his temporary popularity with the failing economy, and Bill Clinton became the new and distinctly unfatherly president. Clinton was the Boomers' own president, a new generation of leadership that, like JFK's years, promised youth, vigor, and hope for a new beginning, but that hope failed, too. In the partisan strife and discord of those eight years, the country was finally torn into two political factions that have evolved into something approximating two separate nations. Now, in the reign of Bush II—with the tragedy of 9/11, followed by the disastrous Iraq War—we have become a nation continually more polarized and alienated from itself.

How has this manufactured mana taken hold in our psyches? How has it caused us, like irritable adolescents whose parents have shown their human fallibility, to expect perfection or nothing from our leaders? If we go back to the media for our answers, we are led particularly to its most powerful influence: television. In his brilliant essay on the effect of the TV image, Keith Polette cites Jung's assertion that the liminal and polyopthalmic nature of mythology and the unconscious imagination "point to the peculiar nature of the unconscious, which can be regarded as a 'multiple consciousness'" (96). Therefore, Polette reasons, "TV eyes are blinded to multiple points of view that exist outside of the rectangular frame of reference. When eyes adopt the TV outlook, they confine themselves to a linear and limited view," thus creating a monoconscious experience that excludes "images of the mythic figures that soar through the imaginal sky of the mind or dwell deeply in the chthonic underground of the psyche" (Polette 96). The rich and ambivalent world of our archetypal imagination is replaced by the synthetic TV universe, with its manufactured mana. Thus, the normal progress of development in which we are able to withdraw our archetypal projections and accept the flaws inherent in all of humanity is halted by unreal expectations that bear no relationship to truth.

Jung speaks of the gods as having "become diseases," through literal interpretations that replace archetypes with stereotypes (*CW* 13: 37). Polette suggests that thus sex replaces love; surgically enhanced duplication becomes a sad parody of beauty; Athena and Ares become senseless violence and mindless vengeance; "Hermes's divine tricks become laugh-track-punctuated sitcoms; and the dark domain of Hades becomes pictures of people killing people" (Polette 106–07).

Unable to construct our own images, to connect with our own myths, we remain fixed in a Peter Pan world, not only unwilling but unable to grow up, and dependent upon Oz to tell us how to feel, how to think, how to live. Our gods are "personalities," constructed, like Potemkin villages, of two-dimensional simulations of real life. Even Andy Warhol, with his prediction of a future with fifteen minutes of fame for everyone, might find himself bemused by the plethora of "personalities" who have achieved the remarkable feat of becoming famous for being famous, à la Paris Hilton.

Since we remain in this puer/puella stage unconsciously, we attempt to give it the semblance of physical reality with the literal trappings that seem to furnish our only clue of what reality might be. A steady parade of teenaged female pop star clones make themselves ridiculous in costumes so brief they seem better suited to toddlers, in a parody of adult sexuality that often shows a pathetic lack of self-awareness. Their male counterparts, in an attempt to simulate the street-smart machismo of the Gangsta/Rapper, also manage to resemble nothing so much as overgrown children in droopy long shorts, backward baseball caps, untied sneakers, and T-shirts with various motifs stretched across fat, baby bellies.

Where are their parents? Right there with them in many cases, turned out like aging toddlers, as well, attempting to stay young with their children. An amusing but distressing current term for this unseemly phenomenon is *teenile*. Youth and age have collapsed into one confused and misbegotten entity in this "Second childishness, and mere oblivion, / Sans teeth, sans eyes, sans taste, sans everything" (Shakespeare, *AYL* 2.7.173–74), because their false gods in the machine have failed to produce a desirable model of maturity.

Since every action produces a reaction, the other cultural extreme has become the fundamentalist right wing. Here the model for maturity, although ostensibly more conventional, is a stubborn insistence on the literal. In *Memories, Dreams, Reflections*, Jung writes about the confusion of his father, the fundamentalist minister whose faith eventually failed him (52–55, 73). It was, in fact, the tension between his mystical mother and his literalist father that seems to have been responsible for much of Jung's early search for truth. Perhaps because he incorporated both of those extremes in his early consciousness, he was able to liberate himself from absolutism.

Puer and Senex: Cowboy and Puritan

Two strains of influence that have contributed to the rise of Christian Fundamentalism are to be found in the national myth of the American in his western incarnation as the pioneer/cowboy/loner, on one hand, and his eastern counterpart in the pilgrim/puritan/Calvinist self-made man on the other.

When pioneers who settled the West glorified the wide-open spaces and the virtues of a simple life, their attitude developed into a defensive posture that devalued Eastern refinement and, by association, the European tradition from which it had sprung. This grew into a shadow projection based on the assumption that, simplicity being good, complexity must be bad. Anti-intellectualism still pervades our cultural mindset, equating youth and simplicity with virtue, thus relegating age and complexity to its opposite, an attitude that is clearly antithetical to individuation.

But let us travel back farther, before the pioneers ventured west. Each November, every American schoolchild is reminded of the Pilgrims who celebrated the first Thanksgiving in that month after having survived the cold, hardship, and disease of their first year in the New World. These refugees, having come in search of religious freedom, quickly fell prey to their own shadow projections in an *enantiodromia* or reversal that began a tradition of religious contradiction that persists as a stubborn vein in the culture. Their Puritan mindset remains embedded in our collective unconscious, documented by tales of religious persecution from the stories of Roger Williams and Anne Hutchinson, who were driven out of the Massachusetts Bay Colony for divergent religious views, to the present day, when those who are not "born again" are consigned to the fires of hell in the tales of Fundamentalist Christians. Such insistence on conformity is fatal to any sense of individual development in the Jungian sense.

These two extremes, the cowboy and the puritan, represent the Jungian dichotomy of the puer and senex. Latin for "old man," senex

> is often mentioned in contradistinction to the *Puer aeternus*. Puer pathology can be described as excessively daring, over-optimistic, given to flights of imagination and idealism, and excessively spiritualised. Senex pathology may be characterized as excessively conservative, authoritarian, over-grounded, melancholic and lacking in imagination. (Samuels 137)

We see this pairing in much of our cultural landscape, particularly in the areas of politics and religion, when the puer, incapable of going through the painful process of individuation—because it involves acceptance of both our shadow and our contrasexual qualities—either cedes his power to the senex in order to remain childlike or becomes the senex, whereby self-doubt and questioning are no longer necessary. In Jung's view, much of the confusion surrounding our contemporary difficulty in passing successfully through the stages of life is due to the lack of initiation rites in our culture, one of the many aspects in which myth once guided the individual in the ways of society. In many cultures, initiation was a public event designed to signal the passage from childhood to adulthood, thus overcoming the child's regressive longing for the safety of infancy and childhood (Stevens 130).

Mythos and Logos: Fact and Meaning

In her excellent study of fundamentalism, *The Battle for God*, Karen Armstrong stresses the separation of *mythos* and *logos* that marks one of the main differences between the worldviews of our early ancestors and of our present thinking. For them, myth applied not to literal reality but to meaning:

> Unless we find some significance in our lives, we mortal men and women fall very easily into despair. The *mythos* of a society provided people with a

context that made sense of their day-to-day lives; it directed their attention to the eternal and the universal. It was also rooted in what we would call the unconscious mind. The various mythological stories, which were not intended to be taken literally, were an ancient form of psychology. (Armstrong xv)

One might speculate that, whereas Europe turned to arts and letters as a return to *mythos* for a balancing of the psyche, the raw young country lacked the capacity to express the psychic disturbance brought on by the fast-paced events that propelled their world of the eighteenth century straight into the coming age of the machine. The similarities of the violent religiosity that sprang up at that time with the corresponding Romantic Revolt seem hardly coincidental. The world was moving too fast, propelled by science that threatened to engulf humanity in a strange and godless universe in which nature is swallowed by the infernal machine.

Like those of their premodern forebears, their creative energies were channeled into religion. In Jung's words, "The man whom we can with justice call 'modern' is solitary. He is so of necessity and at all times, for every step toward a fuller consciousness of the present removes him further from his original '*participation mystique*'" (*CW* 10: 75). This regression can represent a return to childhood, in which individual responsibility is forfeited in return for tribal security.

A nation of immigrants, all leaving behind their traditions and their ties to the past, became not quite the proverbial "melting pot" but a loose confederation of refugees, seeking a better life in the New World. As each new wave of immigrants followed, they suffered the scorn of those who had come before, all attempting to belong in an alien world in which it was necessary to forge a new tribal identity, to fall back into the comfort of Jung's participation mystique.

Lacking the comfort of tradition and the sense of belonging, each new generation has attempted to invent itself anew, to reject the old values of their polyglot forebears and create a fresh, young, independent American persona. We circle back to the national myth of the Western hero here: the lone paladin who, having vanquished the forces of evil, disappears into the sunset. Unlike Joseph Campbell's Hero, though, he never returns but keeps on with his interminable quest, untrammeled by adult responsibility. A truncated archetype, forever young, noble, God-fearing, and inaccessible, he becomes a sort of divine child/savior figure. Thus, a dangerous inflation pervades the national psyche, a grandiosity that convinces us that we have been elected to save the world.

Fundamentalism has served to unite large portions of the country's population as a people still unsure of their identity have retreated gratefully into the refuge of a doctrine that eliminates uncertainty and fear of ambiguity. For them this is the supranational identity that has proved elusive in a constantly changing world. It is a retreat to childhood simplicity disguised as moral certainty—puer qualities that provide welcome retreat from the sense of inferiority that dogs many of those who feel threatened by the complexities of a bewildering post-modern culture.

Of course, the shadow of this attempt at prelapsarian purity grows ever larger and darker. The prurient celebrity mania that pervades our culture titil-lates by demonstrating the Sodom and Gomorrah that one can escape only by foreswearing all the behavior that the pop icon or celebrity *du jour* dangles in front of the saved as a constant reminder of guilty, vicarious pleasure. These two extremes feed each other as reverse mirror images of the *puer aeternus* mentality. Like a giant high school with its cliques and posses in opposition, each side clings to its own participation mystique, terrified of the dangers of growing up and contending with the complexity of coming to consciousness that is essential to individuation in our contemporary world.

Critical to the fundamentalist mindset, in many cases, is the growing End Times movement. As it happens, this movement was largely powered by an Englishman, John Nelson Darby, who was unable to interest many of his coun-trymen in his theories and so came to the United States and toured six times between 1859 and 1877, gaining many converts to his cause in that time. Darby's rationale for his beliefs is a small passage from Paul: "Then we which are alive and remain shall be caught up together with them in the clouds, to meet the Lord in the air: and so shall we ever be with the Lord" (1 Thess. 4.17). This so-called Rapture has become the stuff of which dreams are made on for those who consider themselves among members of the elect tribe. Karen Armstrong describes it as a fantasy of revenge for those who have felt marginalized and ridiculed for their faith:

> A popular picture found in the homes of many Protestant fundamentalists today shows a man cutting the grass outside his house, gazing in astonish-ment as his born-again wife is raptured out of an upstairs window. Like many concrete depictions of mythical events, the scene looks a little absurd, but the reality it purports to present is cruel, divisive, and tragic. (Armstrong 139)

The Great Divide

Tragic is the proper description for the sickness that grips much of American society today in the form of radical, vicious hatred toward those who disagree with their beliefs and their way of life. Such an attitude is exemplified in such a public figure as the Reverend Pat Robertson, who declared that both 9/11 and Katrina were God's vengeance on a nation that did not happen to adhere to Robertson's particular religious beliefs. This attitude is closely allied to the political peculiarities of our times, as well. Thomas Frank, in his thoughtful examination of the great divide in American culture and politics, says,

> In an America where the chief sources of one's ideas about life's possibilities are TV and the movies, it is not hard to be convinced that we inhabit a liberal-dominated world. . . . [Thus,] the backlash sometimes appears to be the only dissenter out there, the only movement that has a place for the uncool and the funny-looking and the pious. (Frank 241)

This sense of alienation accounts in part for the fury of the students who have taken to mass-shooting sprees in schools across the country, beginning with Columbine's atrocity. It is the fury of the outsider, the other, those who feel as if they are on the outside, looking into a world increasingly alien to them. The ubiquitous nature of popular culture, fueled by commercial interests, forces those who feel alien to that world to band together into groups that seem to have some sort of commonality, much like the different groups in contemporary schools; cliques of refugees attempt to form their own tribes in order to be part of a group, one of the most primitive human needs.

For the individual seeking his or her own path—those who follow the path of individuation—all the shadow aspects that drive so much of this tribalism become clear when brought into the light of consciousness. For those who remain stubbornly in an unconscious state, the need for some sort of outside authority is necessary in order to feel secure. Like children, they cling to the notion that there are simple answers to complex questions. Not only anger and paranoia but fear results from this feeling of isolation, and that fear, according to Huston Smith in a recent issue of *Parabola*, is "[t]he underlying cause of fundamentalism . . . the fear that derives from the sense of insecurity, of being threatened. People are scared; the world is scary" (41).

The Cult of Youth Worship

In a frightening world we look for any amulet, any nostrum that might postpone our entry into adulthood, that place where we might be expected to be part of the solution to the world's problems. Thanks to a relentless media machine that imposes conformity masquerading as individualism we have lots of recipes for success: "Assert your independence," "Do your own thing"; all it takes is the magic potion, the hot car, the right shoes, the right home gym, and you can stand out from the crowd of wannabes who are striving for all the same things. Be unforgettable, quirky, bohemian, sophisticated, slim, smart, strong, and young. *Especially young*. Is it then surprising that we have become a nation of perpetual adolescents, *pueri aeterni* and *puellae aeternae*, whose normal attempts at development into adults are thwarted at every turn by the constant assurance that we can stay young forever and, indeed, had better try or be left in the cold, as useless as yesterday's newspaper.

In its definition of adolescence, Webster is not much help, citing merely that it is "[t]he period of life from puberty to maturity terminating legally at the age of maturity." Interestingly, though, Webster's third meaning says: "A stage of development (as of a language or culture) prior to maturity," so we are not bending the meaning by applying the word to our entire culture. That still leaves us with very little in terms of definition, but, like pornography, we know it when we see it, particularly after having gone through the process ourselves. Adolescence is characterized by mood swings ranging from manic happiness to deep dejection, loneliness, self-consciousness, hubris, self-doubt, desire to please, to break away from parents, and most of all, to find validation from peers. Thus are generated the increasingly exclusive cliques, conformity masquerading as nonconformity, and above all an "us or them, with us or against us" attitude.

In order to maintain that pack mentality, we project our shadows on anyone who is not us. Humans are capable of cruelty only when the other is dehumanized, and we see the tragic results of projection and dehumanization not only in our high schools but in our nation, as well. It is necessary to withdraw our shadow projections in order to see the other in the light of rational, humane thought. In a puer society, the life of the mind or of the spirit becomes lost in the narcissistic confusion of the adolescent mentality, in which the ego-centered consciousness often regards either mental or spiritual growth as a further sign of its own unique powers, rather than a gift to be explored and nurtured.

James Hillman writes,

> Relation with any archetype involves the danger of possession, usually marked by inflation. This is particularly true of the puer, because of his high-flights and mythical behavior. Of course, possession through the senex brings an equally dangerous set of moods and actions: depression, pessimism, and hardness of heart. Even a minimum of psychological awareness—that I am just what I am as I am—can spare complete archetypal possession. This awareness is made possible through the reflective, echoing function of the psyche. This function is the human psyche's contribution to spirit and to meaning, which noble as they may be can also be, without psyche, runaway destructive possessions. (*Puer Papers* 30)

So the main puer problem is not lack of worldly reality but lack of psychic reality. Hillman goes on to cite the puer-psyche marriage as the union of "the young and burning sulphur with the elusive quicksilver of psychic reality before it becomes fixed and weighty" (*Puer Papers* 31). In myth, of course, Psyche is personified as female, creating an easy leap of the imagination to Jung's anima, or the contrasexual archetype in the male. Anima also means "soul," and one anima-task is to help the man integrate that quality of soul and to reflect upon meaning, all of which is part of the hero's journey toward selfhood, or individuation.

For the woman, the puella, whose journey must lead her into an integration of her animus, her contrasexual archetype, the problem in our culture is of a different sort. Ideally, a woman's animus can give her strength and foster her capacity for rational thought, but in a society that prizes only physical beauty, those qualities of strength and rationality are not always valued in a woman. With the prevalent media models of the whore and the virgin, the woman is placed once more into the position of object, from which she has been attempting to escape for centuries. The road ahead is obscured by mirrors that taunt and deceive her, showing her neither physical nor psychic reality but mirages and chimeras, impossible dreams of eternal youth and fabulous success.

For both men and women, the media today offer few examples of desirable maturity. But Peter Pan, the emblematic boy-hero, stubbornly maintains his status for men by refusing to grow up, quite literally. The fortunate Peter, of course, has Wendy, who mothers the lost boys and allows them to deceive themselves into believing that they are independent. But what if Wendy had given up and joined the lost boys in their quixotic pursuit of eternal youth? Who indeed could blame her, since her mature feminine qualities of nurturer and caretaker go unrewarded?

Consider, for instance, the current spate of male "buddy" films, of which film critic Manohla Dargis writes, "The movies have long nurtured the arrested development of the American male, serving as a virtual playpen for legions of slobbering big babies for whom Peter Pan isn't a syndrome but a way of life" (1). The writer goes on to note that many women have met this perpetual adolescent and have tried to date him but prefer seeing him in film, where he is more likely to grow up.

What happens if he fails to grow up? Every archetype has its shadow, and Jung warned us that "[t]he only person who escapes the grim law of enantiodromia is the man who knows how to separate himself from the unconscious" (*CW* 7: 73). Enantiodromia, the principle that eventually everything turns into its opposite, applies here: the rugged individualist of American legend has become the perpetual adolescent, still seeking adventure and change at a time when he should be moving into the middle period of his life in which he begins the process of individuation. The narcissistic puer is unable to make the transition from an ego-centered life to one that, in its growing empathy, is able to move toward the archetype of the Self.

Those who simply pass straight from the puer to the senex stage exhibit "[s]enex pathology [which] may be characterized as excessively conservative, authoritarian, over-grounded, melancholic and lacking in imagination" (Samuels 137). All of these qualities are inherent in the disappointment of the puer who suddenly finds himself confined to the sidelines for having committed the unforgivable sin of growing older. Bitterness and disillusion are natural states when one becomes aware that the only goal he has pursued is finally, irrevocably unattainable. Lacking insight and a normal social framework that provides models for maturity, he often fails to see that the positive side of the senex can offer balance, generosity, wisdom, and farsightedness (Samuels 137).

Finding the Hero Within

According to Jung, each of us is born with an archetypal heritage that, given a normal chain of events, "presupposes the natural life cycle of humanity: being mothered and fathered, exploring the environment, playing in the peer group, meeting the challenges of puberty and adolescence" (Stevens 60–61), and so on through the stages of maturity into old age and death. In older societies, and especially in those designated as "primitive" by our Western, industrialized standards, many of these life stages have been marked by initiatory ceremonies, public events that confirmed the individual's entrance into another period of life. These rituals, while easing the transition, also "activated archetypal components in the collective unconscious appropriate to the life stage that had been reached" (Stevens 64). Jung asserted that the virtual disappearance of these rituals has left us without a mythic context that provides meaning.

Jung's concept of the Self was as a sort of organizing genius of the entire personality, the autonomous goal of which was wholeness:

> The Self, therefore, possesses a *teleological* function, in that it has the innate characteristic of seeking its own fulfillment in life. (*Teleo* is a combination word derived from *teleos*, meaning perfect, complete, and *telos*, meaning end; *teleology*, therefore, is about attaining the goal of completeness.) This is the process that Jung calls individuation, by which he meant the fullest possible Self-realization, both in the psyche and in the world. (Stevens 41)

The process of individuation is a lifelong quest that is never completed but is always in progress, working toward our most complete self, and each life takes its own path toward that ever-elusive goal. Unfortunately, in our current society, that journey is often thwarted by a skewed vision of reality constructed by the commercially motivated mass media. Oz is still behind that curtain, assuring us that we need not bother with the tedious business of growing older but can put it off indefinitely by following the Yellow Brick Road that leads us in a circle of self-deceit and keeps us from the natural path to individuation.

This circle is often represented by the image of the uroboros, a circular snake, swallowing its own tail. Until we let go of the past, it is impossible to move forward into the future. Our vulnerability to the blandishments of the commercial youth peddlers is caused in part by a lingering conviction of superiority by virtue of our comparative youth as a nation, the romance of the Cowboy and the Pioneer preventing us from coming to grips with the reality of our present place in the world.

Unsurprisingly, Shakespeare says it best, in *The Tempest*'s familiar exchange between Prospero and his daughter, Miranda:

> MIRANDA: O brave new world,
> That has such people in't!
> PROSPERO: 'Tis new to thee. (5.1.199–201)

Herein lies a bittersweet reminder of the way in which life unfolds for each generation. Prospero's knowledge is appropriate to his age, as is Miranda's dewy-eyed wonder to hers. *The Tempest* can be read as an individuation drama that marks life's seasons in some of Shakespeare's wisest, loveliest poetry. For everything there is a proper time, not only with individuals but with societies, nations, and cultures. As Miranda's naïveté would ill suit her father, so does such an attitude reflect poorly on a nation that remains stubbornly wedded to its own youthful illusions. Like Dorothy, we must find our way back to Kansas, to the reality of a life lived honestly and the rewards of discovering the richness of our individual Selves, the real wizard behind the curtain of our own unconscious.

The Self is the hero within who is neither masculine nor feminine, neither young nor old, but the eternal seeker whose quest, though never complete, remains vital because it is the ontological goal of human life, the search for meaning which is the human striving toward consciousness. Jung believed that this lifelong quest is at once universal and unique to each individual, as are the natural stages of life. If we, as a nation, can pull ourselves out of the morass in which commercial interests and our own history have mired us, we can find the sense of meaning that has been hidden behind the curtain and see the possibilities of life lived to its fullest.

That national transformation will require the difficult work of withdrawing the projections that prevent our seeing others as full human beings, and of accepting difference as part of nature. Consequently, it will require tolerance and patience, along with the will to change ourselves and those parts of the world that can be changed for the better. Perhaps the most difficult part is the resolve to live with ambiguity, resigned to the fact that there are no simple answers to complex questions. Jung believed that the Self is the core of each individual, with the ability to connect us with our own truth, however imperfectly realized. Ultimately, the search, which is unending, results in the grand paradox of finding ourselves simultaneously as unique individuals and as an inextricable part of a whole that is infinitely greater than its parts.

Works Cited

"Adolescence." *Merriam-Webster Online.* 3 May 2007. www.m-w.com.

Armstrong, Karen. *The Battle for God: A History of Fundamentalism.* New York: Random House, 2000.

Campbell, Joseph. *The Hero with a Thousand Faces.* Princeton: Princeton UP, 1968.

Camus, Albert. *The Myth of Sisyphus and Other Essays.* New York: Random House, 1955.

Dargis, Manohla. "You, Me, and Dupree: Guess Who's Coming to Dinner (and Staying)?" *New York Times* 15 September 2006, Arts sec., 1.

Edinger, Edward F. *Ego and Archetype.* Baltimore: Penguin, 1973.

Frank, Thomas. *What's the Matter with Kansas?* New York: Henry Holt, 2004.

Gordon, George, Lord Byron. *Lord Byron: The Major Works.* Ed. Jerome J. McCann. Oxford: Oxford UP, 2000.

Hillman, James. *A Blue Fire.* New York: Harper & Row, 1989.

———, ed. *Puer Papers.* Dallas: Spring, 1979.

Jacobi, Jolande. *The Way of Individuation.* Toronto: Signet, 1965.

Jacoby, Mario. *Individuation and Narcissism: The Psychology of Self in Jung and Kohut.* New York: Routledge, 1990.

Jung, C. G. *The Collected Works of C. G. Jung.* 20 vols. Trans. R. F. C. Hull. Ed. H. Read, Michael Fordham, and Gerhard Adler. Princeton: Princeton UP, 1953–1989.

———. *Memories, Dreams, Reflections.* New York: Vintage, 1933.

———. *Modern Man in Search of a Soul.* San Diego: Harcourt, 1933.

Noll, Mark A. *The Scandal of the Evangelical Mind.* Grand Rapids: Wm. B. Eerdmans, 1994.

Polette, Keith. "Airing (Airing) the Soul: An Archetypal View of Television." *Post-Jungian Criticism: Theory and Practice.* Ed. James S. Baumlin, Tita French Baumlin, and George H. Jensen. Albany: State U of New York P, 2004. 93–116.

Rich, Frank. "What O. J. Passed to the Gipper." *The New York Times* 20 June 2004, late ed., sec. 2: 1.

Samuels, Andrew, et al. *A Critical Dictionary of Jungian Analysis.* New York: Routledge, 1991.

Shakespeare, William. *As You Like It. The Riverside Shakespeare.* 2nd ed. Ed. G. Blakemore Evans et al. Boston: Houghton Mifflin, 1997. 399–436.

———. *The Tempest. The Riverside Shakespeare.* 2nd ed. Ed. G. Blakemore Evans et al. Boston: Houghton Mifflin, 1997. 1656–88.

Smith, Huston. "Why Fundamentalism Matters." *Parabola* 30.4 (Winter 2005): 54–63.

Stevens, Anthony. *On Jung.* Princeton: Princeton UP, 1999.

Strozier, Charles B. *Apocalypse: On the Psychology of Fundamentalism in America.* Boston: Beacon Press, 1994.

Shaken, Not Stirred

James Bond and the Puer Archetype

LUKE HOCKLEY

> The "child" is all that is abandoned and exposed and at the same time divinely powerful; the insignificant, dubious beginning, and the triumphal end. The "eternal child" in man is an indescribable experience, an incongruity, a handicap, and a divine prerogative; an imponderable that determines the ultimate worth or worthlessness of a personality.
>
> —C. G. Jung, *The Archetypes and the Collective Unconscious*

> You have a nasty habit of surviving.
>
> —Kamal Khan (Louis Jourdan) to James Bond, *Octopussy* (1983)

The *puer*-fixations of contemporary American culture have their approximate equivalents in British film culture. The little boy who won't grow up is easily recognizable and familiar in the figure of Peter Pan. In contemporary popular culture that image has been replaced by numerous figures, including that of James Bond. Bond is an "eternal child," albeit one with adult toys, such as watches with built-in lasers, cars that turn into submarines, and a rocket-powered backpack that lets him take to the skies. Though 007 belongs to the United Kingdom, his appeal to Anglo-American culture suggests that movie audiences on both sides of the Atlantic participate in the fantasy of maintaining a perpetual childlike state. This is the condition in which the puer embodies a desire to avoid coming to terms with the complexities and ambiguities of life. Fleming's novels and their film adaptations offer many case studies in British puer-fixation, demonstrating that America is not the only culture that is tempted to look back to an early stage in its history. Unconsciously, this carries with it a psychological attitude that encapsulates the country's identity based on illusion and nostalgia. The other option, of struggling to engage with the realities and difficulties of life, seems an altogether less palatable prospect.

It almost goes without saying that James Bond is a phenomenon. In Britain the Bond films form part of the national consciousness. The now long-standing tradition of network television's Christmas Bond along with turkey, mince pies, and the Queen's speech is an essential part of a "proper" Christmas. Yet this phenomenon is a curious one. There is something striking about the longevity of a character who is sexist, misogynistic, voyeuristic, and who represents the fading vestiges of a colonial empire. Why is it that such a character (to date played by six different actors in the "official" films)[1] has enduring appeal? There is no simple answer to the question. As already hinted, despite their facile appearance Bond films actually act as a psychological container for a series of contradictions and tensions in British self-identity. This chapter is going to suggest that their appeal lies in the unknowing way that the films mediate unconscious fantasies and concerns about changes to our conscious sense of self and to our national identity. Readers from other countries will have different relationships with the films.

This piece is indebted to a number of different authors—the first of these, Umberto Eco, serves as an essential reminder that narratives can be interpreted in a variety of ways. He points to the discrepancy that exists between the apparent and accessible meaning of a narrative and its "deeper," more ideological and psychological values. His view on the psychological worth, or otherwise, of such material forms an important part of this chapter. While Eco's presence is obvious, less clear is the influence of Simon Winder, whose lighthearted and broadly historically based account foregrounds the significance of the British Empire in the everyday life of Britain. As a personal reflection, this essay also points up the shifting nature of the meaning of the films, noting that what was significant for the original audience may well be lost on contemporary viewers. If Eco provides a structural account, and Winder a quasi-historical one, then Jung provides the archetypal perspective through which this article tries to provide some understanding of the enduring appeal of Bond films. These three key themes play off each other throughout this essay as they attempt to articulate the relevance of the puer archetype as a container for these differing perspectives.

Given the success of the films and their sheer scale, it might be tempting to see Bond movies as modern myths. Their exotic settings, the apparent simplicity of the characters, the dichotomy between good and evil, and the heroic image of Bond on a quest to vanquish evil—all seem to prompt such an interpretation. However, alongside the mythological, the films also include fantastical elements more typical of those found in fairy tales. If the films do not quite manage enchanted forests, they do feature an underwater world that provides the hi-tech home of villains. The sea is also where magical devices such as Bond's underwater Lotus Esprit (*The Spy Who Loved Me*, 1977) come to life. In highlighting the mythological and fantastical qualities of the Bond films the intention is not to locate them outside the realm of ideology. As will be demonstrated, a characteristic of the Bond films is their juxtaposition of mythological and ideological motifs. This said, both mythology and ideology embody a belief in something other than the lived experience of the everyday world and so, in their own ways, represent a type of fantasy.

Bond is a quintessential image of the puer. Twenty films on from *Dr. No* (1962), a naturally aged Bond should be sitting comfortably by the fireplace surrounded by grandchildren. But Bond refuses to age: he refuses to grow old, and he refuses to die (which ends up as parody if the actor stays too long in the role, as was the case with Roger Moore in *A View to a Kill* [1985]). As one of the films reminds us, he will "*Die Another Day*." Instead, a series of actors have inhabited the Bond persona without its apparently proving too troubling for audiences, although there is always a bit of a fuss when a new actor takes on the Bond role. The result, however, is an eternally youthful Bond.

The latest Bond is Daniel Craig, who was in the first "proper" film version of *Casino Royale*, released in November 2006. It is worth noting that at least some of the anxiety around this particular change in actor revolved around a disruption to the persona, since this was the first Bond not to have dark hair—Craig was a "blond Bond," although in reality his hair turned out to be light brown. Bond's other persona-elements remain fairly intact, although Craig provides audiences with a tougher, more visceral version of the character. His infatuation with the sensual side of life—with fine clothes, good food, the niceties of how drinks should be served, and above all with meaningless sex—are all, in essence, simple person-pleasures and show how Bond consistently values stimulation over meaning. The audience's identification, then, is with the persona, not so much with the actors who have inhabited the role. In a shift from normal cinematic conventions, the audience finds itself in tune not with the concerns of a character but with a psychological fantasy—a psychological mask that covers the real-life concerns of British society.

Of course, different actors do bring subtly different qualities to the role. It is interesting that John O. Thompson ("Screen Acting") suggests the possibility of applying Roland Barthes's semiotic notion of commutation to film acting. The process involves imagining what it would be like if another actor had played the role. The hope is that this will reveal the signifying, or distinctive, qualities that the actor brings to the role. Later, Thompson revised his original approach, suggesting that the endless possibilities provided by constantly swapping actors rendered the task meaningless ("Beyond Commutation"), a problem compounded by the role of the film theorist who uses his own judgment over the results in deciding what is significant and what is not. Nonetheless, it remains quite possible to envisage a scaled-down version of the exercise in which one Bond actor is swapped for another. While such an activity is outside the scope of this article, what it might reveal is that continuity of persona is more important than the actor's interpretation of this role, suggesting that the psychological nature of the role is more important than the individual qualities bought by the different actors who have played Bond. This provides the first clue that Bond films are somewhat different from more typical action films.[2]

Part of the appeal of James Bond results from the way in which he represents what Lévi-Strauss refers to as an "anomalous character." This anomaly is partly because his Saville Row suits, vodka martinis, and general taste for the finery of life are out of place in the modern world. In 1962, in a relatively poorer Britain, such finery—along with Bond's penchant for travel—were aspirations for many. However, he is also an anomalous character because he straddles the divide between good and evil, and, in doing so, he is as much ambiguous as he is anomalous. This ambivalence is contained within his psychological image as puer: the adolescent who, despite his sexual nature, refuses to grow up. This provides the ideal container for a country that refuses to accept its changing role in the world. Likewise, the Bond films refuse to change in format and style and, in so doing, create a stable cinematic space within which to hold the puer image.

The first of the Bond films—*Dr. No*—premiered in the U.K. in 1962 and was an unexpected success. It was made for less than one million dollars (which, even by the standards of the day, was a modest sum) because its producers were uncertain about the longevity of the "concept" and about the possibility of future films. Admittedly, the second Bond film, *From Russia with Love* (1963), with twice the budget, was already in the pipeline. Estimates vary, but these two films were box office successes, taking close to $140 million between them. The detail is not what is important here. It is enough to note the clear popularity of the films, suggesting, as it does, that something in them was proving a strong attraction for audiences in the United Kingdom and United States alike. The budget for the third film, *Goldfinger* (1964), rose to three million dollars, by which point the Bond films had established themselves as what modern marketing-speak terms as "a franchise." Recent computer games, graphic novels, and fan literature such as Kate Westbrook's *The Moneypenny Diaries: Intended for her Eyes Only* have further added to the Bond oeuvre. The films have also been given a digital makeover; the classic Bond movies have been cleaned up and reissued. Clearly, MGM believes there is still a strong market for the Bond films and the cost of releasing newly packaged DVDs packed with extra features is corporate money well invested.

To understand the appeal of the early Bond films, we might try to cast our minds back to the time the novels were being written, to gain some insight into the mindset of their author. In undertaking this exercise in truncated history, we will possibly see the different levels of psychological material gradually layering themselves one on top of the other. The effect is sedimentary. The meanings are partly social, partly political—some look toward the past, while others face the future. To be clear, this is not an exercise in history; rather, it is an exercise in imagination. As will be explored later, the blurring of the distinction between reality and myth is another of the distinguishing features of the Bond oeuvre. At first sight, the Bond films appear to belong fairly and squarely to the era of the "swinging sixties." This was a period of sexual freedom, designer chic, and international sophistication—all of which seemingly provides an ideal backdrop for Bond and his exploits. The Maurice Binder title sequences in the films[3] only serve to reinforce the image: they feature women in outline silhouette in various states of undress against lurid psychedelic-colored backgrounds; over the title track the women pose, rest, and fly in and around martini glasses, guns, and other trappings from the *mise-en-scène* of the Bond films.

Yet, despite the visual designs and origins of the Bond films, their psychological imagery and their worldview derive their potency from other earlier sources. While the British Empire was now very much over, it had been vast; until recently it had continued to occupy a not-small part of the national consciousness. As Winder notes, one of the curious myths held about the Empire was that unlike those of others countries this Empire was a kindly one; of course, the legacy left in countries such as India gives a rather different impression (17). Yet there was the sense that the British Empire had been a civilizing influence on the world and that there was something quintessentially good about being British—a curious misconception that continues to be perpetuated by the Bond films. Of course, Fleming was writing in the 1950s, not the 1850s; this was a period when Britain was coming to terms not only with the loss of empire but also with the loss of more than nine hundred thousand of its population in World War I. The death toll in other countries was higher. The world in which Britain had led the way via the Industrial Revolution of the nineteenth century and the might of the British armed forces had changed. America had clearly overtaken the U.K., and the cost of the wars was measured not only in lives but in financial terms, too.

The Fleming family had originally made its money in banking as Fleming and Co. The fact that they moved in elite British circles is shown clearly by the obituary in *The Times* for Ian Fleming's father, Valentine Fleming, who had died May 20, 1917, in World War I—it was written by Winston Churchill (Cork, "The Life"). Ian was just eight years old. He was educated in a traditional upper-class British fashion, first at Eton and then Sandhurst Military Academy, although he failed to thrive at either. Eventually, he was schooled at Kitzbuhel. His first employment was for the Reuters news agency, where it seems significant that he covered a "spy trial in Russia" (Cork, "The Life"). Seeking more money, he became a banker and took a flat in Belgravia (22 Ebury Street, London), strangely enough, in part of a converted Baptist church, where he filled his time with sexual affairs, eating, drinking, and gambling. It was in 1939 that Fleming started to work for the Foreign Office; he carried out this work with Bond-style aplomb, dining at the top restaurants in London, including the Dorchester (Cork, "The Life"). After the war, Fleming purchased a house in Jamaica, which he named *Goldeneye* (also the title of one of the Bond films, though not used for any of the novels), and eventually went to live there permanently with Lady Anne Rothermere. Her second husband was Lord Rothermere, owner of the *Daily Mail*, which was and continues to be a right-wing newspaper; it supported the fascist movement pre–World War II, and its stock-in-trade was to make the "other" a matter of concern and anxiety. Anne was now pregnant with Fleming's child, although she subsequently miscarried (Winder 71). It was 1952, and as Fleming waited for her divorce from Lord Rothermere, he started on the first of the Bond novels—*Casino Royale*, which would be published the following year (Winder 71). More importantly for the British, this was also the year of the coronation of Elizabeth II. Just at the point when the British Empire had disappeared, instead of realizing what was going on, the British, in a somewhat contrary manner, chose to look backward to the glories of a bygone era. Clearly there are parallels between Fleming's lifestyle and his hero's. There are also implicit political similarities. Against a background of diminished empire and growing cold war anxieties, Fleming locates Bond in a fictional world where he continues to carry the flag for England and to live out the fantasy that the British (and perhaps Fleming himself) were as indispensable to the world's intelligence communities as they had previously been.

The literary influences on Fleming come from similar ideological territory. The schoolboy heroics of John Buchan's *Greenmantle* novels are one such source. Another is Rider Haggard's *King Solomon's Mines* (of which Jung was also a devotee, as is evident in the quotation below). Both stories feature a white English hero triumphing over villains while he manages to maintain a broadly right-wing and sexist outlook on life. Regrettably, this attitude is still very much alive in the British imagination, as evidenced by George MacDonald Frazer's *Flashman* novels. As Winder notes, Sax Romer's *Fu-Manchu* novels and the exploits of the characters in Captain W. E. John's *Biggles* children's novels (Biggles being a World War I pilot with a general gung-ho colonial attitude) are also important influences (Winder 31–32). It is interesting to speculate what influenced the name Fleming chose for his novel's central character. Fleming claimed to have named his hero after the American author of *Birds of the West Indies*—James Bond (Winder 28). However, given the character's penchant for the finer things in life and Fleming's family interests, perhaps he also had in mind a financial product, namely, the bank bond. Bringing together an interest in watching "birds" and money in the one name seems an interesting accretion of sexual and capitalist values.

The novels mentioned above are not overly psychological, and it may already be clear that in one sense Bond films are somewhat psychologically impoverished. It is certainly the case that the Bond films are not full of obviously mythological or archetypal imagery. This need not prove an undue worry, as the way that the political, racial, and social settings for Bond films are rendered against what was happening in the real world gives plenty of scope to reflect on the psychological relationship between the films and society more generally. Further, Jung drew the attention of his readers to his view that it was in precisely this type of material that it was possible to find some of the most penetrating psychological insights. The problem is in having to dig away to find them, unearthing the layers of sedimented meaning until finally the core of the matter is exposed. Jung's non-elitist approach has great merit and, given the time that he was writing, is unusually perceptive—it serves as an important reminder that psyche does not discriminate about where it makes its projections. In dreams, as in spontaneous creative acts more generally, the unconscious does not make its decision on the basis of aesthetics; instead, it makes psychologically meaningful statements:

> In general, it is the non-psychological novel that offers the richest opportunities for psychological elucidation. Here the author, having no intentions of this sort, does not show his characters in a psychological light and thus leaves room for analysis and interpretation, or even invites it by his unprejudiced mode of presentation. Good examples of such novels are those of Benoit, or English fiction after the manner of Rider Haggard, as well as the most popular article of literary mass-production, the detective story, first exploited by Conan Doyle. (Jung, *Spirit* 137)

Haggard's novels (particularly *King Solomon's Mines* and *She*) share with the Bond films another disturbing quality. The happy side of the relationship is concerned with myth, unwitting psychological exploration, and a general sense of adventure. The less palatable aspect is the racism that permeates both the Bond films and *King Solomon's Mines* (a racism, it has to be admitted, that is also reflected in some of Jung's writing). The psychological marker that may be illuminated here is that in these cases the "exotic" stands for the "other"; it is used to delineate what is "not me," and the worrisome aspect of this device is that it can all too easily deteriorate into a denigration of the "other." Indeed, the Bond films do just that. However, the situation is more complicated than this comment suggests.

Jung's interest in lowbrow fiction was also evident in his passion for detective stories. In one of those rare passages in the *Collected Works* where Jung mentions cinema, he does so linking it with the figure of the detective. In the following excerpt, he seems to be suggesting something close to revelry in the pleasure of vicarious literary induced experience. Perhaps more significantly, he suggests that what he refers to as "symptoms" have the capacity to tell us something about ourselves and also about our culture:

> The cinema, like the detective story, enables us to experience without danger to ourselves all the excitements, passions and fantasies which have to be repressed in a humanistic age. It is not difficult to see how these symptoms link up with our psychological situation. (Jung, *Civilization* 195)

In strict terms, Bond is not a "detective," as detectives work outside the traditional structures of law and order. By contrast, Bond is an institutional figure who works for the British Secret Service—MI6. But, like the detective, he too has a transgressive element to his persona. After all, he is one of the handful of "double 0" agents (007) who are "licensed to kill," and this distinction carries with it a certain illicit quality. In Bond movies death, sex, and the exotic seem to offer a tempting escape from the realities of life. In this respect, both the detective and James Bond have strong puer qualities: they are concerned with the search for the criminal, the quest for truth, and each will bend the rules to get his man. While Bond offers a more charismatic figure than most detectives who seem caught in the confines of rain-splattered, darkened city streets, both figures are concerned with maintaining the status quo. Neither wants to change society; indeed, what both characters want is that life and society stay just as they are. The invitation of Bond as puer is to show us the world, its adventures, and its dangers but with the tacit understanding that nothing will change.

This narrative world of Bond novels is deconstructed by Umberto Eco. It is important to bear in mind that the novels are quite different from the films: Bond's persona is a little less polished; he drinks too much; he has more affectations than his filmic counterpart; and he generally seems to share many of his author's interests in life. Interestingly, Daniel Craig's Bond restores some of these earthier qualities and, in so doing, may be indicating a shift in the filmic Bond toward the Bond of the novels. This said, Eco's comments nevertheless remain as relevant to the main body of the films as they are to the novels:

> In the last pages of *Casino Royale*, Fleming, in fact, renounces all psychology as the motive of narrative and decides to transfer characters and situations to the level of an objective structural strategy. Without knowing it Fleming makes a choice familiar to many contemporary disciplines: he passes from the psychological method to the formalistic one. (Eco 36)

This is an interesting observation, and it is certainly possible to argue that the Bond films are something of a subgenre in their own right. Through their recycling of conventions and motifs, they play on audience expectations. As these are extensive, it is difficult to know where to begin, but here's a partial list of some of the structural elements of the Bond genre:

- Each film opens with the familiar image of Bond framed centrally inside the aperture of a camera iris—he fires his gun toward the audience, and blood oozes down the screen;
- Bond starts each film in danger and escapes it before the main titles—often some way into the film;
- Bond's one-liners are sexually suggestive;
- Technologically sophisticated gadgets are provided for Bond by Q or his successor, R;
- Bond films don't feature England as their main location (*Thunderball* [1965] being the exception);
- Bond is known wherever he goes by that nation's secret service;
- Bond knows how to place the best order for any food and drink;
- Bond must at least attempt to bed every attractive woman he meets;
- Bond does not become romantically involved (the exception being his marriage to Tracey in *On Her Majesty's Secret Service* [1969]).

There are plenty of other examples. To these generic and formulaic elements Eco adds a series of opposites that he rightly identifies as inscribed into the Bond mythos. In his view, such opposites show that Bond narratives are mythologically encoded, which for him is synonymous with the flight from reason and a retreat into what, at best, is a conservative mythological worldview. At worst, such a retreat serves to reinforce prejudice and stereotype:

> Fleming is, in other words, cynically building an effective narrative apparatus. To do so he decides to rely upon the most secure and universal principles and puts into play precisely those archetypal elements that have proved successful in fairy tales. Let us recall for a moment the pairs of oppositional characters: M is the King and Bond is the Knight entrusted with a mission; Bond is the Knight and the Villain is the Dragon; that Lady and Villain stand for Beauty and the Beast; Bond restores the Lady to the fullness of spirit and to her senses—he is the Prince who rescues Sleeping Beauty; between the Free world and the Soviet Union, England and the non–Anglo Saxon countries is realised the primitive epic relationship between the Privileged Race and the Lower Race, between White and Black, Good and Bad. (Eco 45)

However, is Eco right to suggest that such structural concerns render the films psychologically barren? Is there not another challenge here, which is to accept that the shadow of the puer is alive and well in the contemporary psyche? Much as it is tempting to believe that culturally Britain has escaped from the shadow of its colonial past, in fact it is still quite definitely alive, and this might go some way to explaining some of the contemporary attitudes that abound in British society about race and religion.

As already noted, the films do not appear to offer a particularly rich vein of psychological material—at least at first sight. Yet analytical psychology provides a useful reminder that structures in and of themselves are not necessarily without psychological meaning. Quite the opposite: psychological structures can be thought of as containers that are latent with meanings that need to be expressed in appropriate imagery—as in the relationship between archetypal patterns and their associated images. Bond films, precisely in the way they pass off unpleasant qualities as desirable, offer up material that is worth further psychological exploration.

Not surprisingly, Eco is onto this game:

> Fleming also pleases the sophisticated readers who here distinguish, with a feeling of aesthetic pleasure, the purity of the primitive epic impudently and maliciously translated into current terms and who applaud in Fleming the cultured man, whom they recognise as one of themselves. . . . [T]he sophisticated reader, detecting the fairy-tale mechanism, feels himself a malicious accomplice of the author, only to become a victim for he is led on to detect stylistic inventions where there is on the contrary . . . a clever montage of *déjà vu*. (Eco 47)

There are a number of issues to unpack here. Identifying in Bond something of the primitive epic reclothed in contemporary dress does not mean it is also necessary to applaud Fleming's view of culture. However, Eco seems correct to note the authorial link, as clearly there is a circulation of meaning between Fleming's own life and the activities of Bond. Both represent a particularly outmoded and unpleasant view of Britishness, resting as it does on the cultural foundations of a powerful and essentially false myth of a good Empire. This is the view of the child who finds nothing to criticize in the parent. It is the worldview of someone who has yet to move outside his or her own sense of self, to understand the complexities of social, psychological, and political relations. This, then, is part of what Bond offers, an infantile view of our cultural selves—the view of the puer.

Perhaps this thesis offers a partial explanation as to why the Bond films have not, and probably will not, deal with contemporary terrorist issues—

particularly Islamic terrorism. While appearing to be permeable, the world of these films actually has little to do with the real world. Admittedly, the plot of *Casino Royale* (2006) does involve the financing of terrorism. However, the focus is on Bond's skill at playing cards, not on the motivation of the terrorists who, in any case, are amalgamated in the figure of Le Chiffre. The film displays the outlook of the *puer* who gazes nostalgically to the past rather than engaging with the issues of the present day. To keep the Bond myth intact, the real world must be kept at bay. This said, Islamic *characters* do occasionally occur in Bond films. A notable example is Art Malik's character, Kamran Shar, whom Bond rescues from an Afghani jail in *The Living Daylights* (1987). It transpires that Shar is leader of the local Mujahideen. The seemingly insurmountable problem of clashing ideologies between West and East is dealt with via two narrative devices. First, having been educated at the University of Oxford, Shar is almost as English as Bond. When viewers first encounter Shar he is in jail; he is scruffy, and he speaks with a strong local accent. Once back in his palace, however, he speaks impeccable upper-class English. Second, Afghanistan is under Soviet occupation. Having the Soviets as enemies helps to maintain the cold war myth and ideology of the Bond films. Shar's education in the British system suggests the pervasiveness of the Empire and implies that the best foreigners are British underneath. It is so unproblematic for Bond that he assists the Mujahideen by blowing up a bridge and killing a number of Soviets.

There are other ways that this blurring between the real world and the world of Bond films is achieved, creating the suggestion that the films are not entirely fictional. In *Dr. No*, a painting by Goya of the Duke of Wellington is seen on the wall of Dr No's lair. In reality, the painting had recently been stolen, a point that would not have been lost on contemporary film audiences (but now of interest only to Bond aficionados and film theorists trying to deconstruct the Bond *mise-en-scène*). A second type of blurring was mobilized by the figure of Fleming, himself, as it was well known that he had worked for the British Secret Service: this detail raises the possibility in viewers' minds that perhaps a little of what is seen on screen might be true. The audience always has permission to say that, of course, what they are watching is a fiction, a ridiculous fantasy. Yet, at the same time, it is possible secretly to believe that "Yes, Britain is still a great world power," and "Yes, what a fabulous world Bond lives in." It is, after all, a world free from the real challenges and problems of life, oil pipelines notwithstanding.

Perhaps we should not be too hard on ourselves. The temptation to remain in ignorance about the psychological reality of a situation is a powerful force. Indeed, it is a key element of the *puer* archetype. It is as though the psyche experiences at the same time the pull forward to growth and the pull backward into the seemingly safe world of the child *imago*. As Jung has remarked, "The unconscious has a Janus face" (*Archetypes* 498):

> In every adult there lurks a child—an eternal child, something that is always becoming, is never completed, and calls for unceasing care, attention, and education. That is the part of the human personality which wants to develop and become whole. But the man of today is far indeed from this wholeness. (*Development* 286)

But what seems to have happened with Bond is that, far from issuing a call for development and wholeness, he is stuck in a perpetual adolescence. This is interesting for several reasons, not least of which is that Bond films appear to look toward the future. The most obvious aspect of this is the appearance of numerous gadgets in the films, some of which have now become everyday items, as with the Aston Martin DB5 in *Goldfinger* (1964), which features a form of satellite navigation. More subtly, the Bond films offer the promise of a better, more exotic life. In this way, the magical becomes real, suggesting that the fantasies of the Bond film may hold a truth. Today it may strike us as odd that in *Dr. No* Bond needs only to arrive at the airport in Jamaica to be accompanied by the full musical theme. But in '60s Britain, foreign travel was still something that was fairly unusual, and the calypso music of the film would have been relatively unfamiliar to British viewers—it was not easy to reach France only twenty-two miles away from the English coast, never mind Jamaica (Winder 83). The lush tropical scenery, the unusual food, and sumptuous hotels all seem mundane by today's standards. The more recent films, while keeping similar locations bedecked with glamorous women and other standard plot elements required by the genre, substitute the allure of the older films' locations with the visceral excitement of special effects and astonishing stunts. While the original signification of the music and scenery has shifted, the films still subliminally signify the exotic as "other."

Fortunately for Agent 007, the bad guys in the Bond films are as impractical as they are ingenious. Yet it is another disturbing part of Fleming's legacy that the villains in the films are rarely Anglo-Americans. Their country of origin is often unclear, but there is a vague sense that they might be Russian, or at least Eastern European, or perhaps Jewish, and many of them have slight deformities. The villains in the novel *Casino Royale* and in the films *From Russia with Love* and *Goldfinger* were agents for SMERSH (the fictional Soviet intelligence agency) which Fleming replaced with SPECTRE (SPecial Executive for Counter-intelligence, Terrorism, Revenge, and Extortion) in the novel *Thunderball* (1961). SPECTRE's aim was to create conflict between the two world superpowers

(United States and Russia).[4] This was an interesting move on Fleming's part, as in the cold war era SPECTRE served to make the threat general and pervasive. Wherever danger might come from, at least it certainly would not arise from within. The threat was always from the "other":

> If Fleming is reactionary at all, it is not because he identifies the figure of "evil" with a Russian or a Jew. He is reactionary because he makes use of stock figures. The very use of such figures (the Manichean dichotomy, seeing things in black and white) is always dogmatic and intolerant—in short, reactionary. . . . [H]is is the static, inherent, dogmatic conservatism of fairy tales and myths, which transmit an elementary wisdom, constructed and communicated by a simple play of light and shade, by indisputable archetypes which do not permit critical distinction. If Fleming is a "Fascist," he is so because of his inability to pass from mythology to reason. (Eco 46)

Certainly Fleming is reactionary and, in that sense, does divide the world into black and white. But there is also a more subtle sense in which differences and oppositions confusingly run into each other. Jung refers to the reversal of energies as *enantiodromia*, and it is evident in the Bond films, for example, when the real world blurs the fictional or when Bond as a force for good is also a licensed killer. Likewise, it can be seen in the use of sophisticated technology that points us to the future but that is rooted in an outdated ideology properly belonging to the British Empire of the nineteenth century.

Often *enantiodromic* movements indicate a change in the psyche that presages rebirth. But, far from producing a dynamic system, what seems to have happened here is that the myth has become stuck, or to use a term from earlier in this article, sedimented. The myth does not seem to have moved on, quite possibly because there is a very real sense in which British society has not moved on. This is seemingly a silly remark: after all, over the course of the last fifty years or so Britain has become wealthier, with a higher standard of living; it is, enjoyably, much more multicultural; air travel is cheap; technological changes such as the Internet have grafted Britain into the world economy. But, in a psychological sense, the notion that the culture may have not dissolved the shadow of Empire and World War II remains curiously alive in the nation's consciousness. Britain seems to need new enemies to fight.

Yet, would such violence and aggression have anything to do with the childish *puer* archetype? One could argue that the *puer* is a singularly poor archetype to contain such a complicated set of dynamics, but actually this is the appropriate archetype, and Jung draws our attention to the manner in which the child archetype, in another *enantiodromic* movement, is both helpless and powerful:

> It is a striking paradox in all child myths that the "child" is on the one hand delivered helpless into the power of terrible enemies and in continual danger of extinction, while on the other he possesses powers far exceeding those of ordinary humanity. (Jung, *Archetypes* 289)

Curiously, in the films almost nothing is known about Bond's family life. He never becomes a father; his marriage is brief and tragic, and of his parents little is known other than that they died in a mountain climbing accident when he was eleven years old. James Bond is a child, albeit one with sophisticated toys. To all intents and purposes, Bond is an orphan, and it is important to note this parental absence. In most child-myths there is a mother to protect the child in his or her early years. It is also not unusual for her to have a significant role to play in subsequent developments of the mythology—Christianity provides an obvious example. Yet Bond lacks this parental support. The only vaguely parent-like characters in the films are M and Q. M is a rather taciturn individual, who seems more like a headmaster than a parent, while Q is a trickster-like uncle.[5] Yet it is in M's briefings, where 007 is prepared to deal with his mission, that the impending threat of "otherness" is made clear. Is it an accident that M is no longer played by Bernard Lee but by Judi Dench, the only significant woman in the films whom Bond does not try to sleep with? In fact, the idea of Bond's seducing M (whether male or female) is preposterous, as there is almost an inbuilt Oedipal prohibition to the very idea. Having argued that there is little by way of psychological movement in the Bond films, I should now ask, however, is there a sense in which "other" is becoming Mother? If so, is this a good development? M is not a maternal figure—quite the opposite in the films, at least toward Bond—but rather s/he is a part of the institutions of state. It may be that M does not represent the feminine but is just a reworking of the old English fantasy of Britannia—not without female qualities but presented in a rather masculine (some Jungians might say *animus*-laden) manner.

The feminine in Bond films deserves more space than is possible here. Alongside Judi Dench's M, there are such iconic moments as Ursula Andress emerging from the sea, Aphrodite-like, in the first Bond film, *Dr. No.* The sensual, the exotic, the sexual are all linked. And in a curiously English manner these are also matters for which Bond needs to be punished:

> We have discussed the Bond-Villain dichotomy at length because in fact it embodies all the characteristics of the opposition between Eros and Thanatos, the principle of pleasure and the principle of reality, culminating in the moment of torture (in *Casino Royale* explicitly theorised as a sort of erotic relationship between the torture and the tortured). (Eco 43)

The linking of sex and pain in the Bond films is territory that is explicitly explored in *The World is Not Enough*. Sophie Marceau's character (Electra King—who, incidentally, in Bond-villain style, has a deformed ear) traps Bond on a sort of medieval torture rack and kisses him while at the same time she turns the screw. While it is important not to make too much of this, is it coincidental that Bond is in the process of trying to rescue M (Judi Dench) and that she watches as Bond shoots Electra and then gently kisses her as he lays her on the bed? There is something disturbingly Oedipal about the inversion of the "mother" watching the child who happens to have just killed "Electra King"—the Electra Complex being Jung's renaming of what Freud referred to as the feminine Oedipus attitude (Jung, *Psychoanalysis*).

There is nothing particularly political about this scene. It simply serves to remind us that, despite apparent concerns with international intelligence, plots to blow up the world, and such, there is also a concern for the personal and the psychological. This appeals to a childlike level of the psyche that does not want to grow up. Culturally, it is the part that wants to stay in the past and in a secure attachment to something that is recognized and known—even if that relationship is based on a fantasy. What Hillman has to say about dreams speaks equally well of our relationship to Bond films and our curious anticipation and desire for the next film:

> [I]f each dream is a step into the underworld, then remembering a dream is a recollection of death and opens a frightening crevice under our feet. The other alternative—loving one's dreams, not being able to wait for the next one, such as we find in enthusiastic *puer* psychology, shows to what extent this archetype is in love with easeful death and blind to what is below. (Hillman 131)

It was Raymond Chandler who, in his review of *On Her Majesty's Secret Service* in *The Sunday Times* in 1963, quipped that "Bond is what every man would like to be, and what every woman would like to have between her sheets" ("MI6"). That somehow Empire, sex, and Britishness have managed to get themselves mixed up should not really come as much of a surprise. More astonishing is the extent to which Britain seems stuck. Perhaps alongside issues of Empire, somewhere there is also a residual concern about change, about accepting that, just as the international landscape has moved on, so too in microcosm our individual lives need to respond to the challenge of change.

It is a challenge to our national psyche to move on, and it is no less a personal challenge. However, instead of looking to the future, we choose to dwell in the past. Like Bond's famous vodka martini, we might have been shaken but not stirred into change.

Notes

1. The "official" films are defined as those made by MGM and with a least one of the Broccoli family as producer via Eon Productions. This excludes the spoof *Casino Royale* (1967), which featured David Niven and Woody Allen, and *Never Say Never Again* (1983), the result of legal wrangles. By any other measure, this is a Bond film as recognized by the cinema-going public; Bond aficionados may disagree. Barry Nelson's Bond for CBS, in their 1954 *Casino Royale*, is best left unmentioned.

2. It is worth noting that only two English actors have played Bond, and, as such, the role serves to blur this distinction between Englishness and Britishness. Roger Moore and Daniel Craig are English, Timothy Dalton Welsh, Pierce Brosnan Irish, George Lazenby Australian, and Sean Connery Scottish. I am indebted to John-Paul Green for this point.

3. *Never say Never Again* (1983) is a notable exception.

4. As a side note, that SPECTRE has its headquarters in Paris only serves to confirm British suspicions about the French and shore up the nation's Francophobia.

5. Q and his successor R were played by Desmond Llewelyn and John Cleese, respectively.

Works Cited

Bond, James. *Birds of the West Indies.* 2nd ed. Boston: Houghton Mifflin, 1936.

Buchan, John. *Greenmantle.* Harmondsworth: Penguin, 1956.

Casino Royale. Ken Hughes and John Huston, dir. With David Niven, Peter Sellers, and Orson Welles. Columbia Pictures, 1967.

Casino Royale. Martin Campbell, dir. With Daniel Craig and Judi Dench. Metro Goldwyn Mayer, 2006.

Chandler, Raymond. "MI6: The Home Of James Bond 007." 3 May 2007. <www.mi6.co.uk/sections/literary/ohmss.php3>.

Climax! "Casino Royale." William H. Brown, Jr., dir. With Barry Nelson. CBS Television Network, 1954.

Cork, John. "The Life of Ian Fleming (1908–1964)." 3 May 2007. <http://www.klast.net/bond/flem_bio.html>.

Die Another Day. Lee Tamahori, dir. With Pierce Brosnan, Halle Berry, and Judi Dench. Eon Productions, 2002.

Dr. No. Terence Young, dir. With Sean Connery, Ursula Andress, and Bernard Lee. Eon Productions, 1962.

Eco, Umberto. "Narrative Structures in Fleming." *The James Bond Phenomenon: A Critical Reader.* Ed. Christoph Linder. Manchester: U of Manchester P, 2003. 34–55.

Frazer, George McDonald. *Flashman (the Flashman Papers).* London: HarperCollins, 1999.

From Russia with Love. Terence Young, dir. With Sean Connery, Tatiana Romanova, and Bernard Lee. Danjaq and Eon Productions, 1963.

Goldeneye. Martin Campbell, dir. With Pierce Brosnan, Sean Bean, and Judi Dench. Danjaq, Eon Productions, Metro Goldwyn Mayer, and United Artists, 1995.

Goldfinger. Guy Hamilton, dir. With Sean Connery, Honor Blackman, Gert Fröbe, and Bernard Lee. Danjaq and Eon Productions, 1964.

Haggard, H. Rider. *King Solomon's Mines.* London: Cassell, 1885.

————. *She: A History of Adventure*. Serialized in *The Graphic* 1886–87. London: Longmans, 1887.

Hillman, James. *The Dream and the Underworld*. New York: Harper and Row, 1979.

Johns, William Earl. *The Camels Are Coming*. London: John Hamilton, 1932.

Jung, C. G. *Civilization in Transition*. 2nd. ed. Princeton: Princeton UP, 1970.

————. *The Archetypes and the Collective Unconscious*. New York: Bollingen, 1959.

————. *The Development of Personality*. 3rd print., with additional corrections. Princeton: Princeton UP, 1970.

————. *Psychoanalysis and Neurosis*. Princeton: Princeton UP, 1970.

————. *The Spirit in Man, Art, and Literature*. New York: Pantheon, 1966.

Lévi-Strauss, Claude. *The Raw and the Cooked*. London: Cape, 1969.

The Living Daylights. John Glen, dir. With Timothy Dalton, Maryam d'Abo, Art Malik, and Desmond Llewelyn. Danjaq, Eon Productions, and United Artists, 1987.

Never Say Never Again. Irvin Kershner, dir. With Sean Connery, Klaus Maria Brandauer, and Edward Fox. European Banking Company Ltd. et al.,1983.

Octopussy. John Glen, dir. With Roger Moore, Maud Adams, and Louis Jourdan. Danjaq and Eon Productions, Metro Goldwyn Mayer, and United Artists, 1983.

On Her Majesty's Secret Service. Peter R. Hunt, dir. With George Lazenby, Diana Rigg, and Bernard Lee. Danjaq and Eon Productions, 1969.

The Spy Who Loved Me. Lewis Gilbert, dir. With Roger Moore, Barbara Bach, and Bernard Lee. Danjaq and Eon Productions, 1977.

Thompson, John O. "Beyond Commutation." *Screen* 26.5 (Sept–Oct 1985): 64–76.

————. "Screen Acting and the Commutation Test." *Screen* 19.2 (Summer 1978): 55–70.

Thunderball. Terence Young, dir. With Sean Connery, Claudine Auger, and Bernard Lee. Danjaq and Eon Productions, 1965.

A View to a Kill. John Glen, dir. With Roger Moore, Christopher Walken, and Desmond Llewelyn. Danjaq, Eon Productions, Metro Goldwyn Mayer, and United Artists, 1985.

Westbrook, Kate. *The Moneypenny Diaries: Intended for Her Eyes Only*. London: John Murray, 2005.

Winder, Simon. *The Man Who Saved Britain*. London: Picador, 2006.

The World is Not Enough. Michael Apted, dir. With Pierce Brosnan, Sophie Marceau, and Judi Dench. Danjaq and Eon Productions, Metro Goldwyn Mayer, and United Artists, 1999.

A Crown Must Be Earned Every Day

Seeking the Mature Masculine
in High Art and Pop Culture

DARRELL DOBSON

I've recently been enjoying art, both high and popular, that is distinctly "masculine." More than enjoying it, I've been seeking it out and immersing myself in it. From the literary fiction of Michael Ondaatje, the poetry of William Blake, the stories of Arthurian legend, the mysteries of Arthur Conan Doyle and Michael Innes, to the television series *24* and *CSI*, I have been partaking in art made by men or clearly imbued with "masculine" elements. This has been a new phenomenon in my life, as for years my favorite musicians have been the American folk duo the Indigo Girls, and my favorite novelist has been Iris Murdoch.

When I began to reflect on the unconscious motivations behind these emerging aesthetic interests, I realized that I was seeking models of maturity in order to compensate for an omnipresent immaturity demonstrated both individually and collectively in the current social milieu. In this chapter, I offer an original synthesis of Jungian approaches to aesthetic experience, masculinity, self-study, and cultural studies in an attempt to facilitate both personal and social maturation. Through this analysis, I have discovered a context within which I can comprehend my recent experiences with high art and popular culture. At the same time, this investigation suggests that my personal experiences entail meaning and possibility that may be of some cultural interest and significance, since they provide insight into the adolescent nature of contemporary American culture and posit Jungian approaches to both masculinity and aesthetic experience as means of facilitating the further emergence of maturity in the collective.

It would be pleasing to my own literary and academic sensibilities to engage in an in-depth analysis of a single work using these archetypes of maturity as an interpretive lens, to show that the archetypes are manifest in a single work of pop culture or high art and that such analysis reveals an artwork as compensatory for collective imbalances. However, to do so would be to impose an artificial structure or unity that is absent in my actual experience, and the intention here is to investigate that experience, not to apply a theory. This eclectic collection of aesthetic expressions—from a variety of sources and across a full range of aesthetic quality, from sublime art to popular television and all stages in between, each of which is only touched on here—is itself an indicator of adolescent aspects of the collective (and individual) psyche. Each creation provides a fragment; few are able to provide access to images of maturity in its wholeness. We are drawn to them out of a deep-seated need for these images, for the glimpses of the mature magician in *CSI* and the sightings of the healthy warrior in *24*.

Using this mosaic of aesthetic experiences lacks the obvious unity of the traditional literary essay but instead posits that these varied aesthetic experiences as a whole possess a symbolic logic in a manner similar to that of dreams—they seem fragmented and disorderly, but there is an underlying symbolic order and meaning that is here brought to consciousness. I will further consider the nature and relevance of "self-study research" itself below; however, at this point I will suggest that this phenomenological inquiry recognizes that I, and others, may be "haphazardly" and mostly unconsciously constructing a collage of maturity, assembling its elements as if constructing a mosaic, acquiring the experiential pieces that can contribute to the whole. Doing so emphasizes that in an adolescent society, authentic images of maturity are clearly challenging to create and to find. Yet images of maturity do arise as a necessary compensation, for instance, in some parts of *The Lord of the Rings* or *24*, and the public response indicates a collective yearning for these representations as guides and as a reminder that each of us needs to access such energy in our own personal, social, and political lives. My approach accords with Christian Gaillard's assertion that "a painting, a sculpture, or any work of art—or a dream for that matter" should be regarded "not as a punctual, isolated event to be individually interpreted, but as a moment in a process, whose end remains uncertain, but whose manifestations demand to be considered and accompanied at the rhythm, sometimes slow, of their transformations" (344–45).

I must confess that I, myself, remain somewhat wary about the role of pop culture in the individuation process. Keith Polette, for instance, aptly points out the shortcomings of television as a force for individuation. He argues that dives into television are not likely to be plunges into the unlit archetypal realms but are more likely to be "belly flops into puddles lit by flashlights" (Polette 101) because the products of television "dwell in a consciously constructed [and profit-driven] universe, not an archetypally depicted one" (102). He points out that "the bulk of TV's stories and images do not foster an archetypally individuated psyche but instead reinforce the undifferentiated, childish mind of popular culture" (110). Much of what we encounter on television is indeed sterile, simplistic, childish, stereotypical, literal, shallow, animalistic, undifferentiated, mass-minded, reductive, violent, sentimental, mediocre, or unimaginative.

I agree with Polette that it is necessary, therefore, to "shut off the TV in order to exercise the individuating imagination" (Polette 111). There is only limited assistance available from television, and that narrow potential resides not in passive consumption but in one's active response to a charged experience. Though there is significantly more satisfaction to be found in the high arts in this regard, the experiences we have with them, too, are only indicators, not answers. The energy of an aesthetic experience, whether high or low, is an alarm clock ringing out loudly, or softly, in order to encourage a new kind of wakefulness, a further expansion and development of consciousness. The dynamism of an aesthetic experience indicates that that the respondent is ready for further growth of personality. Further development requires looking inward for reflection, analysis, alignment of the actions in the outer world with the needs of the inner world, and altering one's experience of being in the world through symbolic action. One must, therefore, turn off the TV or return the rental DVD. It is also necessary to close the literary novel, finish the poem, close the lid on the piano, clean and set down the paintbrush, or finish the dance, just as one must wake from the dream. The goal is to use each and any of these products of psyche as a means of increasing consciousness and then to enact oneself in new ways, to develop fresh and vibrant experiences and expressions of oneself in the world: this adaptable self, this fluid world; this constant Self, this stable world.

Such deeply committed symbolic action is hard work, for it involves suffering, sacrifice, and courage. Maturity is an ongoing practice of creating and recreating oneself; it is a daily achievement—a crown must be earned every day—and so the challenge of maturity is seldom undertaken and often abandoned. The rewards, though, are powerful, for they are nothing less than the embodied experience of being more fully alive and present in one's life, the daily creation of a better life for oneself and all those with whom one makes contact. These are rewards that are often intrinsic—which is another challenge in an insecure and immature society that seems addicted to seeking external affirmations of worth.

We must not simply project blame for the immature masculine onto others and do nothing ourselves, and so I take seriously my burgeoning inclinations in the high and low arts as a message from my unconscious about the life-giving potential and growth to be found in further integrating the aspects of the mature masculine in my life. It is a message that doing so benefits all of the people with whom I am in contact, including, but not only, those I teach, my family, and myself. Maturity is its own reward in my life, and when I remain stuck in—or return to—the immature shadows, the most painful aspect is actually experiencing myself in those ways. The more I am able to integrate aspects of maturity into my life, the more I *experience* my life as satisfying and meaningful.

Aesthetic Response and the Transformation of Self

My desire to understand my recent predilection for William Blake and Sherlock Holmes leads me to analytical psychology, where I find that Jung suggests both a social and personal role for the arts and aesthetic experience. On the personal level, individual aesthetic response represents a process of self-revelation in the life of individuals. Personal responses to art function in a similar way and with a similar purpose as other manifestations of the unconscious mind, such as dreams, fairy tales, myths, and rituals. Jung wrote, "A great work of art is like a dream" (*CW* 15: para.160), and in his essay, "Ulysses: A Monologue," he analyzes his *reaction* to the novel by James Joyce—which he finds irritating—as if it were a dream. He writes, "A therapist like myself is always practicing therapy—even on himself. Irritation means: You haven't yet seen what is behind it. Consequently we should follow up our irritation and examine whatever it is we discover in our ill temper" (*CW* 15: para.168). The aesthetic experience, positive or negative, is itself an image, a symbol arising from the unconscious to facilitate the further unfolding of personality. Jung also asserts that "when an archetypal situation occurs we suddenly feel an extraordinary sense of release, as though transported, or caught up by an overwhelming power. . . . That is the secret of great art, and of its effect upon us" (para. 128). A charged aesthetic response, whether to high art or popular culture, can signify such an archetypal encounter. The ego-Self axis (Edinger) is activated by the images within the art object or experience; the individual aesthetic response itself becomes a symbol, and a numinous quality can permeate the experience. This numinosity reveals that within the aesthetic encounter "a hidden treasure . . . conceals a fragment of the godhead. . . . [M]an, in addition to being a creature, is also a creative force demanding fulfillment. Wherever it appears this creative force has a character of revelation" (Neumann 168); we can then analyze such an aesthetic experience as a symbolic call for transformation, an opportunity to integrate more of the comprehensive perspective and latent potential of the Self into ego consciousness. For these reasons, the Jungian analyst Ann Yeoman suggests that

> We may turn to art to learn better how to create and continually recreate ourselves, and to remember that the fully and consciously lived life is a life of deeply committed symbolic action. Story, then, confronts us with soul, and storytelling engages us in an activity of soul-making. (119)

This process of soul-making involves incarnating a renewed attitude, informed by the comprehensive wisdom of the Self as encountered here in the symbolic aesthetic experience. This new stance needs to be actualized in the daily enactment of conscious ego in the outer world through literal action that is understood to have symbolic resonance. This is a lifelong, ongoing practice of creating and recreating identity in order to integrate consciously that which is gleaned through numinous archetypal encounters—as available to us through dreams and active imagination—but also through the arts and even, occasionally, in popular culture.

Archetypes of Mature Masculinity

Western society has been deeply immature for thousands of years, as can be seen, for instance, in the practices of patriarchy. However, Moore and Gillette assert, "patriarchy is *not* the expression of deep and rooted masculinity, for truly deep and rooted masculinity is *not* abusive: patriarchy is the expression of the *immature* masculine. It is the expression of boy psychology.... Patriarchy in our view is an attack on masculinity in its fullness as well as femininity in its fullness" (xvii, original emphasis).

Navigating masculinity, creating and re-creating a mature masculine identity, is a complex process in the contemporary era as the oppressive practices of patriarchy still predominate and still exert a colonizing and hegemonic influence on both men and women, and, in an understandable reaction to the experiences of patriarchy, we also regularly encounter an often undifferentiated condemnation of the masculine. Movies, books, ideas, systems, and attitudes are frequently critiqued and dismissed solely on the grounds that they are masculine. It sometimes appears as if everything "masculine" is tainted by patriarchy. We educated men, particularly those of us interested in the arts, have learned implicitly and explicitly that the means of not being patriarchal was to become more feminine, and we have in many ways been rewarded for doing so. This powerful social phenomenon was exacerbated for many men by growing up with either an absent or negative father energy, and the confluence of these trends has often led us to be complicit in the suspicion and condemnation of the masculine. Those of us who have been trying ardently throughout our lives not to be patriarchal, trying in so many ways not to be our fathers, in such a context, can find ourselves alienated from our own mature masculinity and therefore caught in its archetypal shadows.

Accessing each of four archetypes of the mature masculine may well be a means of redressing this balance; these archetypes are the King, the Warrior, the Magician, and the Lover. As Moore and Gillette show (*King*), each of them possesses a bipolar immature shadow, one pole characterized by an active stance and the other by a passive one: for the King, these are the tyrant and weakling prince (63–70); for the Warrior, the sadist and masochist (88–94); for the Magician, the master of denial and the trickster (111–16); and for the Lover, the addicted lover and the impotent lover (131–40). The predominant individual and social tendency to oscillate between the shadowy opposites is a result of not consciously seeking to access the energies and potentials of the mature archetypes. Each of these shadow images is prevalent in contemporary society and each is an enactment of immature psychic energy, of the adolescent behavior that predominates in our culture and in so many individual lives.[1]

This movement toward a more mature masculinity requires first accessing but then transcending the hero archetype, which serves as a means of severing oneself from the domination of internalized parental controls. The hero archetype allows one to differentiate oneself from the complexes and archetypes within, from the universe at large and especially from the parents. Then, "the Ego must pass beyond the heroic stage, the last stage of legitimate grandiosity, to a condition of true humility. It must offer its loyalty to the Transpersonal Other in its form as the archetypal King and Queen" (Moore and Gillette, *King*; see also Shearer). If successful, this process leads to mature selfhood.[2]

King, Warrior, Magician, Lover in High Art and Pop Culture

That the Canadian author Michael Ondaatje appeals to the mature lover in me explains my recent attraction to his work, particularly the novel *In the Skin of the Lion*, a poetic and sensuous story full of beauty and suffering. Also, I can now better understand that my interest in William Blake resides in the strength of his resolve to enact his inner truths in the outer world, the facility with which he plumbs his own depths and portrays the insights derived therein through his illustrations and poetry. In these ways, he is a marvelous amalgam of the Magician and Lover, the artist as shaman—and one cannot read Blake long without also encountering the Warrior, as Blake draws on the Warrior's strength to enact the insights of the Magician and the passions of the Lover. These elements are all evident in some of my favorite excerpts from *The Marriage of Heaven and Hell*:

> Once meek, and in a perilous path,
> The just man kept his course along
> The vale of death.
> Roses are planted where thorns grow.
> And on the barren heath
> Sing the honey bees. . . .

What is now proved was once only imagin'd . . .

The cistern contains: the fountain overflows.

One thought fills immensity.

Always be ready to speak your mind, and a base man will avoid you.

Every thing possible to be believ'd is an image of truth.

The eagle never lost so much time, as when he submitted to learn of the
   crow. . . .

You never know what is enough unless you know what is more than
   enough.

Listen to the fools reproach! it is a kingly title. . . .

The apple tree never asks the beech how he shall grow; nor the lion, the
   horse, how he shall take his prey. . . .

The head Sublime, the heart Pathos, the genitals Beauty, the hands & feet
   Proportion . . .

Truth can never be told so as to be understood, and not be believ'd.

Enough! or Too much. (Blake 66–80)

Through the archetype of the mature Warrior, I can now understand my
interest in the pop culture television show *24*. Keifer Sutherland's character, Jack
Bauer, is an agent in the Los Angeles bureau of the Counter Terrorism Unit. The
character is portrayed as a mature Warrior characterized by his alertness, clear
thinking, and the constant immediacy with which he takes necessary action.
He is consistently appropriately aggressive in protecting others, all the while
displaying a loyalty to something larger than himself and other individuals,
a transpersonal loyalty to the greater good of his society, which often entails
substantial personal sacrifice. Through his relationship with the character of
President Palmer, he acts in the service of the good King, who is himself in
service to the needs of the collective. I realize that my interest in the show is
really about my need for the mature Warrior energy in my own life, in which
this energy is likely to be passive, but the popularity of the show reveals that the
need for models of the mature Warrior is also shared by a present and historic
culture dominated by the shadow Warrior in his active stance, the Sadist.

I can now also appreciate that my intermittent interest in *CSI* is really about
a need to integrate further the mature Magician archetype. Grisholm and
his colleagues, Crime Scene Investigators in Las Vegas, master their scientific
technologies for the social good, solve difficult crimes through the use of close
and careful observation, logical analysis, and laboratory work, an endeavor
that frequently also draws on the energy of the mature Warrior. Again, the
popularity of the series suggests that there is a collective need to access such
archetypal energy. A similar dynamic informs my reading of Sherlock Holmes,

who also implements careful observation, the scientific method, and logic to protect society.

My forays into some of tales of King Arthur and Parzival (Lang; Tennyson; Wolfram; Chrétien), and the appeal of the characters of President Palmer in *24* and President Bartlet (Martin Sheen) in *The West Wing* can now be understood to arise because of a longing to integrate further a mature King energy in my own life—a need to be more generative, to serve as protector, provider, and procreator in both my inner and outer worlds. They are part of a drive to provide ordering against the forces of chaos, acknowledge the worth and virtue of others, and act in service to the community rather than to advance personal wealth, status, or ego.

The mature King is also a mature Warrior, Magician, and Lover. I offer what is likely an unexpected example of the image of the King in Gandalf from the enduringly popular novel *The Lord of the Rings: The Return of the King* (Tolkien) and its contemporary movie (Jackson et al.), which won the Academy Award for Best Picture in 2003, a fact that demonstrates the resonance of the tale in the contemporary collective psyche. At one point in the story, the city kingdom of Minas Tirith faces attack, and its current steward, Denethor, illustrates the way in which one often flips between the immature shadows; one aspect tends to dominate, and, in times of stress, one often flips to the other extreme. It is as a Tyrant that Denethor sends his own son, Faramir, and many of his soldiers on a futile and perilous defensive maneuver, motivated by pride rather than tactical wisdom. Later, when attack on the city is imminent, he advises its citizens to surrender and runs off to commit suicide, a prime example of a Weakling Prince. But at this crucial moment, it is Gandalf who rises to the occasion to access the energy of the mature King. That he is already the mature Magician is well established in the stories as he consistently uses his magical knowledge and insight for the good of humankind—and all the other races of Middle Earth. At this point in the story, Gandalf for a time becomes the mature King, taking on the role of leadership when he must. That, as "king," he is a mature Lover is seen in his affection for the hobbits and in the care he takes to protect the humans, individually and collectively. From this foundation of relatedness, he is able to inspire the citizens to defend themselves. As the mature Magician, here seen as military technician, he orchestrates and leads the defense of the city on horseback, and as the mature Warrior, he takes active part in the battle. Another aspect of his maturity is seen after the battle is won. He does not overidentify with the literal role of king, as had the steward, Denethor, before him. When it comes time to inaugurate Aragorn, the heir and rightful king, he actively supports the transition, puts himself in service to the greater good, and when he is no longer needed, retires gracefully from the scene.

Social Relevance of the Inquiry

Now I understand the role of the recent aesthetic experiences in my own life: they have activated the ego-Self axis in order to provide a more comprehensive and integrative perspective, facilitating my personal maturation. But is this phenomenon relevant to anyone else? I suspect that it might be for at least two reasons. For the first reason, I draw on the theory of self-study research, and for the other I draw on Jung's work on the social role of the arts.

First, as a piece of self-study, this chapter draws on established "Guidelines for Quality in Autobiographical Forms of Self-Study Research," which delineate how it is that self-study transcends purely personal relevance: "When the issue confronted by the self is shown to have relationship to and bearing on the context and ethos of a time, then self-study moves to research" (Bullough and Pinnegar 15). Autoethnography alternately attends to the particular or personal, and then to the cultural or the social; it moves between the two, crossing, even blurring, these boundaries in order to illuminate and differentiate the phenomena at the center of the inquiry, perhaps in an effort to resist dominant cultural interpretations and values (Ellis and Bochner 733–68). I suggest that the commercial success of the pop culture examples and the enduring interest in the high art upon which I draw are indicative of just such a bearing on the ethos and context of our times. It is also clear that the shadowy, immature manifestations of the archetypes of masculinity stalk our lands, for example (but not only) in the questionable justifications for the invasion of Iraq, the Abu Ghraib prison scandal, increasingly frequent reports of soldier misconduct and crime, and the recent spate of corporate fraud including Enron, WorldCom, and Bre-Ex.

Such qualitative methods of inquiry are not rooted in scientific epistemologies about the nature of knowledge and research. Eisner and other researchers argue that science is only one of many species of research, and that inquiry need not be science-based to count as research (see, for instance, Denzin and Lincoln; Eisner and Peshkin; Ellis and Bochner). The difference between conventional research and qualitative research, such as this self-study, is a difference between doing science and doing art (Eisner, *Enlightened Eye* 14). Self-study, like art—and like science—is a mode of inquiry into experience and a means of representing the findings of that inquiry. From this postmodern perspective on research, knowledge is understood to be more of a construction than a discovery. The values, perspectives, criteria, and frame of reference of a research tradition and of a researcher all influence the description of knowledge, and any experience or phenomenon may be described in an infinite variety of ways. This approach generates knowledge that is self-consciously aware of, and values, its subjective aspects.

Questions of merit and relevance in such qualitative research are evaluated without appealing to quantitative methods such as statistical generalizability, reliability, and validity. Self-study as a form of qualitative research instead implements criteria such as apparency, verisimilitude, transferability, authenticity, adequacy, plausibility, narrative resonance, consensual validation, referential adequacy, and structural corroboration (Eisner, *Enlightened Eye*; Clandinin and Connelly; Ellis and Bochner). For instance, Eisner describes the kind of generalizations that arise from such inquiries. People make "naturalistic generalizations" (Eisner, *Creation* 213)[3] all the time when we come to conclusions and form expectations from experience. We derive conclusions about the past and create expectations for the future based on the collection of "data" more subtle, complex, and personally relevant than any resulting from statistical data. Eisner describes the benefit of such qualitative research when he draws a parallel to the "generalizations" inherent in the arts, based on "canonical images" rather than statistical validity:

> The arts provide images that are so powerful that they enable us to see or anticipate what we might not have noticed without them. For example the images of Don Juan and Don Quixote define for us two different ways in which people live their lives. They enable us to recognize these qualities in others—and even in ourselves. The images created by painters like Edward Hopper and pop-culture icons such as James Dean provide what Ulric Neisser calls anticipatory schemata, schemata that help us notice by suggesting what we can look for. Indeed the function of a case study is to learn about more than that particular case, for a case is always a case of something. In short, the generalizations I am describing yield, not so much conclusions, but heuristics for inquiry, which in any case is the function that all generalizations serve. (Eisner, *Creation* 213)

It is my hope that this self-study transcends merely personal relevance by providing just such a heuristic for inquiry into the adolescent nature of contemporary American society and thereby "bearing on the context and ethos of a time" (Bullough and Pinnegar 15).

Second, I suggest that Jung's explication of the social role of the arts provides two further avenues for considering this analysis as research of interest and relevance. Jung posits a vital and subversive social role for the arts when he argues that, just as the one-sidedness of the individual's conscious attitude is corrected by reactions from the unconscious, so art represents a process of self-regulation in the life of nations and epochs. Because the artist accesses the collective (as well as the personal) unconscious, her work is not *merely* personal in nature. It also has relevance for the society from which it originates. As the individual manifestations of the unconscious seek to address an imbalance in the individual, so artistic creations give insight into the nature of the collective psychological situation and so, thereby, function in accordance with the laws of psychic compensation on the social level.

According to Jung,

> By giving [the archetypal image] shape, the artist translates it into the language of the present, and so makes it possible for us to find our way back to the deepest springs of life. Therein lies the social significance of art: it is constantly at work educating the spirit of the age, conjuring up the forms in which the age is most lacking. The unsatisfied yearning of the artist reaches back to the primordial image in the unconscious which is best fitted to compensate the inadequacy and one-sidedness of the present. People and times, like individuals, have their own characteristics and attitudes. . . . [V]ery many psychic elements that could play their part in life are denied the right to exist because they are incompatible with the general attitude . . . Here the artist's relative lack of adaptation turns out to his advantage; it enables him to follow his own yearnings far from the beaten path, and to discover what it is that would meet the unconscious needs of his age. Thus, just as the one-sidedness of the individual's conscious attitude is corrected by reactions from the unconscious, so art represents a process of self-regulation in the life of nations and epochs. (*CW* 15: para.130)

Artistic creations are here understood to serve as a compensation for the inadequacies of social consciousness. This compensatory function can be served through symbols that are complementary, representing that current state of collective values in order to focus consciousness on it. For example, mass media productions most frequently demonstrate and reinforce the prevalent adolescent values of contemporary society. However, symbols may also represent a compensatory image of what needs to happen, such as the creation of a novel, poem, film, or television show that points out a new direction or possibility. I suggest that the high art and popular culture discussed herein represent just such "a process of self-regulation" in the collective values and that my original analysis of these particular works using the archetypes of the mature masculine not only provides a cultural critique of the prevalently adolescent nature of contemporary American society but also suggests possibilities for transcending this immaturity through the models found in the mature archetypes of King, Warrior, Magician, Lover.

Further, what Jung says of the artist can also be true of the academic:

Therein lies the social significance of [scholarship]: it is constantly at work educating the spirit of the age, conjuring up the forms in which the age is most lacking. (*CW* 15: para.130)

As a creative psyche at work, the archetypal depths of the scholar-artist are also capable of responding to the lopsided character of the times by seeking to articulate and enact a more mature perspective—more mature because it is more comprehensive and integrative. Of course, the scholar may also create work that complements the dominant mores of the collective (which is a danger given the intellectual nature of the undertaking and the theory-driven and positivistic values inherent in society and in most scholarship)—but I suggest even this phenomenon can be understood in the same way as art that reinforces the collective mores: it does so with compensatory intent, seeking to draw the attention of consciousness to the specific nature of the asymmetrical perspective in order to effect further development. The creations of psyche, the scholarship-art, themselves function as compensatory images. In the case of this specific inquiry, psyche reaches back to the primordial images of maturity as I am drawn inexorably to the archetypes of the King, Warrior, Magician, Lover. I have acquiesced to psyche's insistence that I create this project, and further that, in doing so, I include both pop culture and self-study, though neither is the surest path to academic respectability. Here, psyche insists that even academic respectability must be risked, as it, too, can become a stagnant aspect of the collective mores, exhibiting the tyrannical qualities of the immature King, qualities that might themselves be affected by this inquiry into these archetypes of maturity. I realize that our epoch and nations desperately require the energy and action of the mature masculine, but the archetypes of maturity themselves reveal that an epoch and a nation are not abstract notions—they are composed of individuals, of you and me. All of us are yearning for an experience of more quality, of more energy, of more joy, of more satisfaction, of more purpose, of more presence, of more *spirit* in our lives—and each of us is capable of making it so.

Notes

1. Driver argues that there is a strong tendency in masculinity to hegemony and that much of what passes for a more enlightened masculinity often reverts to a subtle form of hegemony. I do not argue with his premise. Moore and Gillette would describe this same process by asserting that in such a case, the individual or group has stopped accessing the mature masculine and has again been overwhelmed by its immature shadows. Individuation is an extremely difficult process; consciousness, a daily achievement.

2. For a consideration of archetypal theory in light of postmodern feminism, see my article, "Archetypal Literary Theory in the Postmodern Age." See also Rowland. For a discussion of the implications of their work for women and the feminine, see Moore and Gillette.

3. Eisner credits the term to Donmoyer.

Works Cited

Blake, William. *The Selected Poetry of Blake*. 1790. New York: Meridian, 1981.

Bullough, Robert V., and Stefinee Pinnegar. "Guidelines for Quality in Autobiographical Forms of Self-Study Research." *Educational Researcher* 30.3 (2001): 13–21.

Chrétien de Troyes. *Arthurian Romances Including Perceval*. 1170. London: Everyman's Library, 1987.

Clandinin, D. J., and F. M. Connelly. *Narrative Inquiry: Experience and Story in Qualitative Research*. San Francisco: Jossey-Bass, 2000.

CSI: Crime Scene Investigation. CBS Television Network, 2000-present.

Denzin, Norman K., and Yvonna S. Lincoln. "The Discipline and Practice of Qualitative Research." *The Handbook of Qualitative Research*. Ed. Norman K. Denzin and Yvonna S. Lincoln. Thousand Oaks, CA: Sage, 2000. 1–29.

Dobson, Darrell. "Archetypal Literary Theory in the Postmodern Age." *Jung: the e-Journal of the Jungian Society for Scholarly Studies* 1.1 (2005) : <www.thejungiansociety.org/ Jung%Society/e-journal/Volume-1/Dobson/2005.html.>

Donmoyer, Robert. "Alternative Conceptions of Generalization and Verification for Educational Research." PhD Stanford U, 1980.

Edinger, Edward. *Ego and Archtype: Individuation and the Religious Function of the Psyche*. London: Shambhala, 1972.

Eisner, Elliot. *The Arts and the Creation of Mind*. New Haven: Yale UP, 2002.

———. *The Enlightened Eye: Qualitative Inquiry and the Enhancement of Educational Practice*. New York: MacMillan, 1991.

Eisner, Elliot, and Alan Peshkin, ed. *Qualitative Inquiry in Education: The Continuing Debate*. New York: Teachers' College P, 1990.

Ellis, Carolyn, and Arthur Bochner. "Autoethnography, Personal Narrative, Reflexivity." *Handbook of Qualitative Research*. 2nd Ed. Ed. Norman K. Denzin and Yvonna S. Lincoln. Thousand Oaks, CA: Sage, 2000. 733–68.

Gaillard, Christian. "The Arts." *The Handbook of Jungian Psychology: Theory, Practice, and Applications*. Ed. Renos K. Papadopoulous. New York: Routledge, 2006.

Jung, Carl. *The Collected Works of C. G. Jung*. Trans. R. F. C. Hull. Ed. Sir Herbert Read, Michael Fordham, and Gerhard Adler. 20 vols. Princeton: Princeton UP, 1953–91.

Lang, Andrew, ed. *Tales from King Arthur*. Ware, Hertfordshire: Wordsworth Editions, 1993.

The Lord of the Rings: The Return of the King. Dir. Peter Jackson. With Ian MacKellen and Viggo Mortensen. New Line Cinema and Wingnut Films, 2003.

Moore, Robert, and Douglas Gillette. *The King Within: Accessing the King in the Male Psyche*. New York: William Morrow, 1992.

———. *King, Warrior, Magician, Lover: Rediscovering the Archetypes of the Mature Masculine*. New York: HarperCollins, 1990.

Neumann, Erich. *Art and the Creative Unconscious: Four Essays*. Trans. Ralph Manheim. New York: Harper and Row, 1959.

Ondaatje, Michael. *In the Skin of a Lion*. Toronto: McLelland and Stewart, 1987.

Polette, Keith. "Airing (Erring) the Soul." *Post-Jungian Criticism: Theory and Practice*. Ed. James Baumlin, Tita French Baumlin, and George Jensen. Albany: State U of New York P, 2003. 93–116.

Rowland, Susan. *Jung: A Feminist Revision*. Cambridge: Polity P/Blackwell P, 2002.

Shearer, Ann. "Searching for Adulthood in Homer's *Odyssey*." *Harvest: International Journal for Jungian Studies* 51.1 (2005): 7–21.

Tennyson, Alfred. *Idylls of the King and a Selection of Poems*. New York: Signet, 2003.

Tolkien, J. R. R. *The Lord of the Rings: The Return of the King*. London: George Allen and Unwin, 1955.

24. Fox Television Network, 2001-present.

The West Wing. NBC Television Network. 1999–2006.

Wolfram von Eschenbach. *Parzival*. c.1200. Trans. A. T. Hatto. London: Penguin, 2004.

Yeoman, Ann. *Now or Neverland: Peter Pan and the Myth of Eternal Youth*. Ed. Daryl Sharp. Toronto: Inner City, 1998.

"Protracted Adolescence"

Reflections on Forces Informing
the American Collective

JOHN GOSLING

> I consider the puer aeternus attitude an unavoidable evil. Identity
> with the puer signifies a psychological puerility that could do
> nothing better than outgrow itself.
>
> —C. G. Jung, *Letters*

Introduction

American society appears to be in crisis. This observation has recently been explored by several writers (Chomsky, *Hegemony or Survival*; Chomsky, *Failed States*; Ehrenreich; Frank; Frankin; Moore). The Presidential election results in 2004 confirmed that the majority of Americans supported an administration that misled them about the reasons for engaging in a catastrophic war in Iraq, that seriously curtailed civil liberties in the name of national safety and security ("Civil Liberties"), and that sent the gross national debt spiraling to more than eight trillion dollars (Simmons). Furthermore, personal savings have become negative for the first time since the Great Depression of the 1920s (Sparks para. 8). For the first time in history, Americans owe more than they take home in after-tax income.

In this chapter, I will discuss some reasons for this state of affairs. I will argue that the collective American psyche is developmentally stuck in a protracted adolescent phase of "psychological puerility," unconsciously identified with the negative aspect of the archetype of the *puer aeternus/puella aeterna* (the eternal youth). Gripped by this powerful impersonal archetypal energy, individuals remain in a state of emotional immaturity dominated by the "infantile attitude," as Jung expresses it (*CW* 4: 249; *CW* 7: 59; *CW* 10: 161). In this emotionally immature state, that which is experienced as distasteful and causes emotional discomfort (Jung referred to these aspects as the *shadow* [*CW*: 9.2: 13–19; *CW* 9.1: 248; *CW* 18: 160, 484]) is split off and projected outside of oneself onto an Other in the external world that is perceived to be the problem. The world is clearly demarcated into opposites of right and wrong, good and evil—the evil "others" and the good "us." This mechanism probably underlies the now infamous comment by George W. Bush when referring to the so-called war on terror: "You are either for us or against us" (Fisk).

I will discuss how the activation of the positive aspect of the archetype of the child collectively could possibly facilitate achievement of a maturational phase that would help to counterbalance and eventually overcome the one-sidedness of the powerfully activated negative pole of the puer/puella archetype. I will also point out how, by maintaining a constant level of fear in the collective, the Bush administration rendered individuals vulnerable to activation by the amygdala in the brain—that part of the limbic system that stores memories of all past traumatic events (LeDoux, *The Emotional Brain*; LeDoux, *Synaptic Self*). When activated, it renders individuals in a vulnerable state of neurophysiological arousal and fear in which judgment is impaired. The collective will then agree to all sorts of impositions and undermining of civil liberties if this is done with the assurance and promise of increased safety and security. To override this activation would require a transition to mature adulthood with an increase in awareness and the capacity to question the authority of those in power without perceiving them as parental surrogates or as potential saviors. The solution lies within and requires a redirection of energy to explore the inner world and expand consciousness. This requires a transition from adolescence to mature adulthood, and I am arguing that, collectively, the American psyche is still in the process of mastering this developmental phase.

Identification with the Puer/Puella Archetype

One of Jung's major contributions to our understanding of the human psyche was his discovery of the collective or archetypal unconscious (*CW* 9.1: 3–72). Organs of the pre-rational psyche, archetypes are impersonal; each can manifest both a positive and a negative aspect. They adhere to the structure of the human psyche itself and can manifest in relation to inner or psychic life. Like all archetypes, the puer/puella archetype has bipolar aspects, both positive and negative. It is my contention that, collectively, many individuals in the United States, including President George W. Bush and some of his administration, became possibly unconsciously identified with the activated archetype of the puer/puella, which caused them collectively to remain too long in adolescent psychology and contributed to a state of what I am calling "protracted adolescence."

According to Marie-Louise von Franz, it would seem that Ovid used the term *puer aeternus* in his *Metamorphoses* (4.18–20), where it is applied to the child-god in the Eleusinian mysteries. In the positive associations, he is the god of divine youth, a god of life, death, and resurrection, corresponding to such oriental gods as Tammuz, Attis, and Adonis; however, in the negative aspect,

> In general, the man who is identified with the archetype of the *puer aeternus* remains too long in adolescent psychology; that is, all those characteristics that are normal in a youth of seventeen or eighteen are continued into later life, coupled in most cases with too great a dependence on the mother.... In some cases, there is a kind of asocial individualism: being something special, one has no need to adapt, for that would be impossible for such a hidden genius, and so on. In addition, an arrogant attitude arises toward other people, due to both an inferiority complex and false feelings of superiority.... Accompanying this neurosis is often, to a smaller or greater extent, a savior or Messiah complex, with the secret thought that one day one will be able to save the world; that the last word in philosophy, or religion, or politics, or art, or something else, will be found. (von Franz 1–2)

I would suggest that there is an apparent general belief held by many in the United States that they are "something special"—if not the most special and privileged beings on the planet. If not a conscious belief within individuals in America, this attitude at least manifests itself in a collective energy that is perceived by the global community as a general arrogance toward the rest of the world. Accompanying this is a sort of Messianic zeal. Thus, perhaps not surprisingly, one of the stated goals of the war in Iraq was to "bring democracy to the Middle East" (Basham and Preble)—that is, to save the Iraqis from their own fate. In reality, this endeavor has turned into one of the bloodiest catastrophes in recent history, with many thousands of Iraqi civilians slaughtered and more than four thousand American and other troops already dead, with many more maimed and psychologically scarred for life. And there appears to be no end of this carnage in sight.

Such is the danger when impersonal archetypal energies (in this case, that of the negative aspects of the puer/puella) exert a hostile takeover of the ego of an individual or of the psyches of the collective. Alternatively, the same peril exists when the ego *identifies* with the potentially dangerous impersonal archetypal energy, when a mere mortal *becomes* the god. Jung points out that

> [t]he more clearly the archetype is constellated, the more powerful will be its fascination, and the resultant psychological statements will formulate it accordingly as something "daemonic" or "divine." . . . Such statements indicate possession by an archetype. (*CW* 11: 151)

The BBC reports that, when George W. Bush met with Abu Mazen, Palestinian prime minister, and Nabil Shaath, his foreign minister, in June 2003, the latter allegedly reports that President Bush said to all of them:

> "I'm driven with a mission from God. God would tell me, 'George, go and fight those terrorists in Afghanistan.' And I did, and then God would tell me, 'George, go and end the tyranny in Iraq . . . ' And I did. And now, again, I feel God's words coming to me, 'Go get the Palestinians their state and get the Israelis their security, and get peace in the Middle East.' And by God I'm gonna do it." (BBC)

These statements may indicate that some of Bush's decisions were not only "divinely inspired" but perceived as a direct communication from God, illustrating his possible "possession" by activated archetypal energy (as described by Jung in the above quotation) that has had significantly tragic results in both Afghanistan and Iraq—at least for those who have been massacred or maimed and for those whose lives have been irrevocably devastated by these wars.

Jung notes, "In the collective unconscious of the individual, history prepares itself" (*CW* 18: 163). Furthermore, when one or more archetypes are activated in a number of individuals and begin to manifest by coming to the surface, "we are in the midst of history" says Jung:

> The powerful factor, the factor which changes our whole life, which changes the surface of our known world, which makes history, is collective psychology, and collective psychology moves according to laws entirely different from those of our consciousness. The archetypes are the great decisive forces, they bring about the real events, and not our personal reasoning and practical intellect. (*CW* 18: 163).

We who were in New York on the fateful day of September 11, 2001, were indeed "in the midst of history," as were the rest of the United States and the world, thanks to the advent of satellite communication and television. Our lives, and those of many millions throughout the world, were irrevocably changed. On that day, "the surface of our known world" was changed forever with the collapse of the towering World Trade Center, thanks to the activation of powerful archetypal energies, "the great decisive forces," that brought about these awe-inspiring events. It had all the hallmarks of a numinous event with the ability simultaneously both to horrify and enthrall. Living within a mile of the World Trade Center, I personally have never experienced anything as dreadfully awe-inspiring as that unimaginable event.

In a letter, Jung has this to say about the puer:

I consider the *puer aeternus* attitude an unavoidable evil. Identity with the *puer* signifies a psychological puerility that could do nothing better than outgrow itself. It always leads to external blows of fate which show the need for another attitude. But reason accomplishes nothing, because the *puer aeternus* is always an agent of destiny. (*Letters* 1: 82)

In view of the events that occurred on 9/11, these are ominous words indeed. On that inauspicious day, "external blows of fate" in the form of hijacked planes crashing into the World Trade Center towers and the Pentagon changed the sense of apparent inviolability of all Americans forever.

Following those events, there seemed to be a brief window of opportunity for the leaders and the collective to transition to "another attitude," to outgrow the state of "psychological puerility," and to adopt a more mature attitude capable of the self-reflection necessary to accept responsibility for past actions. However, instead, a regression occurred to an even more primitive mode of being with intrapsychic splitting and projection of the shadow onto perceived threatening "others." The opportunity for any meaningful self-examination or questions as to the reasons this treacherous occurrence may have been evoked came and went. The president, his administration, and eventually the majority of the collective appear to have opted for the primitive psychological mechanism of revenge according to the ancient Law of Talion: an eye for an eye and a tooth for a tooth. In the days immediately following 9/11, an astute individual had tied the following poster to a fence at the site of a shrine that had spontaneously arisen at Union Square in New York: "An eye for an eye only leads to blindness." A transition from "psychological puerility" to a more mature attitude would have allowed those in power and others at least to question what collective attitudes and past behaviors on the part of the United States may have awakened and provoked these devastatingly dark forces, which might have led them to calming and enlightened insights in the midst of such emotional and painful events. Indeed, the Bush administration seemed willing to apply the Law of Talion in the American response but unwilling to accept any suggestion that the attacks had originally been an application of the same law.

Essentially, I am postulating that "an agent of destiny" was at work on that fateful day. By way of explanation, let me cite two of Jung's suggestions relevant to the archetypes and the awakening of the collective unconscious:

[T]he collective unconscious is a very irrational factor, and our rational consciousness cannot dictate to it how it should make its appearance. Of course if left entirely to itself, its activation can be very destructive. (*CW* 18: 161–62)

Mankind is powerless against mankind, and the gods, as ever, show us the ways of fate. Today we call the gods "factors," which comes from *facere*, "to make." The makers stand behind the wings of the world-theatre. In the realm of consciousness we are our own masters; we seem to be the "factors" themselves. But if we step through the door of the shadow we discover with terror that we are the objects of unseen factors. (*CW* 9.1: 23)

Powerful, impersonal, irrational, "very destructive," archetypal, "unseen factors" were constellated in the collective unconscious and rose to the surface to manifest in cataclysmic events on the day of September 11, 2001. The gods were evoked; they emerged from the "wings" and used us mere mortals as their puppets to wreak havoc on the stage of the "world-theatre."

Splitting and Projecting: Klein and Jung

Following the tragic events of 9/11, after the brief window of opportunity to embrace a more mature, responsible attitude of self-examination closed, a collective regression appears to have occurred to a more developmentally primitive mode of organizing experience characterized by splitting and projecting. Instead of the shock, horror, and grief having a salutary effect, it evoked a collective state Melanie Klein coined the "paranoid/schizoid position" ("Notes"). From this perspective, one's experience of the external and internal worlds is split into clearly demarcated opposites, good and evil. We are good, and the bad others "out there," into which our entire undesirable, loathsome, painful, and discomforting affects and attributes are projected. It follows then that the all bad and evil enemy in the external world must be destroyed in the interests of "national security." As one might expect, such a collective attitude often leads to wars.

So it came to pass that the United States decided that the enemy responsible for the devastation of 9/11 was in Afghanistan and proceeded to bomb and invade that country—it seemed to matter little that the actual perpetrators (including the infamous Osama bin Laden) were in fact Saudi Arabian. The fact that significant numbers of civilians and American troops have died in the process, while Osama bin Laden—the alleged mastermind behind Al Qaeda—remains at large, has apparently not led to any substantial individual or collective reevaluation of the situation. If this had occurred, there may have been the possibility of the dawning of what Klein refers to as the "depressive position" (*Contribution*) and what Jung calls the integration of the shadow (*CW* 9.2: 9–10).

With the achievement of this maturational phase of the "depressive position," when the "infantile attitude" is relinquished, there is less tendency for the individual to split off discomforting and distasteful affects and to project them onto others in the external world. This is accompanied by ego's increasing capacity to tolerate simultaneously one's positive affects in addition to those experienced as disagreeable and to mediate these and the instincts more appropriately. In this more mature developmental phase, external reality and the inner psychic domain are no longer perceived in clearly delineated opposites, such as black and white, good and evil, or joy and sorrow. It becomes possible to experience finer-nuanced gradations in shades of gray. The ego is able to tolerate anxiety, ambiguity, and ambivalence instead of seeking sureness and certainty. We are able to recognize and endure the greater complexities of being human without projecting onto others and without unrestrainedly acting out.

Achieving this developmental phase of a more mature attitude toward life requires the willingness to suffer more consciously our own humanity, including those aspects of ourselves that we prefer to deny. We are called upon to acknowledge our own assets *and* limitations, our strengths *and* our weaknesses. In short, we need to accept our own flawed humanity:

> Life demands for its completion and fulfillment a balance between joy and sorrow. But because suffering is positively disagreeable, people naturally prefer not to ponder how much fear and sorrow fall to the lot of man. So they speak soothingly about progress and the greatest possible happiness, forgetting that happiness is itself poisoned if the measure of suffering has not been fulfilled. (Jung, CW 16: 81)

Unfortunately, unless driven to seek help by traumatic life circumstances that are causing so much intrapsychic pain that it has become unendurable, or unless overwhelmed to such an extent as to cause dysfunctionality or psychosis, most humans will avoid confronting their own inner demons—"because suffering is positively disagreeable," Jung reminds us, and most people "naturally prefer not to ponder how much fear and sorrow fall to the lot of man"; nor are most people inclined to undertake a process of self-inquiry that may lead to their taking responsibility for their contribution to problematic situations:

> This only falls to the lot of the man who realizes that he has a neurosis or that all is not well with his psychic constitution. These are certainly not the majority. (CW 8: 208)

It is my contention that most human beings in the world today are unwilling to undertake the journey of self-exploration. Hence, the tendency to project shadow aspects onto "the enemy out there" and the danger of falling prey to unmediated archetypal energies remain ever-present dangers that contribute to the disrupted current state of the world. There is an extremely limited capacity to acknowledge that it is I who has these unacceptable sadistic, murderous, hateful impulses. It is I who has in fact done bad, hateful, cruel, oppressive things to others in the past. Rather, it is the other who is perceived to be at fault and who is persecuting me. I am innocent. It is the other against whom I must retaliate and whom I must destroy.

Jung points out that the

> individual being . . . harbours within himself a dangerous shadow and adversary who is involved as an invisible helper in the dark machinations of the political monster. It is in the nature of political bodies always to see the evil in the opposite group, just as the individual has an ineradicable tendency to get rid of everything he does not know and does not want to know about himself by foisting it off on somebody else. (*CW* 10: 299)

Here Jung eloquently describes the tendency both of "political bodies" and of individuals (that make up these "political bodies") to project their shadow aspects "on somebody else" and to see the evil only in those hated and despised "others" in the external world. To rise above this inevitable unconscious human tendency requires the mutual withdrawal of projections by parties on both sides of the conflictual divide. We can then begin to doubt the rightness of our opinions and compare them to the actual objective facts. Had the president and his advisors, and the majority of the collective, been willing to engage in this inner work, the Iraq war may never have occurred. Instead, the American people allowed themselves to be misled about alleged weapons of mass destruction (WMDs) that apparently posed an imminent threat to the safety of the United States. "Bluff is an illegitimate way of overpowering and suppressing others and leads to no good," says Jung (*CW* 10: 300–01), and the Bush administration's bluff about WMDs in Iraq has certainly led to no good. This war has resulted in the sacrifice of many lives, has resulted in a state of civil war in Iraq, and has cost the American people billions of dollars. The repercussions of this travesty will be felt for many years to come.

However, from a Jungian perspective, any person who does undertake the task of integrating the personalities within and expanding her/his consciousness would be less inclined to project the shadow onto others and is willing to confront this dark "other" within. Such a person would be able to echo the words of Prospero in Shakespeare's *The Tempest* when, at the end of the play, he turns to Caliban, a savage son of a witch (whom Prospero has abused and then rejected, thereby tempting Caliban to murder him), and says: "This thing of darkness I / Acknowledge mine" (5.1.275–76). Such a person is willing to attempt to become aware of his/her own shadow aspects that Jung calls "the inferior part of the personality." Jung refers to this process as the "realization of the shadow" (*CW* 8: 208)—a daunting and quite disagreeable task for most of us. There are then fewer tendencies to project unacceptable shadow aspects onto others in the external world. The enemy is no longer sought without but is now confronted within. The challenge is to learn to accept all of the most hateful, despicable, dastardly aspects that are inherently present in every human being. Then the possibility exists that we may discover that "the most impudent of all offenders, yea the very fiend himself—that these are within me" (*CW* 11: 339).

Once this discovery is made and it becomes clear "that I myself stand in need of the alms of my own kindness, that I myself am the enemy who must be loved—what then?" (*CW* 11: 339). What then indeed? Then it is incumbent upon me to reevaluate all of my previous suppositions about the "axis of evil" being out there, as I discover that the "evil one" is part of my own inner world. For Jung, this inner work is also a very real contribution to the world community:

> If you imagine someone who is brave enough to withdraw all these projections, then you get an individual who is conscious of a considerable shadow.... Such a man knows that whatever is wrong in the world is in himself, and if he only learns to deal with his own shadow he has done something real for the world. (*CW* 11: 83)

If the president and those in positions of authority in the administration were able to acknowledge and take responsibility for just some of the aggressive foreign policies in which the United States has engaged over the past few decades (such as supporting the overthrow of President Allende in Chile, which occurred on September 11, 1973 [an interesting fateful synchronicity with 9/11], while supporting a host of undemocratic and repressive regimes, including that of Saddam Hussein in Iraq for several years before he fell out of favor), and if more individuals would be willing to engage in the painful process of self-examination and withdrawal of projections, then a collective shift in consciousness may occur.

It would be unrealistic and unthinkable to advocate individual therapy or in-depth analysis for everyone. However, I am in favor of promoting greater awareness of these basic concepts of how the human psyche functions, and I favor making this body of knowledge available to greater numbers of people. For example, it may be helpful to include in school and college curricula the rudiments of depth psychological understanding in courses such as "Life Skills Training," or "The Art of Being Human." Perhaps even a book such as this one can help to bring these crucial concepts to a different segment of our population by focusing on popular culture and the aspects of our daily lives that may illuminate Jung's theories more readily for contemporary readers.

A shift in collective consciousness is often heralded by archetypal activations in the psyches of a portion of the collective or by the emergence of a leader that embodies positive archetypal energy. Possible helpful archetypal activations may include that of the child archetype (with the child motif appearing in dreams, in fantasies/visions, in movies, on television, etc.) or the positive aspect of the "wise old man" or senex archetype in an individual or individuals (with the emergence of a leader or leaders that embody wisdom, humility, and insight, such as was embodied in someone like Nelson Mandela) to counterbalance the one-sidedness of the eternal youth. However, I see no evidence of any activation of these archetypes or their embodiments in the American collective or leaders, at least as of the date of my writing this essay.

The child archetype represents the original, instinctive, preconscious aspect of the collective unconscious. It exists in all human beings as a functional system in the psyche, the purpose of which is to compensate "the inevitable one-sidedness and extravagances of the conscious mind" (CW 9.1: 162). Such an autonomous activation of the collective unconscious may point to the potential for future developments and change that leads to the dawning of a new and more integrated attitude. The child motif is a symbol that is potentially redemptive and that unites opposites in the psyche—in this instance the conscious attitude of being "right" and righteous with the unconscious shadow aspect. It is potentially "a mediator, a bringer of healing, that is, one who makes whole" (CW 9.1: 164).[1] It anticipates the possibility of a future, more integrated personality. Thus its powerful potential to acknowledge the transgressive unethical actions perpetrated by each individual, as well as those of the U.S. government on others in the name of "national security" for many past decades, in order to mediate and heal the collective.

Jung maintained that self-realization and the transformation of psychic energy in the *individual* were essential to the processes of individuation and increased awareness. This change occurs in the psyche of *each individual* with a concomitant increase in consciousness and awareness that will ultimately have a beneficial effect on society as well. Jung states that "right action comes from right thinking, and . . . there is no cure and no improving of the world that does not begin with the individual himself" (CW 7: 226). Here, Jung's "right thinking" means increased self-knowledge, awareness of the shadow, withdrawal of projections, familiarity with the unconscious (both personal and collective), and a reconciliation of the opposing energies in the psyche. Without this knowledge, unconscious contents will continue to be projected resulting in dysfunctional relationships, fragmented societies, and wars.

The recent elections (November 2008) indicate a belated increase in awareness in a slight majority of the American collective about the inappropriate destructiveness of the former administration's foreign policy in Iraq. I am, however, postulating that the emergence of the child archetype or the embodiment of the "wise old man" archetype in a leader may ultimately help to foster a more substantial compensation for the one-sidedness of the American collective psyche currently in the grips of the negative pole of the puer/puella archetype and stuck in a state of protracted adolescence. Then there is hope for possibly increasing peace in the world.[2]

Possible Causes of the Collective Archetypal Activation of the Puer/Puella Archetype

American culture is primarily a youth-oriented, youth-consumer, and youth-driven culture. Many corporations specifically target only the youth in advertisements and the media. Pop culture icons such as Michael Jackson, a modern-day Peter Pan, who until recently lived on his "Neverland Ranch" estate, are cultural heroes. This overemphasis on youth predisposes the culture to experiencing collectively an activation of and identification with the negative pole of the puer/puella archetype as I will outline below.

American society has become increasingly technologically driven, and this is resulting in increasing numbers of individuals being separated from their roots, the ground of their being. Children and young adults spend hours playing computer games, surfing the Internet or watching television. Life in the United States and in most of the Western world has become "a life out of balance" from its roots in nature.

Francis Ford Coppola and Godfrey Reggio made an independent film titled *Koyaanisqatsi*, a Hopi word meaning "life out of balance," between 1975 and 1982. The musical score was composed by Philip Glass. The film depicts an apocalyptic collision between two worlds: that of urban living with its technologically dominated lifestyle versus the magnificence of our natural environment (or rather, what is left of it). This film is a remarkable visual portrayal of how we humans have "evolved" away from nature while creating our highly technologically developed artificial environments in which we encase ourselves in concrete jungles. Pollution of various sorts has become ubiquitous in most large cities and their industrialized environs—resulting in a threat to our very survival on this planet as global warming reaches unprecedented proportions ("Global Warming"). The number of recent hurricanes to traverse the Gulf of Mexico, including the devastation wrought in some southern states by Hurricane Katrina in 2005, underscores the consequences of our refusal to deal with the imminent reality of global warming and the threats that it poses to our world (Chomsky, *Hegemony or Survival* 3). Urbanization is continuing to accelerate at an unparalleled rate, as masses of rural dwellers flock to the large cities in the hope of a better life, resulting in increasing numbers of individuals finding themselves unwitting participants in "a life out of balance."

When we become removed from contact with nature and caught up in the maelstrom of technologically driven urban life, a gradual severance occurs for most of us from our roots—our original, unconscious, instinctive, primitive psyche—represented by the archetype of the child (and also by various animal images in dreams). This split-off, vital aspect of our psychic functioning continues to exist in the nether regions of the unconscious where it gains power and inevitably constellates in a more negative form, such as the negative pole of the puer/puella archetype. In the form of a powerful archetypal activation, it is now able to exert a hostile takeover of consciousness. This only *apparently* inactivated split-off part of the psyche

> brings about a possession of the personality, with the result that the individual's aims are falsified in the interests of the split-off part. If, then, the childhood state of the collective psyche is repressed to the point of total exclusion, the unconscious content overwhelms the conscious aim and inhibits, falsifies, even destroys its realization. Viable progress only comes from the co-operation of both. (Jung, *CW* 9.1: 164)

Thus, the stage is set for the possible activation of the negative pole of the puer/puella archetype that I am postulating has occurred on a collective level in the American psyche.

However, the age of technological advancement is here to stay and has become an integral part of the lives of most individuals living in first world countries and the ideal of those living in second and third world countries. Cell phones, computers, the Internet with access to an information highway of knowledge, information at our fingertips that in the past would have taken ages to research, satellite communication that links us via television into one global village where world events can be observed in real time as they are occurring, advances in genetic research—all are unprecedented developments unimaginable a few short decades ago. Is the advancement in the understanding and awareness of our inner psychological condition keeping pace with this rapid technological progress? I fear not. I fear that we are increasingly neglectful of our inner worlds, and, in view of the current technological explosion, this situation is exceedingly dangerous—as is evidenced by the escalating levels of domestic violence, rape, murderous adolescent rampages, atrocities perpetrated by humans on each other and the environment worldwide, areas of unrest, wars, and so on. Martin Grotjahn expresses this dilemma as follows: "It is also likely that if we neglect the inner mastery, the integration of conscious and unconscious mind, the outer technical mastery will be dangerous. It would be like putting bombs into the hands of infants" (197).

Another possible factor that makes us all vulnerable to communal activations of archetypal energy is the capacity by those in power to induce and maintain collectively a chronic state of fear. Following the events of September 11, 2001 the U.S. administration did in fact devise a highly effective system of color-coded warnings related to alleged information "from reliable sources" that a possible terrorist attack was imminent. For months and years after this inauspicious event, the color-coded fear-inducing system would be announced, intermittently and unpredictably. This served as a system of intermittent reinforcement, one of the most powerful behavioral techniques for conditioning both animals and humans. The colors seemed to hover somewhere between yellow and orange, the latter being a state of high alert, with red being the most dangerous scenario. When these color codes were announced, a confusing mixed message was given by the authorities: "We encourage you to be extremely vigilant and to report anything suspicious to the authorities; however, we also urge you to go about your normal activities." This is akin to giving a dog the commands to "stay" and "fetch" simultaneously. Such an animal becomes disoriented and confused. Following these warnings, many analysands would show up for their sessions with me in a highly anxious and often agitated state, disproportionate to the alleged threat.

Joseph LeDoux, an experimental psychologist, has demonstrated that portions of a small nucleus in the brain called the amygdala[3] (a Greek-derived word meaning "almond" because of the shape of this nucleus) are responsible for fear conditioning. Sensory input reaches the amygdala directly, allowing it to monitor the outside world for signs of danger. The amygdala forms part of the limbic system, or "old brain." LeDoux has shown that neuroanatomically there are extensive neuronal connections from the amygdala and hippocampus to the neocortex (the "new brain," and postulated seat of consciousness), but there is a paucity of neuronal input from the neocortex to the limbic system (LeDoux, *Emotional Brain* 165, 303). The reason for this is survival of the species. The limbic system and specifically the amygdala respond to perceived danger to survival and set in motion a cascade of neurophysiological events (such as increased heart and respiratory rates, sweaty palms, increased levels of cortisol, and so forth) that give rise to the "fight or flight" or "freeze" response and are accompanied by intense anxiety, fear, or terror—depending on the severity of the perceived threat. During this autonomous activation, the neocortex (presumed seat of ego consciousness) is incapable of overriding the input from the amygdala (because of the paucity of input from the neocortex to the amygdala and the limbic system) and initially simply responds automatically (LeDoux, *Synaptic Self* 121–23).

I am postulating that, similar to memories of personal or inherited traumatic experiences that are encoded in the amygdala, complexes[4] (that are also the result of personal or inherited traumatic events), and possibly also the archetypes themselves may be encoded in the amygdala and/or the limbic system.[5] LeDoux poses the following question:

> How does the amygdala achieve this alteration of consciousness, this transformation of cognition into emotion, or better yet, this hostile takeover of consciousness by emotion? The answer, I believe, is that emotion comes to monopolize consciousness, at least in the domain of fear, when the amygdala comes to dominate working memory. (LeDoux, *Synaptic Self* 226)

Could this possibly be translated into the experience of either when a *complex* is *activated* or when powerful *archetypal energy* is constellated and invades and takes over ego-consciousness? Either of these activations results in a situation where "the unconscious content overwhelms the conscious aim and inhibits, falsifies, even destroys its realization" (Jung, *CW* 9.1: 164).

By intermittently reinforcing a state of fear via the color-coded warning system and the media, the administration has at times successfully maintained a collective state of chronic amygdala activation that manifests as anxiety and even panic. I am postulating that this state of heightened arousal results in many individuals' extreme vulnerability to activations of related complexes and/or archetypes. In this state, judgment is impaired. Under these conditions of chronic amygdala activation with the concomitant state of hyperarousal with increased fear and vulnerability, a state of collective regression may also be induced. Consequently, many in the collective will tend to turn to the perceived "good parent" (projected onto the president and his administration) for reassurance and safety. Jung points out that in times of great instability, upheaval, and disorientation, such as has been occurring in the United States for the past few years, the archetype of the savior becomes activated and is also projected onto the leaders (*CW* 18: 161). As a result of these psychological mechanisms occurring en masse, there can be a tendency to agree to all sorts of impositions and undermining of civil liberties, all done with the assurance and promise of increased national safety and security. This occurred repeatedly over the past few years in the United States to the extent that one of the fundamental premises of the Constitution, namely freedom of expression, became threatened. Criticism of the administration was not tolerated; those who dared to question any actions were labeled "unpatriotic," a disturbing phenomenon explored in depth by Glenn Greenwald in "How Would a Patriot Act?"

Yet to overrule this activation of the amygdala requires much psychic effort. As LeDoux has demonstrated, there are sound neuroanatomical reasons why it is so difficult to override activations of the amygdala (which I am asserting may be akin to activations of a complex or archetype). Those of us who have ever been in the grips of a truly powerfully activated complex or archetypal energy can certainly attest to the verity of this observation. Jung further illustrates this point regarding the autonomous nature of complexes and their ability to usurp the ego: "Everyone knows nowadays that people 'have complexes.' What is not so well known, though far more important theoretically, is that complexes can *have us*" (*CW* 8: 96). A prerequisite, then, for transition to mature adulthood would require the willingness at least to attempt to become aware of and to override such activations. A level of maturity is necessary to question the authority of those in power without perceiving them as parental surrogates or saviors. This would require a transition from a state of immaturity or adolescence to mature adulthood, and I am arguing that, collectively, the American psyche has not achieved this developmental phase. Therefore, a majority of Americans have failed to challenge until very recently the premises and activities of the Bush administration. However, this has indeed been a very serious situation, since recent policies have gradually eroded many hard-won civil liberties that have been among the outstanding achievements of American society over several decades.

Conclusion

It is my contention that the majority of the American collective is experiencing a state of protracted adolescence—akin to Klein's paranoid/schizoid position and Jung's projection of the shadow. The hope is that increasing numbers of individuals will be moved to engage in the difficult process of becoming more self-aware, an *opus contra naturam* (a work against nature), as Jung puts it (*CW* 16: 262). It is against our natural inclinations to confront our own inner selves, especially our shadow aspects, and this requires considerable courage and fortitude. It involves, among other tasks, the difficult process of "how he is to reconcile himself with his own nature—how he is to love the enemy in his own heart and call the wolf his brother" (*CW* 11: 341). If we are able to continue working to disseminate and make more accessible the body of knowledge about how the human psyche functions, especially to the youth, there is hope for a better future for all to achieve a life that may contribute in some way to the possibility of greater world peace.

Notes

1. Jung equates the child motif with the Self. He points out that it can be expressed by roundness, the circle or sphere, or else the quaternity—all symbols of the Self. The child motif, like the Self, can indicate a synthesis of the personality in the individuation process.
2. The uniting symbol of the child or other symbols of the Self has the potential to bring about a greater unity of the personality, resulting in the warring opposites finding greater peace.
3. Although there are two amygdalae (plural of amygdala), one in each half of the brain, they both perform the same functions. For the sake of simplicity, I will thus use the singular, amygdala, throughout this paper.
4. Jung describes complexes as psychic fragments or nodes of energy that have split off, owing to traumatic life events or tendencies that are incompatible with the personality. They can be activated by external events or internal thoughts. Once activated, they disturb consciousness, impair memory, are often highly emotionally charged, can lead to obsessions, and appear and disappear as if by their own unpredictable volition. They are also referred to as "sub-personalities" (*CW* 8: 121).
5. I will explore this hypothesis—that complexes and/or archetypes may be situated in the limbic system—more fully in a future paper.

Works Cited

Basham, Patrick, and C. Preble. "The Trouble with Democracy in the Middle East." Cato Institute, 2003.

British Broadcasting Corporation. "God Told Me to Invade Iraq, Bush Tells Palestinian Ministers."<http://www.bbc.co.uk/pressoffice/pressreleases/stories/2005/10_october/06/bush.shtml>.

Chomsky, Noam. *Failed States*. New York: Metropolitan, Holt, 2006.

———. *Hegemony or Survival*. New York: Metropolitan, Holt, 2003.

"Civil Liberties and Human Rights Eroded by Changes to U.S. Law and Policy." New York, 2003. *Human Rights First*. 27 June 2006. <http://www.humanrightsfirst.org/media/2003_alerts/0311.htm#>.

Ehrenreich, Barbara. *Bait and Switch*. New York: Holt, 2005.

Fisk, Robert. "We Are the War Criminals Now." *The Independent* (2001).

Frank, Thomas. *What's the Matter with Kansas*. New York: Metropolitan, 2004.

Franken, Al. *Lies and the Lying Liars Who Tell Them: A Fair and Balanced Look at the Right*. New York: Dutton, 2003.

Global Warming News Update—June 15th, 2006. 27 June 2006.<http://www.saveourwetlands.org/globalwarming.html>.

Greenwald, Glenn. *How Would a Patriot Act?* San Francisco: Working Assets P, 2006.

Grotjahn, Martin. *The Voice of the Symbol*. Los Angeles: Mara, 1971.

Jung, C. G. *The Collected Works of C. G. Jung*. 20 vols. Trans. R. F. C. Hull. Ed. H. Read, Michael Fordham, and Gerhard Adler. Princeton: Princeton UP, 1953–1989.

———. *Letters Vol. 1: 1906–1950*. Ed. Gerhard Adler. Princeton: Princeton UP, 1973.

Klein, Melanie. "A Contribution to the Psychogenesis of Manic-Depressive States." 1935. *Love, Guilt, and Reparation and Other Works*. London: Karnac; Institute of Psychoanalysis, 1992. 262–89.

———. "Notes on Some Schizoid Mechanisms." 1946. *Envy and Gratitude and Other Works.* London: Karnac; Institute of Psychoanalysis, 1993. 1–24.

LeDoux, Joseph. *The Emotional Brain: The Mysterious Underpinnings of Emotional Life.* New York: Simon & Schuster, 1996.

———. *Synaptic Self: How Our Brains Become Who We Are.* New York: Viking Penguin, 2002.

Moore, Michael. *Stupid White Men . . . And Other Sorry Excuses for the State of the Nation.* New York: HarperCollins, 2001.

Shakespeare, William. *The Complete Works of William Shakespeare.* New York: Avenel, 1975.

Simmons, Gene. "The National Debt Is $8.4 Trillion!" 2006. *National Debt Awareness Campaign.* Ed. Gene Simmons. 27 June 2006. <http://66.249.93.104/ search?q=cache:6UDe3At5 DPkJ:www.federalbudget.com/+national+debt+trillions&hl=en&ct=clnk&cd=2>.

Sparks, Allister. "Is Bush America's Worst Leader?" *Cape Times* 3 May 2006, sec. Opinion.

von Franz, Marie-Louise. *Puer Aeternus.* Santa Monica: Sigo, 1981.

Senex and Puer in the Classroom

A Conflict of Consciousness in Education

KEITH POLETTE

Only in the kingdom of doubleness
do voices sound
undying and tender.

—Rainer Marie Rilke, *Die Sonette an Orpheus* (Sonnet IX)

Were Orpheus alive today, we would most likely find him seated in a classroom, lost in the reverie of a secret daydream during a lecture on the chief heroic figures of Greek mythology. In such a desk-locked position, he would certainly have to ask for a hall pass before he could descend into Hades to try and redeem his beloved Eurydice—so long as he had a note from his parents and agreed to return before the lunch bell sounded!

And the merits of his adventure would not be judged on how well his song could stir the heart, quicken the mind, fire the soul, and quiet the caustic intellect, but on how well—and how quickly!—he could bubble-in the right answers on a standardized, high-stakes test over such things as the difference between a half note and a whole note, the correct definitions of rhythm and tempo, the right name of the inventor of the lyre, the geographic placement and geological makeup of the ancient Greek underworld, and the exact arrival dates and causes of death of all the shadows haunting Hades.

His test would then be shunted to an Olympian-like building to be sorted, scanned, scored, and stacked. Flattened onto paper, corralled by blackened circles, and measured by a machine, Orpheus would suffer a transformation worse than anything that Circe or Medusa could conjure: he would become a number, a bloodless cipher. Reduced to a digit and lodged in a neat row of numbers whose raison d'être is to feed the cold god of statistics with data to devour, Orpheus would find himself with no song to sing, no quest to tackle, no Hades to harrow—his underworld lyrics replaced by the upper-world, mechanized voice of the scantron. And the scantron's soulless song would certainly sing of Orpheus as one significantly *below the mean*—the Orphic imagination deadened by mechanical evaluation.

Flagged as a failure, Orpheus would find no happy home in our current system of education that prizes and rewards correct answers, convergent thought, codified cognition, rule-bound behavior, practicality, rationality, and predictability. And he would certainly not be proffered an invitation to join the bright ranks of the National Honor Society. More than likely, he would be labeled as *learning disabled* and consigned to the dull rooms of ditto-sheeted remediation. And if he displayed any resistance to the psychic downsizing of the lessons he was forced to eat and regurgitate—by bursting forth with spontaneous song—he would be re-labeled as *behavior disordered* and put into the straightjacket of stimulus-response-driven behavior modification techniques. And if this did not quell his vigorous voice, he would be labeled yet again as *attention deficit disordered* and, most likely, loaded up with daily doses of Ritalin!

Rank Education

Such a scenario, which we might entitle "The Deconstruction of an Orphic Way of Knowing," is not as far-fetched as it might seem. Although it is, in some ways, a fiction—and an exaggerated one at that—it is designed to amplify and clarify the structural dynamics informing the current conflicted system of American education, and to dramatize how this system is shaping the minds of children.

The structural dynamics of this system come into sharper focus when we consider these remarks from an editorial in a recent issue of the *English Journal:*

> For whatever reasons, in the United States, we are a testing, ranking, and measuring society. . . . We seem obsessed with the top ten, the twenty worst, the decade's average. . . . And in education . . . there seems to be no lessening of hunger to test and measure and put into stanine rankings. In fact, many members of the public feel that testing is the only way to insure any kind of consistency, any kind of quality control regarding teaching and learning and what goes on in school. (Chistenbury 11)

As this description aptly points out, ours is indeed a "ranking and listing" culture of self-inscribed itemizers whose collective psyche is encoded to collect and catalogue. Our national liturgy, *the list*, arises from a creedal belief in the epistemological sense that understanding is predicated on the ability to group things hierarchically. The groupings, moreover, then form their own exclusionary categories of how we view the world and what we value in our top-down worldview.

Implied in our *list-o-mania* is the notion that if something cannot be measured and ranked, it must hold even less value than those items at the bottom of our myriad lists. Consequently, we ignore or banish any rank-resistant item as we reconnoiter the world for more facts to feed our ravenous hunger for lists. (As such, the vital experience of Orpheus's melodic manner and song-fed imagination is shunned and repressed: a mode of being that has no place in the list-driven consciousness.) Indeed, our mania to test and rank has become so habitual and so pernicious that we fail to see it as an ingrained habit; we merely assume that it is the natural, and therefore national, way to think.

If, however, we are to free ourselves from this pervasive, national way of thinking, we must locate the source of our one-sided measure-mindedness. Such a one-sidedness, such a consciousness moved by one way of thinking, certainly points to a consciousness ruled and dominated by a powerful archetypal constellation. This move to identify the source of our measure-mindedness is grounded on Jung's notion that we are moved not so much by the will of the ego but by the constellation of archetypal energies not under our conscious control. When ignored and not consciously reflected upon, these energies rise up and dominate the ego. These unconscious energies—what Jung calls "archetypal figures"—are living entities inhabiting the psyche, fueling its functions, and in-*forming* all of its various conditions. Jung states: "We derive our psychic conditions" from "archetypal figures" (*Alchemical Studies* 247). He adds:

> *We are still possessed by autonomous psychic contents as if they were Olympians.* Today they are called phobias, *obsessions*, and so forth; in a word, neurotic symptoms. The gods have become diseases. (*Alchemical Studies* 37; emphasis added)

Following Jung, we must look to—and *through*—our "symptoms" and our "diseases" to catch sight of the "archetypal figures," the "gods," who possess us—and, by extension, our educational cosmos. Such a *looking through* moves us away from the literal, away from the outwardly causal, and into the mythic and metaphorical. For Jung reminds us that we best understand the psyche's functions and effects when we think mythically and metaphorically. And so, to find the primary god—the chief archetypal figure—who is the root of our educational "disease," we must use the method of equivalences, of metaphorically measuring like with like.

Such a measuring must also be mythic because it follows Jung's notion that "all mythical figures correspond to inner psychic experiences and originally sprang from them" (*Four Archetypes* 136). To catch sight of and find ways to relate to the source of our obsession, we must thus look to the mythic figure—"the inner psychic experience"—who generates it. To think mythically, then, is to discover that behind everything we think, do, and say is a mythic figure, an archetypal entity, in a word, a god. James Hillman writes:

> We can imagine nothing or perform nothing that is not already given by the archetypal imagination of the gods . . . [T]he necessary is that which occurs among gods, i.e., that myths describe necessary patterns . . . If the gods are the true background to human life and we are made in their images, then our sickness too has divine origin; not merely sent by the gods . . . but background and foreground, they and we, conform in archetypal infirmity. (*Facing the Gods* 4)

Following Jung and Hillman, we will use the mythic method of discovery; for if we do not identify the mythic figure that drives us and our educational system into extreme one-sidedness, we will fail to penetrate the core of patterns that give rise to our ideas, fantasies, actions, and fixations.

To make known the "god" of education, we must remember that this god is not a literal, distant deity reigning somewhere beyond the topmost cloud layers. No, this god is a mythical figure, a psychic experience, an imaginal source of education's divine affliction, and a constellation of energies that both dwells *within* each of us and energizes us into unconsciously driven action. Should we ignore this figure, we will continue to be besieged and will continue, unthinkingly, to follow his/her stanine dictates. Without coming to grips with the deity that drives us and our educational system to rank and measure, our attempts to make effective changes will fail because these attempts will continue to be directed by the unconscious deity. The result would simply be a stultifying closed loop of action and intention.

Before we can even think about re-devising our approaches to both pedagogy and the structure of our educational system, we must consciously confront the god who has remained hidden from our sight but at whose altar we have been unconsciously worshipping for years. To discover the god of our obsession and infirmity, then, we will be best served if we compile a list of symptomatic attributes and pinpoint the god who manifests them. Therefore, we seek to identify the god of absolutes who craves clear categories; the god who renders rank-induced judgments; the god who demands the consistency of quantifiable knowledge; the god of cold facts; the god who demands the use of standardized tests; the god who speaks in terms of right and wrong; the god who upholds hierarchies; the god who separates high from low; the god who controls behavior by means of inclusion and exclusion (behavior modification techniques); the god who issues decrees of *either/or*; the god who enforces razor-sharp rules; the god who sees children as entities to be controlled, dominated, and directed into a rigid fantasy of adulthood.

Education's Deity, Education's Dis-Ease

James Hillman writes: "*The high god of our culture is the senex god*; we are created after this image with a consciousness reflecting this structure" (*Blue Fire* 208; original emphasis). Hillman defines the senex as the archetypal constellation of a psychic disposition that is manifested in "a style of life and thought characterized by a sense of time and history, a concern with order, a love of tradition, and a tendency toward the abstract and the regulated" (*Blue Fire* 4). As Hillman points out, the archetypal figure who dominates our culture—the manifestation of constellated energies—and the god of our disease is Saturn, the mythical mode of the senex consciousness. Because, as a culture, we collectively bow down at Saturn's orderly altar of "ranking," "measuring," and "listing," we have accordingly designed our schools to be temples to the senex. Hence, it comes as no surprise to discover, for example, that most states employ a high-stakes standardized test as the chief tool for determining how much their students have "learned."

But an education that is centered on, and constrained by, the senex's ways of testing and measuring the acquisition and retention of quantifiable knowledge is one that seeks to establish a consistent point of view—a standard of eyes—through standardizing. Such a system would have us all look at schooling in the same way, and would have us imagine that the notions of "measurability," "consistency," and "quality control" must rest at the heart of all teaching and learning. But such a system blatantly ignores, for instance, Emerson's reminder that "consistency is the hobgoblin of little minds" ("Self Reliance" 137).

Such a system is also rooted in the notion that children must fit into a preexisting construct sired by the senex notion of *progression*. At the heart of this concept is the image of children learning in ways that are consistent with the standardizing norms the senex has established—norms that are a codified reflection of the senex's constellated consciousness. In this view, children will move heroically up and out, will acquire new and better information and leave behind the old and outworn, will drop subjectivity for objectivity, will exchange fecund fantasies for sturdy facts, will move spatially and sequentially through education's ladder-like system—so long as they don't flunk, drop out, or get kicked out—and will jettison all traces of childishness, ignorance, and dependency as they progress steadily into the sanctified realm of adulthood, fact-based knowledge, and independence.

A central problem with the senex preoccupation with *progression*—and the corresponding view of children and learning based solely on cognitive psychology—is that it generally snubs the philosophical distinction between "being" and "becoming." In the *progressive model*, uneducated children "become" educated adults by passing through a quantifiable series of discreet stages. In other words, children "be" to "become." As such, the *progressive model* implies a conscious aiming at a final goal, an ultimate stage, an end result, a finished product, and a perfect finish. The educated adult is fantasized as a planned and perfect product.

Additionally, in the progressive model, human beings are fantasized as passing through the same developmental stages—unless they exhibit a physiological disorder. Consequently, many people who adhere to the progressive model believe that children can and must be taught with quantifiable, replicable, programmatic methods that are designed to promote and ensure the notion of progress. But Jung reminds us that a large part of the psyche does not adhere to the progressive strictures laid out by the senex consciousness in love with the fantasy of progressive development. Jung tells us that in each person there lurks "something that is always becoming, is never completed, and calls for unceasing care, attention, and education" (*Development of Personality* 170). And the kind of education that Jung calls for is one that teaches each person how to realize his or her innate quirks, eccentricities, and peculiarities—those constant psychic "beings"—rather than one that merely trains the intellect to jump through the serial hoops held by the senex. He states:

> Personality is the supreme realization of the innate idiosyncrasy of a living being. It is an act of high courage flung in the face of life, the absolute affirmation of all that constitutes the individual, the most successful adaptation to the universal conditions of existence coupled with the greatest possible freedom for self-determination. (*Development of Personality* 171)

But the current system of education most often leads students away from their own eccentricities and the quirky path of individuation. It wants consistency, not irregularity—predictability, not peculiarity. As such, it reveals another aspect of senex-consciousness in its psychic disposition, which pays tribute to the notion of omnipotent omniscience.

Hillman reminds us that "Saturn . . . attends to childbirth so as to be able to eat the newborn, as everything new coming to life can become food to the senex. Old attitudes and habits assimilate each new content" ("Senex and Puer" 18). Like the Old Testament deity—the senex writ large in antique form—who hid from sight and issued inflexible commands and unbreakable edicts for the "good" of his people, the senex-system of education deploys "old attitudes" to "assimilate new content." In this way, it tells its students that it knows *what* they need to know, *how much* they need to know, and *when* and *how* they need to know it. In so doing, the senex ignores the newness of its students and devours their imaginations that would seek out new things to discover, new things to explore, new songs to sing. Consequently, the senex's distant Yahweh-like ideas have become codified into curricula, and students are imagined and treated as knowledge-hungry, empty-headed supplicants who come to school begging for the redemption of education. And to make certain that students do come "to know" the right facts, and the rites of facts, in the right way—that they reach the "promised land" of reasoned right answers at the end of the long trek through the progressively oriented desert of acquired knowledge—the system has armed itself with a battery of objective tests, tests that do not nourish but instead devour the bud of individuality and the newness of imagination.

These tests are designed to discover if students are indeed "measuring up" to those objective, knowledge-specific standards that fall under the larger rubric of "predictability," "rationality," "practicality," "consistency," "rankability," and "quality control"—a rubric that the students have not chosen but that has been imposed upon them nonetheless. In this way, the educational covenant drawn up by the senex mind of education is actually an imposition foisted as a choice. What the makers and foisters of this covenant have failed to see, or have willfully and willingly ignored, is that knowledge is not equivalent with a thing known, and that an educational system that lives only to be tested, measured, and ranked is akin to little more than counting dead bugs in a jar—or deadened minds into the stomach of Saturn.

When knowledge is equated with facts, those facts are the carcasses of what were once enlivened events. We must remember that what we call knowledge is actually a *way* and *means* of knowing. To consider "knowing" only as a noun is to lose sight of its underlying dynamic properties, its interior active agency, its undercurrents and orienting energies. Knowing nominalized (as knowledge) obviates its generative spirit and occludes us to the fact that prior to all knowledge are the foundations of the mind that give birth to the ability to know. Jung writes that "the psyche creates reality every day" (*Psychological Types* 52) and that "archetypal explanatory principles, that is, psychic premises . . . are a *sine qua non* of the cognitive process" (*Psychology and Alchemy* 288-89). He adds that

> intellectual understanding is not sufficient. It supplies us only with verbal concepts, but it does not give us their true content, which is to be found in the living experience. . . . No understanding by means of words and no imitation can replace actual experience. (*Psychology and Alchemy* 349)

An educational system that insists upon only one kind of knowing—objective, consistent, practical, standardized, rational—is, in fact, enforcing nothing less than a monotheistic perspective that obliges its students to use only one "archetypal explanatory principle" and to understand facts without the deeper "experience" to which these facts point and to which they might also lead. This monotheistic perspective, by locking all means of knowing into one clearly defined precinct, seeks, like a jealous god, to banish all other "archetypal principles," all other ways of knowing, that do not submit easily or happily to being tested or measured by the quasi-scientific yardstick of statistical averages and predictable behaviors and outcomes. Jung writes:

> Under the influence of scientific assumptions, not only the psyche but the individual . . . and, indeed, all individual events whatsoever suffer a levelling down and a process of blurring that distorts the picture of reality into a conceptual average. We ought not underestimate the psychological effect of the statistical world-picture: it thrusts aside the individual in favour of anonymous units that pile up into mass formations. (*Civilization in Transition* 252)

Hence, we can conclude with Jung that "our modern education is morbidly one-sided" (*Civilization in Transition* 153). By operating from the "statistical world-picture" of senex consciousness, education emphasizes correctness over curiosity, control over spontaneity, knowledge over uncertainty, measuring over musing, cognition over imagination, compliance over resistance, consistency over idiosyncrasy, research over in-search, imitation over initiation, silence over song, and tests over trials. As such, it does not "lead" students "out" of themselves and toward potent but denigrated and unrealized ways of knowing; rather, it "keeps" them contained "in" the system's systematic, non-Orphic thinking. In other words, senex consciousness wants students to know information *about* songs, but it doesn't want them to throw their heads (and hearts!) back and sing.

Being one-sided, however, "our modern education" also casts a strong shadow. Jung writes:

> human nature has its black side—and not man alone, but his works, his institutions, and his convictions as well. Even our purest and holiest beliefs rest on very deep and dark foundations; after all, we can explain a house not only from the attic downwards, but from the basement upwards. (*The Practice of Psychotherapy* 64)

One result of education's shadow manifests itself in children's resistance to becoming what the senex would have them become. Rather, children rebel against the senex's strictures, decrees, and admonitions. And rather than become the "perfect" *adults* that the senex would have them become, they stay mired in a sphere of *childhood* from which they rarely, if ever, dislodge themselves.

Education's Shadow

To perceive the subaltern shadow-site of education, however, we must, like Orpheus and Odysseus, descend into its underworld. Here we must scout for that educational figure whom the senex has made into a pariah—because s/he displays a consciousness subversive to the senex's ways and means. By dropping our line of sight from an upper-world perspective, which sees only from above and from afar, we will strive to locate what is subcutaneous to the senex. And so we will look *beneath* the senex's skin to see what *gets under* its skin.

Our task, then, must be subjunctive and insubordinate if we are to illuminate that which the senex strains to keep subordinate. And so we must seek out the god who cannot be contained by senex methods, the god who evades being cast into the mold of facts, the god who adroitly dodges tests and measures, the god who refuses to be ranked, the god who revels in inconsistency, and the god who blurs all categorical distinctions: the god whom the senex can neither contain nor control.

To identify this god, we might first ask: Why does the senex keep his school rooms so well lit? Why does he pack his ceilings with so many florescent lights so as to allow no room for shadows to fall? What shadowy figure does he wish to banish? These questions are important, for to ignore the archetypal figure that the senex wants to white out is to lose sight of the power that gives birth to its shadow and informs its activity. Failure to investigate this figure and to make it conscious is to invite it to continue in secret to seize and secure the unlit side of the senex psyche and direct it to do its bidding.

Additionally, when we think mythically, we remember that archetypal conflicts are familial and that the gods of psychic contention are always related to one another; we realize that we must look close to home. If the senex consciousness is a manifestation of the archetype of Saturn, what archetype gives rise to its shadow? Jung offers our first clue when he writes: "Saturn is the father and origin of Mercurius, therefore the latter is called 'Saturn's child'" (*Alchemical Studies* 227). He also writes: "Mercurius, following the tradition of Hermes, is many-sided, change-able, and deceitful . . . He is duplex and his main characteristic is duplicity" (*Alchemical Studies* 217). And he adds, "Hermes is a god of thieves and cheats, but also a god of revelation" (*Alchemical Studies* 233). Hillman amplifies Jung's description:

> Hermes/Mercury is the God of messages . . . And he is the God of . . . language, interpreter of invisibilities, audacious liar, artful craftsman and easygoing thief with a special relation to the Underworld. His arrival is instantaneous, a flash of inspiration; innovative, cunning. (*Kinds of Power* 234)

And Karl Kerényi tells us that the "activity of Hermes refers to alternatives of life, to the dissolution of fatal opposites, to clandestine violations of boundaries and laws" (7). Because he is "Saturn's child," Mercury bears special relation to his father, but it is not one of *like-father-like-son*. As we shall see, Mercury is precisely everything that Saturn cannot bear to acknowledge.

Saturn's Scion

Being the antithesis of Saturn, Mercury/Hermes is everything that our educational system likes to lock up, white out, and shut down. Because he is the god of lies and alternatives who violates boundaries and is home to invisibilities and changeabilities, he darts through Saturn's orderly world in ways that the senex consciousness cannot fathom. He—or she!—can neither be kept out of Saturn's realm nor contained by Saturn's devisings. Too quick to catch and too slick to hold, Mercury evades even the most well-wrought senex plan to nab and negate him. (Remember: Mercury/Hermes is the *only* god who can move in and out of the realms of the other gods.)

Being the offspring of Saturn, Mercury gives rise to a consciousness that *springs off* its own distant dad, which is to say: just as Saturn fathers-forth Mercury, so too does the senex procreate its antithesis—the puer. Hillman states that the puer archetype often manifests itself as

> the King's Son . . . Mercury-Hermes, Trickster. In him, we see a mercurial range of . . . "personalities": narcissistic, inspired, effeminate, phallic, inquisitive, inventive, pensive, passive, fiery, and capricious. . . . The puer cannot do with . . . timing and patience. . . . The puer therefore understands little of what is gained by repetition and consistency, that is, by work, or of the moving back and forth . . . which makes for subtlety in proceeding step by step through the labyrinthine complexity of the horizontal world. These teachings but cripple its winged heels. ("Senex and Puer" 23–24)

The puer, then, in its style and orientation of consciousness, is everything that the senex is not: where the senex is cold, the puer is hot; where the senex is distant, the puer is near; where the senex is rule-bound, the puer is freewheeling; where the senex is predictable, the puer is surprising; where the senex is systematic, the puer is spontaneous; where the senex is historical, the puer is futuristic; where the senex plans, the puer erupts; and where the senex tests, the puer experiments.

Because, as Hillman writes, "the polar division between senex and puer . . . is all about us" ("Senex and Puer" 6), we find that the senex-puer relationship in our current system of education is not a happy one. Such a relationship is structured on division, not cohesion. The lines of demarcation are clear, especially on the human realm: administrators and teachers are unconsciously forced to do the senex's bidding, while the students are left to play the only role left to them—that of the puer. Such an unconscious Saturn/Mercury constellation gives rise to two conflicted modes of consciousness: senex and puer (or senex *versus* puer).

In the senex-dominated world of education, the puer necessarily causes fits. He is wood dissolving into water at the touch of a nail, for he will not be built upon with Saturn's sturdy tools. In the classroom, for instance, the puer refuses to conform, won't give straight answers, cares nothing for lists and tests, cavorts in inconsistency, abhors rows and desks, can't sit still during "worksheet time," passes notes in class to pass the time, drifts into daydreams rather than listen to a lecture, causes trouble via spontaneous eruptions, asks strange questions, bristles at the sight of "comprehension questions" after stories or chapters in textbooks, becomes numb in the face of assigned readings, deplores the dictionary-driven weekly vocabulary word search, harbors a deep resentment against the fill-in-the-blank mentality that has assigned him homework, and purposefully bubbles in the wrong answers on standardized tests.

But to the senex-minded education system, the puer is not merely a nuisance; he is a threat. And education tries to rid itself of all puer energy because it sees such energy as toxic. Furthermore, the senex's one-sided laws are also constructed to give the puer no room to move, no air to breathe, no place to make himself known. Robert Bly reminds us, however, "that every part of our personality that we do not love becomes hostile to us. We could add that it may move to a distant place and begin as a revolt against us as well" (20). But in suppressing and repressing the puer, however, the senex-sanctified education secretly and unconsciously strengthens and encourages it.

When education under senex's sway neither honors nor loves nor makes room for the puer in its students, it actually invites and incites them to revolt. But the puer, following the movements of Mercury, never revolts through a direct, frontal attack; no, he is not the mighty Hercules or the fierce Achilles. Rather, he is more Odyssean (notably, Hermes makes his first significant appearance not in the *Iliad*, but in the *Odyssey*); he is wily and works his magic through deception by blinding the one-eyed power that would seek to control him. As such, he lies, cheats, and steals; he says one thing but does another; he offers illusions in the guise of actualities; he twists facts into fantasies and fantasies into facts; he confounds the intellect and befuddles the imagination; he appears one time as water, another as fire, one time as male, another as female. Because he is outlawed, he becomes an outlaw. In other words, Mercury reads Saturn's edict of banishment as an inducement to ply his—or her!—cunning crafts. And so he wings through Saturn's realm and delights in duping the father who offers him neither love nor respect. And just as he pilfered Apollo's golden cows, so too does Mercury steal from the father that which the father holds sacrosanct. And in his acts we see the shades of revolt.

Giving the Deities Their Due

But if the senex's system of education eternally incites a puer-driven revolt, what are we to do? To move single-mindedly toward one side or the other will do no good, for to adopt the attitude of one over the other is to create a one-sided approach, or what Jung calls a "neurotic" perspective. It is not a matter of either/or, not a matter of a substituting one monocular vision of education for another, whether it be Saturnine or Mercurial. We cannot opt for senex at the expense of the puer; nor can we adopt the puer and jettison the senex.

What is called for, in this case, is to give each god what s/he is owed. And what is owed is a conscious recognition of, and an active participation with, both the Saturnine and the Mercurial figures who move us and our ideas about teaching and learning. I am not endorsing cheating, plagiarism, or any acts of academic thievery. I am arguing that as individual teachers we must find ways to reach the puer, to create a harmony—bridges of association—between senex and puer. I am arguing that the educational system must rethink its senex-obsessed orientation so as to meet the young where they are, respecting the creativity and free-flying mayhem of the puer, while teaching them the concepts of valuable play. In so doing, we will craft and discover a song that includes both, a melody that blends each voice, a rhythm that creates distinction without division.

Our first task will be to broaden the educational imagination so that as administrators and teachers we begin to center—or *decenter!*—our pedagogy on strategies that offer a clearly delineated territory for the senex to rule while simultaneously allowing for the vast and unconstrained free play of the puer: we need to remember education's etymological design, "to lead out." This leading out must move our students from one-mindedness to many-minded-ness. To this end—or these ends—we must practice *paradoxical pedagogy* and construct, for example, laws for lying, guidelines for inconsistency, and decrees for transgression. Thus, we must, for example, create trials instead of tests and rituals instead of repetitions. We must swap lectures for stories, worksheets for work-play, grammar for *glamour* (its original "magical" meaning), history for *memoria*, and math for magic. We must employ senex-oriented facts in the service of the puer's unpredictable movements—and puer movements to discover senex facts.

We must, for instance, see and identify a turtle shell as a turtle shell (which Saturn bids us do) but transform it into a lyre (as Mercury urges us to—and as he did). In other words, we must, metaphorically speaking, find ways to "teach without words" as that Saturnine-Mercurial teacher, Lao Tzu, instructed us to.

For example, instead of a research paper on some aspect of history, we might ask students to travel back to a specific time and place, spend five to ten days in that locale and create five to ten journal entries that tell what they did, whom they met, where they went, and what they discovered. Their entries must successfully combine fact and fiction; that is, the students must know what the senex would have them know but must also use that knowledge in puer ways, imagining themselves in a new time and place and using the facts they have discovered to give a senex foundation to their fantasies of fictional participation in an era that has sprung to life in their puer-playful minds.

Instead of a traditional "report" about an area of nonfiction, we might ask students to investigate the origin of an invention, for instance, and then write three reports: one report must contain the "truth," while the other two reports must be convincing lies. In this way, students will conjoin the senex's penchant for facts with the puer's love of deceptive fictions. In other words, by asking students to hand in something beyond a report, we stop them from being able to "copy" facts from a reference book; instead, we require them to synthesize what they have read. And when we ask them to create fictions that sound like the "truth," we are requiring them to attend to such things as the tone and structure of nonfictional prose—and thus to incorporate this tone and structure into their own writing.

Instead of a paper explicating a piece of literature, we might ask students to create a talk show script where the characters are the invited guests. As such, students must construct questions and answers that explore, for instance, the enigmas of *Death of a Salesman*, *Hamlet*, *Great Expectations*, or *The Old Man and the Sea*. To be successful, students must have both a senex's understanding of the literature and a puer's expression of it.

Instead of the grudge and grind of grammar worksheets where students must identify adverbial clauses, adjectival clauses, participles, gerunds, and absolute phrases, we might ask students to write and illustrate a book for children—in the styles of Chris Van Allsburg, Jon Agee, Anthony Browne, or Judy Barrett—in which they consciously and playfully use adverbial clauses, adjectival clauses, participles, gerunds, and absolute phrases. In this way, students will come to know the senex side of grammar and usage in a puer-oriented context.

Instead of listening to a lecture on the movement of molecules, we might ask students to enact a drama that displays the varieties of attractions and repulsions of those molecules. To do this, students must know which molecules are attracted to, and repulsed by, one another—and under what conditions these erotic connections and repulsions are made. They must then be able to take this knowledge and transform it into puer play.

Thus, our education may both "be" and "become" an education of transformation, not progression, an education that starts where students are, not where
it wants them to be. Such an education must also honor the puer and grant
him/her room to move and breathe. When we invite Mercury to make himself
known, to emerge from a Saturnine eclipse, he may then instruct us by giving
us strange signs; and these signs may then lead us out of the senex's schoolhouse
and into the larger domain of the puer's imagination—and, ironically, through
the puer's imagination and back into the senex's schoolhouse.

By finding ways to enact and give expression to both senex and puer
consciousness, we are, in effect, giving birth to an Orphic way of knowing. For
when we, as administrators and teachers, find new songs to sing and new ways
of singing them, we will, in turn, give our students ways to sing with double
voices, voices whose songs are indeed "tender and undying."

Works Cited

Bly, Robert. *A Little Book on the Human Shadow*. New York: HarperCollins, 1988.

Chistenbury, Leila. "From the Editor." *English Journal* 86.1 (1997): 11.

Emerson, Ralph Waldo. *Ralph Waldo Emerson: A Critical Edition of the Major Works*. Ed.
    Richard Poirier. Oxford: Oxford UP, 1990.

Hillman, James. *Blue Fire*. New York: Harper Perennial, 1991.

———, ed. *Facing the Gods*. Dallas: Spring, 1994.

———. *Kinds of Power*. New York: Doubleday, 1995.

———. "Senex and Puer." *Puer Papers*. Ed. James Hillman. Dallas: Spring, 1979.

Humbert, Elie. *C. G. Jung: The Fundamentals of Theory and Practice*. Wilmette, IL: Chiron,
    1993.

Jung, C. G. *Aion*. Trans. R. F. C. Hull. Princeton: Princeton UP, 1959.

———. *Alchemical Studies*. Trans. R. F. C. Hull. Princeton: Princeton UP, 1967.

———. *The Archetypes and the Collective Unconscious*. Trans. R. F. C. Hull. Princeton:
    Princeton UP, 1959.

———. *Civilization in Transition*. Trans. R. F. C. Hull. Princeton: Princeton UP, 1964.

———. *The Development of Personality*. Trans. R. F. C. Hull. Princeton: Princeton UP,
    1954.

———. *Four Archetypes*. Trans. R. F. C. Hull. Princeton: Princeton UP, 1969.

———. *The Practice of Psychotherapy*. Trans. R. F. C. Hull. Princeton: Princeton UP, 1954.

———. *Psychology and Alchemy*. Trans. R. F. C. Hull. Princeton: Princeton UP, 1953.

———. *Psychological Types*. Trans. R. F. C. Hull. Princeton: Princeton UP, 1971.

Kerényi, Karl. *Hermes: Guide of Souls*. Trans. Murray Stein. Dallas: Spring, 1976.

Rilke, Rainer Maria. *Sonnets to Orpheus*. Boston: Shambhala, 2004.

Insanity by the Numbers, Knowings from the Ground

Outgrowing and Outloving the Cult of Quantification

CRAIG CHALQUIST

Expectations that are merely statistical are no longer human.

—James Hillman, *Suicide and the Soul*

Distinct visions are coming together: the understanding that nature is a source of meaning encounters the hope for a just society. There is no simple name for what is occurring. But certainly a familiar habit of mind, already frayed, is dissolving.

—Susan Griffin, *The Eros of Everyday Life*

It should not surprise anyone that a civilization whose economies of mass consumption, distraction, and destruction regard Earth as a lifeless pile of matter should repress our sense of our surroundings. The perspective of *terrapsychology*, the study of the animated presence of place, evolved to bring this sense back into focus through on-site fieldwork, reexamination of indigenous descriptions of the world's sacred character, emphasis on wounds shared between dwellers and the land, and Terrapsychological Inquiry, a research perspective being designed to explore symbolically rich parallels between human and environmental states of being: islands of greenery and islands of sanity, locked-down minds and locked-up frontiers. Terrapsychological research does use numbers and measurements, but always with a wariness of how easily they anesthetize our deeply felt contact with the animated world we study, care for, and delight in. Naturally, this practice calls into question a religious mentality dominant in the United States: a ritualistic obsession with facts, figures, and numbers. We think of this form of fundamentalism as the cult of quantification.

From the standpoint of terrapsychology, literal-minded reliance on quantitative evidence regardless of fit with a given research topic not only increases the researcher's emotional distance from what is being studied but reveals itself as an unintended gap in psychological immaturity. In mythological terms, behind the epidemic frenzy for measurable results hides a clingy divine child tugging at the skirts of Saturnian scientism (called "peanitis" below) for tokens of categorized certainty. Because peanitis is packed with unconscious theocratic and authoritarian assumptions that reinforce alienation of self from world, a compensatory earthiness resurfaces in supposedly objective abstractions even as empirical operations reveal themselves as mythically tinged. A psychological alternative to this "project of disembodiment" in which intellect futilely seeks to rule the natural world from which it evolved rejoices when the presence of what we study breaches the conceptual levees and pours into the undefended heart.

The Parentification of Fact

As every parent and psychoanalyst knows, children pass through an irritating but relatively brief developmental phrase in which they expect everything to stand infallibly demonstrated as fact. *Yes, honey, the sun comes up every morning.* "Prove it." *Don't rub the cat's fur backward, she doesn't like it.* "How do you know for sure?" *The little mailbox emblem on the screen means that someone has sent us an e-mail.* "But if you didn't actually watch them send it . . . ?"

The sale, deployment, and evaluation of mainstream science remains stuck in this phase in the United States, that haven of many fundamentalisms, where anxious hordes will disbelieve the evidence of their senses unless a study provides confirmation. People who never suspect themselves of harboring superstitious impulses will bypass the practiced and seasoned expert to entrust themselves to bland-faced, white-coated technicians armed with certificates; take hastily tested medications advertised as cures; and change the wise dietary habits of a lifetime because a research project whose sources of funding they have not investigated advises one potion over another. So entrenched is this habit that insurance companies now get away with paying no benefits for anything but "evidence-based" psychotherapy, as though psyches were trains that could be made to run on time: self as corporate cubicle.

This socially sanctioned madness also carries dire ecological consequences. Inuits in the Arctic say that polar bears are drowning and ice floes vanishing in the heat of global warming? "Prove it." Mexican families coughing their lungs out in the barrio claim that toxic fumes from local industries are suffocating their children? Fisher folk, naturalists, ecologists, indigenous hunters, and traditional healers the world over insist that planetary systems now spin radically out of balance? "Prove it, prove it." Unfortunately, the proof hasn't been invented that can sway emotionally defended convictions. The rules are fixed before the studies are even conducted.

What might be called the authoritarianism of evidence, or *factism* (Bortoft 144), also reveals itself in *who* holds the power to demand it. Instead of the burden of proof resting squarely where it rationally belongs—on business and political practices known to deplete landscapes and pollute the ecosphere with the abandon of a protracted and neurotic adolescence—it falls on those who sound the alarm. *They* must make their case to the world. The demand is analogous to requiring a family to prove their home really is burning down before thinking over the wisdom of pouring on more fuel.

C. G. Jung was at pains to point out that because the *mythic* dimension of psychological life receives short shrift in our literalistic age, its motifs and images return through the cultural back door. As more than a century of deep psychology has demonstrated, the story unrecognized has a way of degenerating into the story involuntarily acted out. Behind the double standard of "objective" evidence cleansed of subjectivity and shaved with Occam's Razor hides not only the impatient figure of the puer, the spoiled divine child ("Make it, make it, *make* it fit my yardstick!"), but the parental shadow of cynical old Saturn, sickle-wielding senex of limitations and rules. We would know him for who he is if courses in mythology fit somewhere into no-divine-child-left-behind curricula overloaded with math better done by computers. As it is, we only begin to suspect the leaden presence of the famous eater of children in suggestive hints, like the soul-mowing exam so aptly named SAT.

The totalitarian stretch of his shadow now darkens every formerly open vista on which the cult of objectification has planted its Cartesian crosses, from education to foreign policy, psychotherapy to socioeconomics. So shrill is the demand for "objective," certified, quantified data that the sickle of Saturnian authority threatens virtually every novel perspective and innovative paradigm to come before the public. No study will ever uncover how many creative voices have fallen silent for fear of being dismembered by inappropriate standards whose senexian superstitions they cannot placate and whose razor-edged umbras they cannot get out from under.

Sold as the only legitimately rational instrument through which to peer at the world, could the crosshairs of objectification instead actually blind the critical eye trying to focus on its surroundings? To find out requires a brief consideration of a troubling syndrome hiding behind the missionary zeal to quantify. Its emotional fallout is diagnostically revealing.

Peanitis

Girolamo Cardano (1501–76) is known for his work on the laws of probability. That he cast horoscopes was not particularly strange, in his day or ours, although they were usually wrong, and some deliberately so, such as the one he did for his enemy Martin Luther. His own foretold his death at age seventy-five, and for once his prognostication was correct, if only because he killed himself that year. Ludwig Boltzmann (1844–1906), co-inventor of statistical mechanics, would also commit suicide, as would Allen Turing (1912–54), a founder of computer science and artificial intelligence. He ate an apple laced with cyanide in an odd reprise of the expulsion from paradise his work did so much to advance even farther. Like Cardano, Abraham de Moivre (1667–1754) accurately computed the day of his own death, but by the less violent means of mortality statistics.

Georg Cantor (1845–1918) revived set theory discovered in Asia centuries before his efforts. He also categorically believed that Christ was the son of Joseph of Arimathea, and he took the trouble to say so in print. Between bouts of mathematical research he moved in and out of mental institutions. Leonardo da Vinci (1452–1519) drew tank prototypes, hid them, and worried that a great flood would inundate the world. David Hilbert (1886–1943), creator of fundamental algebraic axioms, was obsessed with proving that things could exist. Augustin Cauchy (1789–1857) discovered more than one infinite set and touted another by encouraging passersby to convert to Catholicism. He might have teamed well with that lover of axioms Guiseppe Peano (1858–1932), who was removed from an Italian professorship at Turin after forcing his students to communicate only in mathematical symbols. They might have diagnosed his condition as a bad case of "Peanitis."

Karl Feuerbach (1800–34), co-inventor of homogenous coordinates, was a recluse. Gregor Mendel (1823–84) was the discoverer of Mendelian heredity but was crippled into illness by test anxiety. Wilhelm Roentgen (1845–1923), discoverer of X-rays, felt too X-rayed himself to speak in public. Kurt Gödel (1906–78) was a paranoid hypochondriac who dreaded being poisoned. Sir Isaac Newton (1642–1727) suffered a breakdown in 1693. Georg Riemann (1826–66) suffered a breakdown in 1851. Wolfgang Pauli's (1900–58) breakdown came in 1931. Ernst Stueckelberg (1905–84) had too many breakdowns to mention but was always armed with all the books he might need wherever he happened to convalesce.

Paul Dirac (1902–84) combined quantum mechanics and relativity theory with so Spockian a personal literal-mindedness that telling him, "I did not understand that question," as happened once in a seminar, could elicit the response, "That was not a question; it was a statement" (Veltman 20). André Weil (1906–98), the brother of activist Simone Weil, lacked any vestige of her humility. "If it were true," he sneered about a mathematician's proposed theorem, "*he* wouldn't know it" (Landsburg). And of course let us not forget Werner Heisenberg (1901–76), whose Uncertainty Principle did not include doubts about heading the atomic research of his fellow Nazis; Erwin Schroed-inger (1887–1961), who thought up wave theory during a rollercoaster affair in Switzerland before moving his wife in with his mistress; and Albert Einstein (1879–1955), who liked to sail but could scarcely find his way home.

Did the weight of their extreme brilliance destabilize these men? No. The gifted are as apt to be as outgoing, sociable, and commonsense approachable as anyone. Nevertheless, these unstable geniuses did share a cluster of psychological qualities exemplified by intellectual giant Isaac Newton.

He was born in a Woolsthorpe Manor on Christmas Day of 1642. An emotionally abandoned loner soothed by the presence of machinery, he was well educated mentally but not joyfully or organically, and he was remembered after his death as depressive, suspicious, fearful, rageful, envious, shielded, and cold. Newton shared with the mathematicians listed above a psychological *project of disembodiment* whose symptoms include an overemphasis on intellect, a diminished capacity for spontaneity, a sense of personal unreality, self-doubt masked by arrogance, resort to the defense of schizoid withdrawal when injured or angered, stiff detachment, an obsession with control, unexpected bouts of impulsivity, and a fervor for objectivity rising to a religious intensity. Emotionally, these wounded people never grew up, never melded the violent swings between puer and senex, impulsivity and rigidity, into an adult sense of balance.

What David Berlinski says about Newton applies to the entire project of disembodiment, its peanitic gleam flashing forth from the adamantine sickle of Saturn:

> His version of things was intensely *global*. The world's ornamental variety he regarded as an impediment to understanding. Nothing in his tempera-ment longed to cherish the particular—the way in which wisteria smells in spring, the slow curve of a river bed, a woman's soft and puzzled smile, the overwhelming *thisness* of this or the *thatness* of that. (8)

Emotionally gappy Descartes sailed under the same globalizing banner. A dream on the Feast of St. Martin of Tours convinced him that God wanted His French mathematician to unify the sciences, if not his emotional lacunae. (God did not actually put in an appearance; Descartes was judging by the holiday, since St. Martin of Tours was a bishop who saw evil demons. His conclusion also does not explain why a stranger in the dream responded to a comment about paths in life by saying, "Yes and no" and dissolving.) Psychohistory bears it out: scratch a totalizer and find a self-perceived exile struggling to compensate for a sense of incompleteness.

Mirroring the monotheistic division of heaven from earth and tame from wild, binary-obsessed rationalism—peanitis—marks the beginning of modernity in all its dreamlike aspirations for living better and nightmarish obsessions with verifiability. It is no accident that in 1619, the year God spoke to Descartes after whirling him around and dreaming him into vertigo, He offered mandates as well to the British, who helped themselves to India and to Virginia; to Jamestown, which received the first shackled Africans to arrive in the Americas; and to Frederick II of Germany to take up the mantle of Holy Roman Emperor for the charge he led during the Counter-Reformation. Conquest was in the air, but first it was in the spreading calculations of inhumane detachment. Columbus made use of it to cross the ocean before sending captive Tainos back to Spain to amuse the royal court. One day soon thereafter his carefully planned *encomienda* system would turn them out, starving to death, into the roads of Hispaniola.

Not their genius but their disembodied one-sidedness, their emotional immaturity, their wild swings between puerile childlikeness and senexian parentalism, and the resulting sense of exile from a touchable, sensible world: these qualities made the missionaries of objectivity vulnerable to being tipped over. Lack of common sense for them echoed lack of contact with the common ground. Simply the juvenile repression of feeling by intellect would be enough to drive mad any less sturdy intelligences: witness young Oppenheimer flipping in an instant from laboratory coolness to uncontrolled rage as he tried to strangle a colleague. An incompetent psychiatrist diagnosed Oppenheimer with schizophrenia, but a babyish tantrum over his own clumsiness with instrumentation would have been a more accurate assessment given his passion-caging persona of icy detachment. Any Church Father would have recognized at once his determination to scrub science clean of the filth of human subjectivity.

Of course, piously tinged psychological instability neither detracts from nor explains away a scientific achievement. That Newton had a breakdown did not prevent his theories from building the basis of physics and mechanics. However, the project of disembodiment does raise the possibility that research science contains more under the hood than a history of uplifting results. Left uninterpreted, the suspiciously bare fact that gravity does indeed decrease with the square of the distance between two objects admits little, if anything, about the social, psychological, ecological, or mythical forces at work behind emotionally distant Newton's famous equation. That science actually works does not spare the requirement of a deeper look at *how* it works inside its many mentalist mansions, some assembled—to paraphrase Paul Shepard— by those whose stance toward the world is that of masters rather than guests (6).

It must now be asked: Aside from the quirks of pioneers, is mathematical exactness, that prince of standards among disciplines held to be objective, really the pure, clean, orderly, rational realm so many believe it to be—or does the senexian missionary shadow lurk even there? Because if it does, then how might it contaminate less methodically exact sciences, including those that would study people and their ailing world?

The(object)ocracy

Many of what now sound like neutral technical terms derive from words and phrases originating in the untidy realm of authoritarian social relations. A fundamentalist zeal to hack and shrink and simplify existence into *formulae* (from a Latin term denoting precisely worded prayers) reveals itself etymologically in some of the most common mathematical terms. For example:

- Axiom: from the Greek *axioma*, "authority" and *axios*, "worthy, weighing as much."
- Rule: from the Latin *regula*, "straight stick."
- Law: from *lagu*, Old Norse for "layer, measure," possibly cognate with the Greek *logos*, "law, language, measure."
- Abscissa: Latin *abscindere*, "to cut off."
- Minus: from Latin *diminuare*, "to lessen."
- Proof: "worthy, good, upright, virtuous," possibly cognate with the Greek *pistis*, "proof, persuasion, faith."
- Multiply: Latin *multiplicare*, "many" + "fold" (a pen for fruitful sheep).
- Divide: "to separate," same Latin root as "widow" (*vidua*). Long division as an act of symbolic divorce.
- Fraction: Latin *frangere*, "to break." Fractions are rational numbers; dividing, halving, and breaking come with its brand of rationality.
- Right, as in a right angle, rightist, or the right stuff: "move in a straight line," from the Latin *rectus*, a term related to "correct," "erection," "rectangle," and "rectum."
- Number: from Latin *numerus* going back to the Proto-Indo-European *nem*-, "to divide, distribute, allot," and also related to "Nemesis"—another interesting mythic figure. Nemesis is the goddess who rights imbalances, sometimes violently.

The history of numerical discovery is equally suggestive in its ascension skyward from whole (counting) numbers to the real, rational, irrational (order-loving Greek scientists were so offended by the square root of two that they refused to dignify it with any name at all), imaginary (Descartes' derogatory term for numbers that refuse to fit on a number line), complex (hybrids of real and imaginary), surds (expressions too "deaf, silent, stupid" to finish themselves neatly) . . .

This metaphorical departure from wholeness into fragmentation and dematerialization kept to a religious vocabulary revealing of what Lyotard would have identified as a comprehensive mathematical "meta-narrative," in this case one of smuggled-in binary values: equality, inequality, Golden Mean, alpha, omega, continuum, conversion, ordinate, correspond, radical, infinite, transfinite, transcendental . . .

In step with this simultaneous progression and spiritualization, the emphasis on origins, centers, and points gradually abducted the quality of presentness from locales vanished into numbers. ("Daddy, are we there yet?") Spaces and places between intervals simply vanished. Haviva Pedaya's remarks about a particular historical development within the esoteric system of Kabbalah apply as well to the religious roots of mathematics, a system developed in Christian monasteries prior to the advent of university departments of science:

> Existence is seen as the departure from a primal point, redemption as the return to that very same point. Moreover, the reference, at times, is expressly to a point as the smallest possible unit of space. The return to the One in Neoplatonism is the arithmetic analogue of the geometric image of the point. (Pedaya 92)

One self-sufficient point, one atom under Democritus, one compartmented individualist self, one nucleus, nation, master plan, and Planner and Meta-Narrator. All these ideas standing in for reality exhibit an unwavering divinization of singularity overseen by a self-knowing and self-justifying Head, an Axiom of axioms.

Whither this central authority? From points extend lines (whose essence, according to Richard Dedekind, resides only in their severability) to colonize a featureless plane where the mathematician arrives at the perfect otherworldly polygons of Euclidean geometry, the subordination of concrete place to coded space, the subversion of natural being by design, and, after Descartes, the replacement of living locale by coordinates:

> The edges and surfaces of the natural world tend irresolutely toward the blob-like; immersed in birth and decay, the biological world is filled with warm and annealing surfaces, swelling up, curved, amorphous, the whole of creation organized but chaotic. A straight line has the purity of any object that does not deviate. There the thing hangs, severe as a swordblade. (Berlinski 40)

A swordblade? *Colonize* a plane? What has mathematics to do with colonization aside from the occasional Joseph-Louis Lagrange (1736–1813), officer of
artillery who collaborated with whatever government (including Napoleon's) he
lived under? Or a John Napier (1550–1617), whose logarithms simplified trade,
exploration, and colonization (1614)? Does calculus colonize infinity by limiting
it? Ernest Rutherford (1871–1937), destroyer of nuclei, proved an exception of
a sort. He did not colonize the infinitely small; he atomized it, like a child
smashing a Christmas ornament to find out what's inside of it. Scientists under
Oppenheimer placed bets on whether the first atomic bomb would atomize the
globe in a final victory of light over darkness. "Mathematics is taught in school
as a coherent set of propositions, theorems, axioms. One forgets that these have
appeared successively in the course of the history of mathematics and of human
society—in short, that they are cultural objects subject to evolution," explains
neurobiologist Jean-Pierre Changeux (18), who could have added: subject to
psychology too, particularly a psychology blind to the power of myth.

As Carolyn Merchant remarks about the mechanical model's ascendance
during a time of rising industrial power and political authoritarianism:

> Living animate nature died, while dead inanimate money was endowed with
> life. Increasingly capital and the market would assume the organic attributes
> of growth, strength, activity, pregnancy, weakness, decay, and collapse
> obscuring and mystifying the new underlying social relations of production
> and reproduction that make economic growth and progress possible. Nature,
> women, blacks, and wage laborers were set on a path toward a new status
> as "natural" and human resources for the modern world system. Perhaps
> the ultimate irony in these transformations was the new name given them:
> rationality. (Merchant 288)

They are also abstractions that founder in the rising seas of what they would
hold at bay.

Nature as Nemesis

Mathematicians who have escaped scientistic peanitis to question the purity
of its premises include Henri Poincaré (1854–1912), who called Euclidean
geometry a convention and who disbelieved in absolute space and time before
Einstein did; Nikolai Lobachevsky (1792–1856), subverter of Euclid's fifth
postulate about parallel lines never diverging; Gottlob Frege (1848–1925), who
described math as a higher geography; Philip Kitcher (1947–), for whom its
ideal agents derive from actual agents in the world; and, going back to the

thirteenth century, Leonardo Pisano (1170–1250), or "Fibonacci" as he was nicknamed, and his famous sequence that traces natural patterns of growth in rabbit proliferations, honey bee populations, snail shell patterns, leaf arrangements. The number represented as e (roughly 2.7) is an irrational that also expresses organic growth.

The most common abstractions of mathematics reflect this stubborn resurgence of the natural world no matter how they try to escape it:

- The symbols 1 and 10: possibly an evolution of the rope used by surveyors who worked in the Nile River valley (Teresi).
- Calculus and calculate: from the Latin *calx*, "pebble" or "limestone."
- Algebra: from the Arabic *al jebr*, "reunion of broken parts."
- Graph: from the Greek *graphikos*, scratchings on clay tablets.
- Grid: from *craticula*, Latin for "griddle" and "grill."
- Figure: from *fig-*, an Indo-European root for "knead."
- Equal: from "flat," the Latin *aequus*, as on a horizontal plane.
- Cardinal: having to do with the four points of the compass; also from *cardo*, a door hinge.
- Operation: *operatio*, Latin for "work, labor."
- Scale: Old Norse *skal*, "cup."
- Circle: Latin *circulus*, "A small ring."
- Rhombus: a Greek word for "bull-roarer."
- Sine: from the Sanskrit *jiva*, "bowstring."
- Vertex: Latin for "whirlpool"; "to turn."
- Tetration (square of a square of a . . . cube of a cube of a . . .): from the Greek "four" and "wing."
- Zero, the set without numbers and therefore different from mere nothingness: from *sunya*, the Indian word for the Buddhist "void" but also meaning "desert."

As for abstract shapes, a square (four sides) is a reconfiguration of the cardinal directions. A triangle (three) is the square divided diagonally. A line separates (two) one side from another. Like divisions, circles enclosing a central point (one) abound in nature, as close as the shadow circling a sundial, as far as the distant horizon.

Probably not one of the mathematical terms listed in the section above lacks an etymological connection to nature if the inquiry reaches back far enough. Even higher math cannot get entirely away from the world: "partition," for instance, as in "partition theory," from the Latin *partitus*, "to separate"; "topology," from "place" and "write." "Matrix" in Latin means "a pregnant animal."

If all this unplanned earthiness troubles the peanitic mindset, recent discoveries from several developing fields undermine it so thoroughly that its totalistic stranglehold on research clutches at the tiller in vain. What growing numbers of researchers now face will not confine itself to their arena anymore. Like Nemesis, who redresses what has gone out of balance, it spins a web of information prying apart the pillars of the Newtonian-Baconian obsession with cause and order, stability and control. To sum up this counterparadigm: the visible matter studied by Western physicists since before Galileo is now believed to compose only a small fraction of the universe, like a luminous crest on a dark wave of immeasurable vastness. In fact, within the most perfect volume of the hardest vacuum, a nothingness walled off from everything else, pairs of subatomic particles blink into existence, mate, and vanish. Where do they come from? No one knows. Where do they go? No one knows. Physicists call this ferment "quantum foam," but its sources—and ours—remain invisible.

When seen through this perspective, orderly laws and calculations, touted for centuries as the uprights of a rationally ordered cosmos, shrink to exceptional eddies in a universal sway of uncertainty, complexity, turbulence, unpredictability, unsolvable nonlinearities, quantum entanglements, rolling soliton "memories," fractally curving strange attractors, and bits of order surfacing now and then from an ultimately unfathomable sea of natural indeterminacy. As Einstein foretold against his will, there is no fixed hitching post in the universe anymore—a universe in which the last word will always be nature's:

> Chaos is like a creature slumbering deep inside the perfectly ordered system. When the system reaches a critical value the sleeping monster sticks out its jagged tongue. (Briggs and Peat 62)

Chaos, a firstborn among the earliest Greek gods: as with all useless strivings for peanitic certainty, math is myth after all, an emplaced subjectivity taken objectively, only to lose itself in a measureless plenum where the cracks forever outgrow the cobblestones. Where is the white ideal purity of numbers now, and its parentified, mechanistic, senexian worldview? Sunk into the ground of being, with only its fading afterglow left behind: the dragons of Chaos have pulled it down, and it will never rise.

Fortunately, the buoyant tools it has left behind float on the surface like letters bobbing in some vast terrestrial bowl of alphabet soup. They will not do for a worldview, least of all an "objective" one, but their limited industrial-patriarchal-religious vocabulary can be of further use if not confused for an organically evolved philosophy of nature devoid of cultural assumptions or political influences.

Quantity and Quality

To appreciate a tool means understanding its shortcomings. The cult of quantification most clearly demonstrates the need to keep our eye on its sickle-shaped shadow when it encroaches where its tools are of limited use, then arrogantly insists that the data are at fault, even when they open themselves up to other, less rigid, more human scientific approaches.

A man dreams that a blonde he dated in Los Angeles approaches him seductively. Upon awakening he wonders whether some news from that city will arrive today. He has not been there in several years and has not kept in regular contact with anyone who lives there. Later that morning the phone rings to announce an unexpected telecommuting job offer from a company based in the City of Angels. "Coincidence," blurts a quantification cultist. "Assuming that no clue of this event arrived subliminally or otherwise: he could not have caused the job offer, and the job offer could not have caused his dream. There can be no causal connection; therefore it must be a coincidence."

No causal connection, perhaps, but the world has known since before the philosopher Hume of more things joined in heaven and earth than are dreamed of in human causality. What the factist is really saying is that the dreamer's sense of a meaningful linkage between the dream and the offer is illusory. The issue here is not whether the dreamer is correct or not but the factist's swift and final rejection of any data falling beyond his yardstick. He does not know it, but he reacts exactly like ancient Romans who unthinkingly attributed all such occurrences to Fortuna, blind goddess of chance. The god Coincidence has become a contemporary, catchall Fortuna.

Even should he suspend judgment long enough to study, let us say, the symbolism of the dream for clues, his approach would still be from the outside. He could time the dream, measure the dreamer's heart rate, even graph brainwaves, but the "Ah ha" sense of meaning would elude his instrumentation. *Exclusively quantitative explorations of the subjective realm reduce it to externalized data and therefore miss its experiential essence and rob it of its self-generating context of meaning through presence.* The fault is not in the data but in the criteria used to evaluate them. An orange peeler turned loose on an apple does not make that apple an orange. This is not to say that quantitative approaches should never be used to explore the inner world. If their limitations are recognized, such approaches can supplement methodologies better adapted to the symbolic life that enlivens and interpenetrates the material dimension of being. It would be interesting to know the precise chronological timing of the dream in relation to what it symbolized, but grasping its fuller significance nevertheless requires more finely tuned tools.

A psychotherapy client on his first visit presents the following in session: a fear of loud noises, an exaggerated startle response, flashbacks to memories of being tortured, phobic avoidance of images or events that symbolize the torture, nightmares and night sweats, irritability, suspiciousness, and distraction. To a trained therapist, the likely diagnosis is post-traumatic stress, but—and this is the point—no symptom studied by itself would definitively demonstrate the diagnosis, for the obvious reason that the same internal state gives rise to different responses in different individuals, or even the same individual at different times. Only by considering all the symptoms together *as a pattern* could the researcher discern the syndrome they comprise. The number of correlations increases the clarity of the syndrome's outline.

Yet even correlational tools meet their limits when one is dealing with subjective realities. Graphing the occurrences of a set of symptoms might prove diagnostically useful, but it would miss what being in the room with the individual might communicate to a trained and sensitized awareness—such as the significance of certain repeated metaphors (looking behind oneself as "watching your back") and the sense of how the individual addresses the witness. Even the witness might have trouble explaining why a single behavior with *no* statistically significant repetitions still gives off the sense of a discernible syndrome. The evidence is not in numbers but in the interpretive skills of the researcher at the scene.

In fact, quantitative projects in the human sciences very often defend against such direct contact with what is studied. Advertising research roars ahead, but how many of its specialists ever sit down and listen to glassy-eyed children spouting sales slogans? How many stop to identify the brand name they help sell emblazoned on the face of a plastic container discarded in a meadow? How many oil companies out to convince the public that global warming is not real send their scientists to visit destitute coastal villages as part of their investigations?

Qualitative research risks these and other hard questions in its cultivation of naturalistic findings and direct participation. A quantitative approach records what brain waves do during an ethical dilemma, but a qualitative approach inquires rigorously into the dimensions of the dilemma for the person caught in its full reality. Examples of qualitative research include person-to-person dialogs and interviews, action studies geared toward social change, analyses of recurrent themes in personal narratives, ethnological examinations of social groups by entering into them (e.g., studying homelessness by becoming homeless), interpreting "texts"—political speeches, urban art, local legends, religious rhetoric—and feeding the findings back into their sources, and investigating a healing modality's effectiveness by supplementing quantified data with direct impressions and descriptions of personal transformation, something no measurement-based approach could fathom in any depth.

Research dominated by an agenda of factist measurability does not work as either a worldview or a general philosophy of science. Here we see its limitations in the realm of mind, as well, a pliers grasping after the flow of subjectivity but fastened instead onto an earlobe.

If the cult of quantification opens its chapel doors only to aspects of reality passive enough to be grouped, groped, and measured (which in the case of human beings means those least psychological because least fluid, unpredictable, creative, and alive), can it exert *any* legitimate authority in the world of nature stretching beyond its quaint nineteenth-century parish? If not, what are the alternatives?

Nature as Co-Researcher

Johann Wolfgang von Goethe (1749–1832) is best known as the nineteenth-century German poet, dramatist, and philosopher who penned a profound version of the Faust legend and whose influence extended over several fields, including European Romanticism, literature, and music. His scientific work in botany and optics is usually deprecated by factists even though it extended over decades of systematic, thoughtful labor. What Goethe sought was another set of explanations not for how plants grew or colors formed but for a nonquantitative, systematic, highly disciplined exploration of them rooted in, but not limited to, direct perception. In other words, he was engaged in *phenomenology*, a form of qualitative research.

Goethe found that if he tended the presence of a plant without raising a screen of conjectures, a moving image formed in his imagination, not as a generalization from the details his eyes took in, but as an experiential outgrowth of them. This movement-image he named the *Ur-plant:* a flow of living becoming similar to what Aristotle thought of as the Form or potential or essence of a thing, its innermost tendency to actualize its being—very different from Plato's conception of an eternal Form standing outside the sensory world. In the eye of *anschauung,* or exact sensorial imagination, the depth that revealed itself lived not below or behind leaf and stem and blossom but within them, just as the "meaning" or richness of a sonata floats *through* the music rather than hiding somewhere behind the composition (Bortoft 21).

As Coppin and Nelson mention in their book on depth-psychological research, inquiry is a *relational* art, one in which researchers and the researched influence one another. In a state of phenomenological attentiveness such as that with which Goethe experimented, consciousness bypasses the subject-object split by partaking from what it examines within a field of relational interdependency. Whatever hypothesizing emerges arises gingerly, even humbly, out of the encounter instead of trying to quantify or categorize it, impose a grid on it, manipulate it, or reduce it to a static lifelessness residing more in the researcher than in the researched.

Researchers really should have suspected long ago—and the Carolyn Merchants and Susan Hardings and Susan Griffins of science philosophy did suspect it, as did Goethe himself—that shrinkage of depth to surface, lack of inwardness, fear of movement, fear of freshness, and repetitive mechanicality belong not to the natural world but to the institutionally sanctioned psychopathology of the quantifier putting it on the rack, as Francis Bacon counseled, to wring from it its secrets.

Perhaps this calls for another Axiom, then, the Axiom of Saturnian Cannibalism: *A commitment to quantification beyond its use as a tool of partial knowledge is an index of its soullessness.* Soullessness is bureaucratic, and bureaucracy is sociopathic. We should have learned that from Trinity, Enron, the Berlin Wall, Gitmo, and Abu Ghraib. We should have learned it forever at Nuremberg. Is it any wonder, then, that studious environmental researches darkened by this degree of self-objectification and inner deadness have failed to revive the ecosphere? That smashing the pretty ornament will never help reconstitute it? As research method, quantification has legitimate uses *when grounded in an adult psychology of responsible participation*, but as ideology (and therefore as blind as any ideology to its shadows, invisible assumptions, and authoritarian implications) it perpetuates the dangerous emotional distance that allows well-meaning people to contribute cheerfully, under the pleasing banner of progress, to the destruction of their own terrestrial home.

Goethe's experiments bring to mind the ancient and indigenous view of psyche as a dimension of being, a view our civilization abandoned in step with the expanding dependency of its economies on terrestrial despoliation. (How long would the CEO of Exxon keep his job if he deeply experienced Earth as a living entity?) This view of universal interiority persists in societies not yet forced to house tourist resorts or military bases. In the West it left the hands of Aristotle and Neoplatonism to weave its way underground through alchemy, panpsychist philosophy, nature lore, and various revivals of paganism before resurfacing in Jung, archetypal psychology, and deep-reflective styles of environmental activism. Today we sort through these tangles of symbolism for silenced *truths* (from the same root as *trees*) to unearth.

Factism did its level- and literal-headed best to disenchant the world of its elves and trolls, sprites and naiads, mermaids and sirens, calliopes and Pan pipes, but is it possible after all that the old stories pointed as much to the future as to the past? What if these figures could be re-dreamed as wily bits of animated matter on the lookout for human research partners?

An approach that transcends the split between qualitative and quantitative methodologies seems particularly fruitful when working on the plane of the symbolic.

To the Places Themselves

I have argued that careful tending of geographical locations reveals "placefield traumas"—points of ecological, cultural, and personal wounding inflicted in particular places—radiating outward in "returns of the ecohistorically repressed" in which symbolic manifestations of the original traumas repeat again and again along several dimensions of human experience. The motif of contamination, for example, recurs multidimensionally throughout the history of San Luis Obispo County, California, from alien species invading Morro Bay to broken oil pipes below Avila Beach to sewers malfunctioning in Los Osos to dreams of this motif before and during my investigations of this place.

From ecopsychological fieldwork and historical research I documented extensive recurrences of placefield syndromes for all twenty-one Mission cities and fourteen Mission counties of California on the assumption that the more I could find, the stronger the surmise of an interactive or intersubjective field joining the injuries of the land with the psyches of its inhabitants. This is a key working premise of terrapsychology, the deep study of the animated places we inhabit. Whether or not these correlated motifs can be operationalized, quantified, and subjected to a statistical analysis, the personal learnings, senses, affects, "ecological countertransferences," and dreams of researchers register them nevertheless.

"But qualitative research isn't scientific!" intones the cult of quantification even as its Newtonian lenses fog in an overheating atmosphere (not yet conclusively calculated to be unseasonably warm: the polar bears know it, but the yardstick wielders must fight it out).

Of course it's scientific. The only question is which version of science is most suitable for a given inquiry. Comparative, phenomenological, hermeneutic, heuristic, ethnographical, ideographic, narrative, depth-psychological, ecopsychological, terrapsychological, and participatory-action studies are examples of research concerned with context, natural settings, and learnings mentored by what is studied. Numbering and measuring generate impressive graphs, can be used to control collective behavior, receive more funding and more public attention, and can calculate precisely the quantity of propellant for a newly machined missile but not a clear feel for the paranoia in the aimers, who have themselves lost the feel for important consequences.

Perhaps that is the point: the numbness of mere numbers, division and separation, reduction and doubt, as scientifically justified narcissistic defenses against the numinous power of the world's animated interconnectedness. Narcissism cannot tolerate relationship. Its envy of spontaneous displays of aliveness elicits dampening and deadening moves referred to in the psychoanalytic literature as "spoiling" and "analization." The more inwardly dead the investigator is, the higher the investment in projecting that deadness outward onto people, places, and lively things.

Within the perspective of terrapsychology, quantified numbers and facts do have their place, but as reconciling metaphors and imagings of earthly forms of address. These emanate from the whole—inside and out—of what guides the study. Calculable tectonic stresses account precisely for slippage rates along the San Andreas Fault but can be reimagined as metaphors of psychic pressures that divide communities the length and width of Alta California, from the relative liberalism of Encinitas versus the conservatism of the Inland Empire up to West County yurts versus Irvine-like Rohnert Park and its calculated displays of architectural giantism. The state as a whole reflects this division: witness the sharp difference of cultures between coastal California and the Central Valley. Regarding the San Andreas as an earthquake fault jostling more than the literal ground eschews the overworked proof paradigm of explanations—"Are places living or aren't they?"—to invite a change of perceptions from arid externalism to revivifying animism without reducing outer to inner or vice versa.

Someday the relationship between vanishing islands of greenery and bluery and vanishing sectors of human joy might lie exposed by the lines on a grid, assuming that someone survives to compute it, but for grasping it now we have qualitative tools, the grounded adult sensibility of those who care about the world, and recovery of trust in subjective earthly knowings: pushed to the edges of culture and consciousness, knowings nevertheless are arising once again from the depths of things within, between, and around us. Just as we need no Index of Anger to tell us that pitting students against each other fills them with frustration and fear, and no Paranoia Scale to uncover the state-supported hatred that unceasing warfare and surveillance express, we need not wait—must not wait—for statistical boxes no better at trapping Earth's astonishing reactivity than at catching any insight into our own. The cult of quantification is itself a paranoid symptom, a pathological longing for certainty and control that in a truly rational scientific establishment would disqualify itself as a matter of course. Although a dream in which Earth shows up as a personified figure in pain and anger should not be accepted at face value uncritically (return of the puer), neither should it be ignored for failing to bring a table of numbers with it (revenge of the senex).

Jung often used a word he got from the old Greek philosopher Heraclitus: *enantiodromia*, the conversion of one extreme into another—rebel into aristocrat, senex into puer, puer into senex, rationalist into mystic, Saul into Paul. *Enantiodromia* expresses the psychological equivalent of Nemesis, fearful settler of accounts. But Jung also wrote about the *transcendent function:* the synthesizing factor that arises when the opposites are kept simultaneously in view. This function evokes the aspect of Aphrodite, the universal energy in every attraction, from matter's cohesion to cosmic gravitation.

The disciplined openness that is our last, best hope reappears when the researcher steers a clear course between Francis Bacon's project, torturing Nature for her secrets, and the other extreme, regarding her as our New Age billboard of omens. Between scientism and pseudoscience, literalism and lunacy, peanitis and Peter Pan, this openness balances fact and fantasy in an aphroditic elegance that recalls the heart—not just a literal pump in the chest but the felt psychic core of the fully adult researcher—back to a sense of responsibility and deep love for people, places, and things spoken into being as kinetic verbs by the world's endlessly imagistic speech.

Works Cited

Balaguer, Mark. *Platonism and Anti-Platonism in Mathematics.* Oxford: Oxford UP, 1998.

Berlinski, David. *A Tour of the Calculus.* New York: Pantheon, 1995.

Bortoft, Henri. *The Wholeness of Nature: Goethe's Way toward a Science of Conscious Participation.* New York: Lindisfarne, 1996.

Briggs, John, and F. David Peat. *Turbulent Mirror: An Illustrated Guide to Chaos Theory and the Science of Wholeness.* New York: Harper and Row, 1989.

Chalquist, Craig. *Terrapsychology: Re-engaging the Soul of Place.* New Orleans: Spring Journal Books, 2007.

Changeux, Jean-Pierre, and Alain Connes. *Conversations on Mind, Matter, and Mathematics.* Trans. M. B. DeBevois. Princeton: Princeton UP, 1995.

Coppin, Joseph, and Elizabeth Nelson. *The Art of Inquiry: A Depth Psychological Perspective.* Putnam: Spring, 2005.

Davis, Philip, and Reuben Hersh. *Descartes' Dream: The World According to Mathematics.* New York: Harcourt Brace Jovanovich, 1986.

Griffin, Susan. *The Eros of Everyday Life: Essays on Ecology, Gender, and Society.* New York: Anchor/Doubleday, 1995.

Hillman, James. *Suicide and the Soul.* New York: Harper, 1973.

Landsburg, Steven. "Andre Weil." Cornell University. <http://people.cornell.edu/pages/ jc353/Andre%20Weil.htm> 25 January 2005.

Merchant, Carolyn. *The Death of Nature: Women, Ecology, and the Scientific Revolution.* San Francisco: Harper and Row, 1983.

Pedaya, Haviva. "The Divinity as Place and Time and the Holy Place in Jewish Mysticism." *Sacred Space: Shrine, City, Land.* Ed. Benjamin Kedar and R. J. Werblowsky. London and Jerusalem: Macmillan, 1998. 84–111.

Shepard, Paul. *Nature and Madness.* Athens: U of Georgia P, 1998.

Teresi, Dick. *Lost Discoveries: The Ancient Roots of Modern Science—from the Babylonians to the Maya.* New York: Simon and Schuster, 2002.

The Marriage of the *Puer Aeternus* and Trickster Archetypes

Psychological Rebirth for the Puer Personality

CHAZ GORMLEY

Setting the Stage for Union

Introduction

The *puer aeternus* personality constellation shoots across the contemporary American landscape like a fiery comet whose progress seemingly can't be stopped, changed, or understood. These energetic, creative firebrands have fascinated people for thousands of years, yet their tendency toward extreme self-absorption and early death leads people to keep them isolated and at arm's distance. As Robert Bly has argued, the increasing numbers of modern *pueri aeterni* emphasize the cultural fascination with this archetype, speed up the culture, and herald a change in the structure of society that goes hand in hand with a social and psychological regression. American popular culture celebrates this event, while the institutions of society suffer from the lack of grounded, mature adult energy. This suggests that American society, itself, has a *puer aeternus* psychology.

The one-sided instability of the *puer aeternus* expresses itself in a heightened quest for psychological meaning, or an overt or sublimated search for religious experiences. The frequent failures of these quests often lead people into self-destructive behaviors, suicidal impulses, early burnout, or death (von Franz, *Puer Aeternus*). If pueri live through these without finding healing, an *enantiodromia* (i.e., reversal into an opposite) into the senex pattern typically occurs. As no society can, seemingly, base itself on masses of people living an unstable psychological pattern that breeds an early death or burnout—even a pattern charged with excitement and powerful energy—an archetypal answer must be found that incorporates the high creativity and genius of the puer archetype (Conforti) into a sustainable, mature, and healthy lifestyle pattern.

An Archetypal Methodology

Many have sought to study and find ways to transform the *puer aeternus* life-style into a stable psychological pattern, without losing the energy, creativity, and charm of the original (see Bly; Hillman, "Senex and Puer"; Jung, *Symbols*; von Franz, *Puer Aeternus*). I will examine these questions, expressed so vividly in these studies: *How can one safely bring the puer down to earth (i.e., daily life) without destroying him? How to manifest the coniunctio and birth a new Self-image within the puer personality?* and *What are the aids and hindrances to such an unconscious healing process?* In this chapter, I propose an answer to these rhetorical questions: *by marrying the puer aeternus to the trickster archetype*. I explore the ramifications that such an attempt at an archetypal marriage brings up.

In this essay, I will try to perform a "therapy of an archetype" (Hillman, "Senex and Puer" 9). All archetypes have a typical set of symbols, energies, and images that tend to cluster around them (Conforti). They proceed out of the unconscious and only later come to conscious knowledge. To understand and integrate archetypal patterns, one must circumambulate them—circle around them and view their central dynamics from multiple positions in order to bring them more fully into consciousness (Jung, *Psychology and Alchemy* 145–48). The chaos and creativity of the puer archetype cannot be understood or integrated through a linear, rational exegesis alone. Therefore, I will move around and between the archetypes of the puer and the trickster, looking at their symbols, their images, their energies, and their behavioral patterns to study and bring them alive, bringing them into clearer focus as I proceed. I will then move into an exploration of a prospective union of these two powerful archetypes in a single personality pattern. Finally, I will attempt to demonstrate that a successful maturation for the puer personality involves a constellating and eventual integration of the trickster archetype within the personality.[1]

The Personalities of the Trickster Archetype
and His Relation to the Puer Aeternus

Trickster stories are among the oldest mythological stories that people have told. Exemplifying this, he is called "First-born" by some Native American tribes (Radin 19). Like the puer, the trickster archetype embodies a transgressive energy, that is, he willingly and easily crosses personal and social boundaries (Hyde), meanwhile maintaining a joyful participation in earthbound activities. The trickster does not attempt to escape Earth, like the spirit-loving puer, but rather seems to find a home in any element in which he places himself. Those in his community see him as good-natured and entertaining, if a little dense. His immense skill at adaptation comes through a full acceptance of all parts of life (Radin). He symbolizes humanity's creative, life-generating power when in a fluid relationship to nature. Our modern pueri love of flight, speed, and careless wasting of earth resources shows the absence of the living trickster archetype in our consciousness. Pueri, instead, find it easier to live and create when disconnected from earthiness.

Pueri aeterni are often victims of significant early psychological trauma, which can constellate their fear of matter (Conforti). The psychological darkness of this trauma can produce an extreme, long-term preference toward the light and spiritual, and the creative and energetic, while simultaneously birthing a profound fear and avoidance of the mundane and ordinary, and the dark and earthy. The trickster doesn't suffer from this drastic psychological split. He readily finds spirit in nature, and he connects with deities of light through involvement with dark matter. The trickster travels between realms, including between the realms of the puer and the senex; he is related to the transpersonal, is against domestication, is pleasure-seeking, promotes spiritual and conscious development, is sometimes hermaphroditic or asexual, and is sometimes considered a "young brother" (Radin), all like the *puer aeternus*. The senex is a psychological opposite to the puer and represents the rigid, static aspect of spirit, with a significant unconscious tie to the material realm (Hillman, "Senex and Puer"). Like the senex, and in opposition to the puer, the trickster is completely earthbound; he sometimes finds himself in positions of authority (a typical goal of the senex archetype) and is sometimes called "old man" (Radin), which is a common name for a strong senex type. This combination of the opposites within a single personality is typical of the trickster.

The trickster archetype seems to be an expression of a primitive mechanism of moving archetypal contents from the unconscious to consciousness. As Jung describes, "[T]he civilizing process begins within the framework of the trickster cycle itself" ("On the Psychology" 206). On a higher cultural level, this civilizing process is typically conducted in organized religious or ritual contexts, or by birthing the divine child—the *puer aeternus* archetype (Jung, *The Archetypes* 22, 151–81). The trickster acts according to his instincts, particularly those connected with sexuality and physical hunger. This behavior leads him into countless difficulties and mistakes, which paradoxically help him to become ever more conscious of himself, as well as adding consciousness to his community (Radin 142, 168). The puer also suffers a profound hunger, but it is one of a transpersonal nature. If he succeeds in satisfying this hunger, through a new birth of the transpersonal, his achievement is likewise a blessing for the community (Conforti). A mythological motif common to many creation stories is that parts of the trickster's body become parts of the Earth and food for people to eat (von Franz, *Creation Myths* 93–107).

The trickster rises to the level of cultural hero, world creator, and savior, or he sinks down to the level of exiled and despised fool whom nobody trusts and everyone avoids, according to the psychological needs of the culture. He solves problems, generates life, and heals people, often unconsciously or accidentally. He combines the divine, human, and animal simultaneously (Jung, "On the Psychology"). This specific archetypal multiplicity is what has allowed for the worldwide appeal of trickster stories (Hyde 9–10). The trickster's psychological pattern coincides with a typically weaker ego consciousness (Jung, "On the Psychology" 201). Paradoxically, this weakness proves a spiritual strength in helping the trickster channel unconscious energies without the interference of the ego and without concern for inner or outer boundaries. The ability to break taboos and go well beyond important boundaries is inherent in the trickster, as it is in the puer.

This interest in crossing boundaries, or eliminating them, is a clear parallel to life in the twenty-first century: airplanes that quickly cross borders, the World Wide Web that recognizes no borders, media that easily travel around the world, and so on. Contemporary technology can create and destroy virtual worlds with a few clicks of a keyboard. Our increasingly single world community may be the ideal playground for the trickster. The trickster's tremendous flexibility and openness to such a community contrast sharply with the puer, who prefers a sharper focus and a solitary existence (von Franz, *Puer Aeternus*).

The trickster's embodied ambivalence is lived in both the inner and outer aspects of his character—both psychologically and materially (Diamond xiii, xvii). He contains both sides of the various archetypal opposites of human existence. He is whole in himself, traveling through a world that expresses wholeness. Through his wholeness, he brings culture to the community, which is also an effect of the individuated person (Jung, *Civilization*). The trickster creates and destroys, takes and gives, tricks others, and willingly plays the tricked fool. This latter behavior puts him in a deeply compensatory relationship to the cultured puer, who seeks intelligence and genius, particularly despising collective stupidity (Conforti). This compensatory dynamic suggests a natural affinity between the two archetypes. This affinity, paradoxically, seems implicitly understood in the trickster cycles. These mythic cycles show the close connection between the trickster and the search for the divine. As Diamond remarks: "[A]mong primitive peoples, all antinomies are bound into the ritual cycle. The sacred is an immediate aspect of man's experience" (xxi). Unlike the puer, the trickster does not have to be rational, powerful, or intelligent to be effective—rather, he is considered effective to the degree that he embodies and expresses new tribal realizations, or to the degree he expresses emerging archetypal patterns, imaged as the will of nature, or the Creator's will (Radin 126, 156, 166). This concern with the sacred expresses a marked similarity with the puer.

The trickster embodies a starkly primitive amorality, differing widely from the puer and the senex patterns: "He knows neither good nor evil yet he is responsible for both. He possesses no values, moral or social, is at the mercy of his passions and appetites, yet through his actions all values come into being" (Diamond xxiii). Pueri typically have a strong desire to birth new cultural values and forms (von Franz, *Puer Aeternus*), yet they fail more than they succeed. The trickster revels in the seemingly senseless energy of life, in the chaotic play of the opposites. Frequently acting in a markedly unconscious state, he has a penchant for cutting off, losing, burning, eating, and talking to parts of his body. His excesses and stupidities are rather appalling to the modern ego, with its tendency to take things literally. Over time, as his consciousness grows, he reclaims these cut-off parts of his body into his identity, realizing that they are not separate beings (Radin 135). This reintegration of body parts is a clear analogy to the reintegration of psychic parts that psychologically minded people are so necessarily concerned with today. It is a seeming schematic for Jung's process of individuation. The need for such integration is particularly obvious for the typically one-sided puer who believes he can make it through life bingeing on the volatile energies of extreme weightlessness and spirituality. The puer unconsciously calls out to the trickster archetype.

Trickster as Twenty-First Century Hero

The trickster's ease of translation to contemporary times, and our ability to update his stories to a modern psychological context make him an archetypally living figure, uniquely suited to the demands of a twenty-first-century multicultural world. He represents a new style of hero. Historically, the trickster archetype seems to predate the hero archetype, and it is most prevalent in very primitive societies (Radin 164). The traditional hero arises out of a specific cultural atmosphere, to which he returns (Campbell), while the trickster is a boundary crosser, committed to no single culture, habitat, or relationship, presaging many *pueri aeterni*. Paradoxically, the trickster often becomes a cultural hero as a result of the adventures constellated during his journeys; these adventures can include boundary creation, as well (Hyde 7). It is precisely this chaotic, nonlinear heroism that seems so fitting for post-Newtonian twenty-first-century culture. Reflecting our new sciences of complexity, the trickster is an embodiment of "sacred complexity" (Hyde 7), a psychic style that might call attractively to wounded pueri. A contemporary cultural example is the trickster heroes in the *Matrix* film trilogy. These heroes, dressed only in black, move between different realms of existence, even different "realities," knowing that retreat, redirection, escape, and even death are as necessary to the process of world (and personality) creation as standing and fighting. The enormous popularity of these films and characters expresses our unconscious hunger for trickster stories and motifs.

The trickster is the world creator that both the puer and the senex long to be (Hillman, "Senex and Puer" 26–30). He is a cultural hero with an, initially, utterly unheroic, unique style. Unlike the warrior heroes so common in Western myths (i.e., Hercules, St. George, Rambo, etc.), the trickster in Native American myth is seen as the opposite of the warrior, even to the point of being a coward. Initially, the trickster fails at everything he does. Despite his seeming distaste for fighting and heroism, in other stories he performs the heroic action that saves people in his community, brings new tools, weapons, culture, and so forth, to humans desperately in need of them (Radin 166). In some stories, the trickster performs the archetypal heroic task of cutting himself and others out of the belly of a monster, symbolic of freeing the ego from its immersion in the unconscious. Through this action, he grows himself to a more complex level, symbolically revealing the growth of the local communal consciousness (Campbell 90–93). As a cultural hero, he domesticates the wilderness for people, and the unconscious for the ego. In a time when the globalization of international culture progresses ever more rapidly, and even the ecological parameters of life are changing, having such an adaptive energy readily available might be a necessity.

The trickster's travels are a mythological analogy to Jung's process of individuation. At the end of the trickster's journeys, the level of consciousness that the trickster represents has dramatically increased, and a new being with a differentiated psychological configuration and environment has arisen (Radin 142, 166, 168). This has been the archetypal promise all along. The late trickster figure in Native American cycles has begun consciously to benefit the associated tribes through his once despised behavior, to articulate a system of values out of his amorality, and to develop a sense of social and moral responsibility out of his previous anarchistic, irresponsible preferences. However, in a sort of refutation of the *puer aeternus*'s spiritual goal, some undeveloped archetypal darkness always clings to the trickster figure. The trickster adds the elements of chaos and disorder into a situation expressing a rigid order, thus expressing both sides of the archetypal opposites and making a psychological whole. His timeliness for a sibling society of *pueri aeterni* (Bly), who in their lack of care for earthy things are destroying the planet's ecology, and the political and psychological culture that it took many centuries to build up, could hardly be more apparent.

The Marriage of *Puer Aeternus* and Trickster

The Effect of the Trickster on the Puer Aeternus

The *puer aeternus* archetype often expresses the most advanced aspects, knowledges, and skills of a particular society (Conforti). The puer creatively gives birth to them, advocates them, integrates them through his lifestyle, and enjoys them. Wolfgang Amadeus Mozart, Percy Shelley, Thomas Jefferson, and Albert Einstein are just a few positive examples of the lived genius and cultural importance of the successful puer. Rather than controlling his high archetypal energy through repression, the developed puer must instead accept the chaotic energy as essentially irrational. The very energy of a nascent Self-image creates an unstable situation fraught with dangers for the individual manifesting a *puer aeternus* pattern (von Franz, *Puer Aeternus* 23–30). This instability can set up the puer's problems and pathologies discussed above. A psychological crash sacrifices the puer's ongoing connection to the transpersonal for an exclusive and collective connection to earth- and time-bound reality—for example, the hippie becomes a stockbroker. The puer must move his efforts toward manifesting a new Self-image as a lived outer reality, and he must experience the new content as an inner, numinous image beyond ego control. This demands sacrifice and acceptance. In this effort, the trickster archetype can provide the path for the *puer aeternus*; he demonstrates a faith in ordinary life without sacrificing the connection to the transpersonal.

Despite the puer's notable cultural sophistication, the trickster expresses the unconscious differentiation that the puer still so desperately desires. The trickster pulls the puer beyond his one-sided spiritual orientation. The trickster teaches the puer relatedness to the various manifestations of life on earth; he teaches him that conflict is a centerpiece of this life, a conflict that frequently pulls one in two opposing directions. Pueri fight mightily to avoid the knowledge and experience of the tension of the opposites (von Franz, *Puer Aeternus*). Psychological ambivalence is one of the puer's largest fears about life (Hillman, "Senex and Puer" 30), as it reflects his early emotional wounding. In a contemporary landscape where such traumas are widespread, a mediator that leads one out of ambivalence and wounding can be a necessity. Healing for the puer will not come from further conscious or cultural differentiation, though he believes it will. Rather, the puer must face his inner, irrational opposite in order to grow to the next level.

The trickster also serves as an archetypal channel for the collective consciousness, balancing its rigidity, and providing a means for it to access the irrational psyche, reaping the riches that remain in the instinctual background of life. The puer, often so far ahead of the collective consciousness of his milieu, builds up his own rigidities over time, becoming a rather static, collective type eventually,

if he cannot embody new archetypal energies (von Franz, *Puer Aeternus*). If
needed by the personality, the trickster archetype creates accidents that force
a new adaptation to the environment. Sometimes, only such new trauma can
wake up the puer from his innocence. Because of the early trauma, the puer,
with his keen sense of intuition (Conforti), strives mightily to avoid any situations that could constellate a crisis that would force a change. By connecting
himself with the instinctual and archetypal psyche, via the bridge of the trickster
archetype, the puer finds a means to experience the new image of the Self he
has so long sought. But it takes a sacrifice of his puer's wounded adaptation
to life in order fully to access this new, unconscious energy. The attitude that
arises from this puer-trickster partnership is one that, on the puer side, can see
beyond the present at how events are likely to develop and end, yet be willing,
through the trickster side, to commit itself to the experience, nonetheless, even
when it may seem foolish.

The Sacrifice of the Mother Complex

The puer's infantilism and regressive tie to the mother (von Franz, *Puer
Aeternus*) are at the centerpiece of what must be sacrificed for growth to occur.
When timely, sacrificing the mother complex adds strength and power to
the conscious personality (Neumann 152–69). Pueri seem to have a problem
with accessing the power archetype in a healthy way. As with the trickster, the
destructive and constructive tendencies are closely related in the puer, though
the puer hides this knowledge from himself. The puer generally tries to push
the opposites apart and identify with the constructive, light, and peaceful
side. Hillman ("Betrayal") discusses the creative need for a deep experience of
betrayal to break through the puer's identification with the archetypal light.
He suggests that a suffering of a large deception, so well promoted by the
trickster, can constellate a painful experience that loosens the puer's habitual
attitude to life and pulls his psyche into a progressive, if initially very dark,
archetypal development. The frequent neurotic problems and psychological
dangers of the *puer aeternus* (Baynes) may be trickster-like attempts by the
unconscious to spur the puer into doing needed psychological work. Here again,
the trickster's willingness to do whatever work lies before him can be a symbolic
model that helps. The trickster may, in fact, be a personification of a tendency
in the unconscious to force such work into consciousness. Unless the ego is
cooperating with the unconscious and its instinctual layers, the ego is too weak
to pull away from its previous infantilism expressed in the mother complex
and to face the creative possibilities that life ever brings it. It needs a relation
to the potentially wounding power archetype. The trickster also manifests an
awareness, desperately needed by the puer, that contact with the unconscious

may overwhelm the ego but that one can still come through such an inundation safely. Rather, pueri typically fear such an unconscious inundation because it can significantly wound the puer's fragile ego (von Franz, *Puer Aeternus* 27, 53, 112). Archetypal development necessarily has periods in which the ego is eclipsed and fails, and preventing such eclipses can also prevent mature development (von Franz, *Projection* 58,187–88). Accepting such a risk, the ego must descend into the unconscious to free itself from the mother tie and connect to the inner center (Jung, *Symbols*). An archetypal descent tends to bring a ritual death followed by a rebirth experience and the breaking of the former regressive tie to the unconscious.

This difficult psychological experience is expressed in modern mythological figures' (such as Attis, Dionysus, or Christ) being dismembered, torn apart, or crucified before being reborn (Jung, *Symbols* 423–25). Integration of dismembered elements must take place in the ego, not in the Self—that is, in the god-image, or in the projections onto outer institutions—if maturation is to occur. This is an important modern change from the style of psychological healing expressed in Western religions, in which individuals were healed collectively via participation in an impersonal god-image. Breaking the tie to the mother also allows an individual development of the anima that brings a safe, reliable means of connecting with the unconscious and with life (Hillman, "Senex and Puer" 30). Instead of such a bridge, the mother complex typically tends to make the puer project Self-images onto outer women, or feminine ideals and contents, which he then, in a compulsive and energetic fashion, seeks to attain, conquer, or worship. A man's Self-projections should properly be placed upon other men or masculine elements, which helps stabilize the male ego. Projecting Self-images upon women tends to weaken a man's sense of commitment to reality and exaggerate his attachment to fantasy (Jung, *Symbols* 298–300). Worse, without a progressive development of the anima, the one-sided energy of the *puer aeternus* can lead to insanity or death (von Franz, *Puer Aeternus*).[2]

Birthing a New Self-Image

The unstable pattern of the puer's religious search for meaning, which easily transgresses borders and moves from the heights of ecstasy to the depths of darkness, resembles the variegated spiritual path of the trickster's physical wanderings. The ability to break taboos and go well beyond important boundaries is common to both pueri and tricksters. In the trickster's case, there is always a commitment to, and appreciation of, the momentary place and time; however, the puer's alternations are a result of trying to escape such a commitment, trying to escape the limitations of space and time, and thinking that some place beyond the here and now will hold the desired transpersonal meaning (Conforti). This style of psychological flight must be sacrificed:

> [E]very encounter with the unconscious [begins with] the complete break-down of the former activities, the goal in life and, in some form, the flow of the life energy. Suddenly, everything gets stuck; we are blocked and stuck in a neurotic situation, and in this moment the life energy is dammed up and then generally breaks through in the revelation of a new archetypal image. (von Franz, *Puer Aeternus* 27)

This is what the puer most fears. I suggest it is the trickster archetype that is trying to break through both in the psyche of the puer and in the culture. This is partly expressed culturally in the rise of comedy as a profitable art/entertain-ment form. It is seen in rock and roll music, which from Elvis Presley onward has shown a fascination with the primitive and often a sort of trickster persona. Like confidence men of old, contemporary musicians are willing to appropriate others' goods or skills, to increase their profits and fame (legend has it that Presley "borrowed" some of his hit songs from black musicians without credit or payment), and they are ready and able to show people the face that they are seeking. One senses this trickster energy in the Rolling Stones, called the world's greatest rock band and certainly one of the most profitable; they are a band whose persona has repeatedly changed as years and fashion have changed, going all the way from street revolutionaries to corporate CEOs. One also finds it in hip-hop and rap music which unashamedly samples (i.e., steals) others' music while loudly proclaiming (with a wink and a nod to those in the know) the primitive gangsta or street thug persona (i.e., living dangerously on the dark earth—home of the primitive trickster) who needs help from no one else. Lest we forget Hollywood, the movie industry is rife with trickster energy, celebrating the continuous flickering of ever-changing images of desire. The modern cult of celebrity may itself be a trickster phenomenon. Both rock concerts and movie houses provide a sort of temporary sacred or luminal space to audiences, offering an unconscious promise of a religious experience or initiation that justifies the high prices. Afterward, as the lights come up and consciousness returns, the quasi-magical feeling fades and nothing has changed—except the size of the celebrity's bank account (Moore and Gillette 142). The corporate and political worlds daily proclaim trickster motifs in the mass media, such as Enron "gaming" the California energy market, causing needless deaths and bankrupt-cies, or the "selling" of the Iraq war, whose raison d'être changed according to the political winds and popular opinion.

Repeatedly, the puer short-circuits the attempted birth of a new Self-image because it is so fraught with extremely intense energies (von Franz, *Puer*

Aeternus). A fundamental question of our time is: *To what extent can conscious-ness participate in directing this process?* By bringing forth the idea that there is a natural partnering between the *puer aeternus* and the trickster, I am positing a means of regeneration for the puer personality whose life pattern is no longer working, and a way of being consciously involved in this unconscious process. I am suggesting a new archetypal direction in which the puer's considerable conscious and unconscious energies and talents can be creatively contacted and directed before the psychic shortcuts that try to reduce inner tension—physical flight, drugs, self-destructive or suicidal behaviors—manifest, producing regret-table and often permanent results. This path of conscious involvement has its dangers, too, for the ego and the Self cannot meet without there being a mutual wounding (von Franz, *Puer Aeternus* 112; Edinger 37–42). Such a wounding can disrupt or destroy the personality. However, if the person stays in the presence of the archetypal wound without fleeing from it and can absorb its traumatic energy, s/he participates in the healing of both ego and Self (Jung, *Psychology and Religion* 355–470). Transformation, however, can only come for the puer when he agrees to commit fully to the present situation, even when painful. The marriage to trickster energy can help him develop a renewed capacity for committing to the situation of the moment, and it can give him skills to adapt well to the chaos. As Hillman details, this marriage also opens up the puer to a much wider differentiation of feeling, with the possibility of achieving true wisdom ("Betrayal" 67–68, 81).

I think that this trickster-puer figure is uniquely suited for the archetypal needs of the moment, and I can imagine a partnership between them as not only thinkable but likely to erupt in a variety of unconscious ways, if not consciously picked up and developed. The great value of the individual's participation in this creative work is that new levels of consciousness can erupt only in the psyche of an individual (Edinger 155–67). New consciousness does not spontaneously erupt in groups, even though American society, with its love of mass media and collective entertainment, seems to believe this, even cherishing it as a great ideal. If this archetypal breakthrough can be related and integrated by the ego, a new archetypal center arises.

The Unified Puer-Trickster Composite

If the energy of the puer is understood and properly integrated into conscious-ness, it can "bring a healing message of love, freedom, and devotion to one's task" (von Franz, *Puer Aeternus* 291). This is the puer's great blessing when his energy is flowing freely. Such a message evokes the typical feeling-state of the trickster archetype. A prospective union between these two figures would likely move between chaos and order without disintegrating or falling back into infantilism. The composite figure would express the ability to channel archetypal energy through the Earth—in a grounded way, adapted to outer circumstances—into facing the needs of the moment, a skill at which the *puer aeternus* is often so poor. Both the *puer aeternus* and the trickster archetypes are seeking to transform meaninglessness into a more meaningful order in a life situation. Both the puer and the trickster seek the divine, but they have very different expectations about, and relationships to, matter. Both archetypes embody woundedness and suffering, and thus they have the ability to heal woundedness and remove suffering from people (Jung, "On the Psychology" 196). Only those who have suffered archetypal wounding can heal others' psychological wounds (von Franz, *Puer Aeternus* 111).

One expression of this combined archetype is the classical shaman or medicine man, perhaps most completely articulated by the Celtic figure of Merlin (Jung and von Franz 347–99). Merlin embodies the archetypal, magical, and spiritual interests so dear to the *puer aeternus*, as well as the Earth energy, hairiness, and instinctuality of the trickster. Merlin acts as an appropriate symbolic bridge between the two archetypes, for he possesses both an expert knowledge of the practical world and a profound understanding of the relations among the invisible aspects of life. Contemporary literary/film examples of this highly popular composite figure, also with Celtic overtones, are the characters Gandalf from the *Lord of the Rings* trilogy and Dumbledore from the *Harry Potter* books/movies. These composite figures embody a strength and power needed by their respective communities. This creative connection to the power archetype, so different from senex power dreams, seems to be a result of the puer-trickster marriage.

The Western unconscious seems to have realized the inner archetypal need to combine the puer with the trickster during the medieval era. In fact, the Grail Cycle of stories may be an expression of this movement within the European person (Jung and von Franz): from an innocent *puer aeternus* in the form of Parzival, to the worldly experienced and powerful, yet mystical and creative, combined *puer aeternus*-trickster in the form of Merlin (or from Harry to Dumbledore in *Harry Potter*). Merlin is the embodied goal of the Grail Legend: he reveals to us the layer of the psyche that combines archetypal opposites—god and animal, the above and the below, the trickster and the puer, and so forth. To constellate this symbolic layer of life, to reach Merlin, one must surrender one's modern style of conscious adaptation and connect with the primitive layer of the psyche. This archaic side still resides within the personality and is seeking expression. It can remain very active and creative. It is sometimes very problematic and disruptive to outer adaptation. The first experience of the emerging Self often has an archaic form (Neumann 5–38). The trickster may be a common face of the emerging Self on the primitive level, with Merlin, or a Merlin analogue, being the corresponding figure on the more human level. Part of the puer's problem is that he has forgotten or rejected this primitive side of the Self, so he receives reminders—often in the forms of accidents, woundings, and so on—from the unconscious trying to lead him back to knowledge of it. The fact that the Self-image—Merlin—disappears at the end of the Grail Legend is a potentially ominous anticipation for the Western consciousness that this composite solution to the puer's dilemma has been born in the Western conscious psyche but may slip back into the unconscious (Jung and von Franz 390–99).

A highly intuitive, combined expression of these two archetypes that I have pieced together from a variety of sources and images, and many hours of self-reflection, is the idea and image of the *Midnight Sun*. It expresses an acceptance of both the earth and the heavens. After envisioning it, I discovered that Persian mystics anticipated my thought and had spent much energy, over the course of centuries, on developing this same image (Corbin 4–7, 45–48). As I understand it, the Midnight Sun arises out of the interior of the earth to its height, rather than crossing the sky to its summit. Symbolically, the Midnight Sun parallels the psychological rise of consciousness out of the unconscious (which the trickster is so concerned with), but it is expressive of a new transpersonal content (which the *puer aeternus* is so concerned with). This new content arises from the unconscious, and is achieved, or released, through a descent to the "underworld and to the gods below. . . . [It is] an experience of the Self, which one can only have by accepting the unconscious, the unknown in life, and the difficulty of living one's own conflict" (von Franz, *Puer Aeternus* 156). The combination of these two archetypal patterns, the puer and the trickster, seems uniquely to combine in this impersonal form. The Midnight Sun image expresses an acceptance of both the light and the dark planetary sides of the transpersonal—the sun and earth, or sun and moon (Jung, *Mysterium Coniunctionis* 92–110, 129–83). This acceptance of the two-facedness of the archetypal world, and the fashioning of images that express its ambivalent energy in a psychologically digestible form, is necessary to heal the *puer aeternus*. Crossing both sides of the contradictory opposites also forces the puer to accept the irrationality of life, with which the trickster is so comfortable. The image of the Midnight Sun is sufficiently paradoxical and imaginative to express this irrationality. Any new and healing Self-image that is to be born, or borrowed, must include these contrary opposites and elicit psychic energy from the unconscious to be effective and healing.

Life after the *Coniunctio*

In our time when the patriarchal sky Father Gods continue to recede into the psychic background, I think that the combined *puer aeternus*-trickster archetype is a developing central myth of our time. Ours is a time that demands accep-

tance of the dark and the light aspects of life if we are to survive. Our time will
be psychologically pregnant for an increasingly growing part of the population.
Our society seems now to breed pueri and will probably continue to do so,
unless a new god-image arises out of the unconscious and is fashioned into a
form or mythic image digestible by the contemporary ego. We are not likely to
see another one-sided, heavenly, spiritual, sun god spontaneously erupt out of
the collective unconscious. Such a pattern might seemingly suit the puer, but
such an all-compassing, patriarchal sky god doesn't seem to reflect the diversity
and the dark, earthy, and ecological needs of the present moment. Likewise,
the chaotic primitivity of the trickster archetype, by itself, would never be
acceptable to modern consciousness, with our highly sophisticated and complex
cultures. Together, the two constellate the *coniunctio*, or union of opposites,
that Jung defines as necessary for individuation (*Mysterium Coniunctionis*). As
archetypes are expressions of unconscious dynamics (von Franz, *Projections
and Recollections* 90-91), I have focused my own questing on the unconscious
issues surrounding the subject because this marriage between the puer and the
trickster cannot be accomplished through conscious means. Ego consciousness
and the rational brain are helpers, at best, during this process; oftentimes, they
seem serious obstacles to it. For the *puer aeternus* to transform, he has to move
through an experience of archetypal darkness, or a descent into the unconscious,
in a way that does not simply wound the puer ego but allows the puer to face
his own darkness before opening up to new energies embodied by trickster
dynamics within the psyche. After the experience of the archetypal Darkness
comes the reborn Light. The secret knowledge with which the puer returns after
his confrontation with dark psychic elements is precisely the knowledge that
allows the expression of new Self-energy, which was his goal from the start. This
is the energy that can heal and mature the *puer aeternus.*

Through a full embrace of the trickster archetype in his deepest psychological
being, the puer personality finds the depth, the fullness, the energy, and his
place in life for which he so desperately longs. Only in this place of wholeness
will the *puer aeternus* find sustainable health and life. In his embrace of the
trickster, the puer finds the meandering road to healing, a new inner image of
wholeness, and a renewed experience of life.

Notes

1. Note on language used: as, mythologically, the *puer aeternus* pattern exemplified the
   young, dying male god (von Franz, *Puer Aeternus*), and since the great majority of
   puer aeternus personalities seem to be male, I have retained the masculine pronoun
   "he" and the masculine term "puer" in this essay; however, there does not seem to
   be an appreciable difference in the behavior of the male *puer aeternus* and female

puella aeterna (Baynes; Conforti; von Franz, *Puer Aeternus*). To avoid confusion and particularly not to constellate the *coniunctio*, or marriage archetype (Jung, *Mysterium Coniunctionis*), when it is not intended, and since the trickster seems to have a male slant in tribal cultures, I use "he" for the trickster figure, as well, though the trickster's gender is often ambiguous and sometimes changes within a single story (Radin 22–23).

2. For the female puella, this parental dynamic is reversed, and the necessary sacrifice is the father complex. This particular reversal is probably the place of greatest difference between the mother complexed–puer and the father complexed–puella. See Linda Leonard's outstanding work, *The Wounded Woman*, for a detailed discussion of specifically designated puella dynamics and woundings in relationship to the father.

Works Cited

Baynes, H. G. "The Provisional Life." *Analytical Psychology and the English Mind and Other Papers by H. G. Baynes*. London: Methuen, 1950.

Bly, Robert. *The Sibling Society*. Reading, MA: Addison-Wesley, 1996.

Campbell, Joseph. *The Hero with a Thousand Faces*. Princeton: Princeton UP, 1949.

Conforti, Michael. *The Role of Space and Time in the Puer Aeternus Archetypal Configuration*. Audiocassette. Portland, OR: Oregon Friends of Jung, 1997.

Corbin, Henry. *The Man of Light in Iranian Sufism*. Trans. N. Pearson. 1971. New Lebanon, NY: Omega, 1978.

Diamond, Stanley. Introduction. Radin xi–xxii.

Edinger, Edward F. *Ego and Archetype: Individuation and the Religious Function of the Psyche*. Baltimore: Penguin, 1972.

Hillman, James. "Betrayal." *Loose Ends: Primary Papers in Archetypal Psychology*. Dallas: Spring, 1975. 63–81.

———. "Senex and Puer." *Puer Papers*. Ed. James Hillman. Dallas: Spring, 1979. 3–53.

Hyde, Lewis. *Trickster Makes This World: Mischief, Myth, and Art*. New York: Farrar, Straus and Giroux, 1998.

Jung, Emma, and Marie-Louise von Franz. *The Grail Legend*. Trans. Andrea Dykes. 1960. 2nd ed. Boston: Sigo, 1986.

Jung, C. G. *The Archetypes and the Collective Unconscious*. 1959. Trans. R. F. C. Hull. 2nd ed. Princeton: Princeton UP, 1968.

———. *Civilization in Transition*. 1964. Trans. R. F. C. Hull. 2nd ed. Princeton: Princeton UP, 1970.

———. *Mysterium Coniunctionis: An Inquiry into the Separation and Synthesis of Psychic Opposites in Alchemy*. 1955. Trans. R. F. C. Hull. 2nd ed. Princeton: Princeton UP, 1963.

———. "On the Psychology of the Trickster Figure." Radin 195–211.

———. *Psychology and Alchemy*. 1944. Trans. R. F. C. Hull. 2nd ed. Princeton: Princeton UP, 1968.

———. *Psychology and Religion*. Trans. R. F. C. Hull. New York: Pantheon, 1958.

———. *Symbols of Transformation*. 1952. Trans. R. F. C. Hull. 2nd ed. Princeton: Princeton UP, 1956.

Leonard, Linda Schierse. *The Wounded Woman: Healing the Father-Daughter Relationship*. Boston: Shambhala, 1982.

The Lord of the Rings: The Fellowship of the Ring. Dir. Peter Jackson. With Ian MacKellen and Viggo Mortensen. New Line Cinema and Wingnut Films, 2001.

The Lord of the Rings: The Return of the King. Dir. Peter Jackson. With Ian MacKellen and Viggo Mortensen. New Line Cinema and Wingnut Films, 2003.

The Lord of the Rings: The Two Towers. Dir. Peter Jackson. With Ian MacKellen and Viggo Mortensen. New Line Cinema and Wingnut Films, 2002.

The Matrix. Dir. Andy Wachowski and Larry Wachowski. Warner Bros. Pictures, 1999.

The Matrix Reloaded. Dir. Andy Wachowski and Larry Wachowski. Warner Bros. Pictures, 2003.

The Matrix Revolutions. Dir. Andy Wachowski and Larry Wachowski. Warner Bros. Pictures, 2003.

Neumann, Erich. *The Origins and History of Consciousness.* Trans. R. F. C. Hull. Princeton: Princeton UP, 1949.

Radin, Paul. *The Trickster: A Study in American Indian Mythology.* 1956. New York: Schocken, 1972.

Rowling, J. K. *Harry Potter.* Series 7 vols. New York: Scholastic, 1999–2007.

von Franz, Marie-Louise. *Creation myths.* 1972. Rev. ed. Boston: Shambhala, 1995.

———. *Projection and Recollection in Jungian Psychology.* 1978. Trans. William H. Kennedy. New York: C. G. Jung Foundation for Analytical Psychology, 1980.

———. *Puer Aeternus* (2nd. ed.). 1970. Boston: Sigo, 1981.

Little Girl Lost

Sylvia Plath and the Puella Aeterna

SUSAN E. SCHWARTZ

> I sit
> Composed in Grecian tunic and psyche-knot,
> Rooted to your black look, the play turned tragic:
> Which such blight wrought on our bankrupt estate,
> What ceremony of words can patch the havoc?
>
> —Sylvia Plath, "Conversation Among the Ruins"

Each of us harbors within our inner universe a number of characters, parts of ourselves that can cause conflict and mental distress when not understood. We are relatively unacquainted with these players and their roles and yet they are constantly seeking a stage on which to perform their tragedies and comedies both personally and collectively. Although the puella, the female version of the puer, is absent from Jung's *Collected Works* (Harvey), like her masculine counterpart she is easily recognized both in life and in literature. Descriptions of puella are particularly clear in the work of poet Sylvia Plath, who killed herself in the early 1960s. Plath herself went through a Jungian analysis; her life and works will be analyzed here as an extreme example of the puella. Her poignant and violent psychological struggle illustrates the cultural and trans-generational shadows of the puella archetype. She is also an apt example because, like many poets, her work reveals the shadow life within an individual and a culture, at both personal and archetypal dimensions.

Plath's life was shaped by many of the personal and cultural factors puella women bring into consulting rooms today. In her Journal she expresses the problem of forging a coherent self from the warring fragments of her psyche that is typical of many puella women: "Each day an exercise, or a stream of consciousness ramble? Hates crackle and brandish against me" (*Journals* 181). Although the puella character can form within the psyche in various ways, it tends to generate from the effects of the absent father, the absorbing mother who is emotionally distant, and the puella who is without sufficient connection to her own ground of being, especially the feminine aspects. The phenomenon described here also occurs in the psyches of men who likewise face the problem of understanding and integrating their own puella characteristics consciously.

The puella can be described as a fascinating woman with a free and childlike vitality. Her presence lights up a room as she performs for the adulation and praise of others. She does not like being restrained, enslaved to rules or convention, or inhibited in any way, particularly by reality. Her freshness, indomitable energy, and zest for the unusual embody perpetual youth and creativity. Naïve fantasies of youth, beauty, and power lift her out of daily life, which she considers dreary and common. In this self-constructed world, she flees from her shadow, which represents the descent to earth necessary for actualizing the creativity and life that can make her whole (von Franz 128). A shadow side of puella manifests in narcissism and difficulty in taking herself seriously because she identifies as a girl, not as a woman. Out of touch with her own femininity, even though she may look the part, she does not find satisfaction in being a woman and does not feel solid within herself.

The puella conforms to outer norms; she is mirrored in the lives of many contemporary women who struggle to feel secure in their bodies and their talents. She is compromised by the cultural value that women are desirable only when young. Unable to be young enough, thin enough, smart enough, she is caught in the personal and cultural pressures of these values that encourage us to worship the unattainable, unrealistic, and inhuman forms of women, a system of values that contributes to the lack of mature female models in our society. The puella nature has a virginal quality, representing a deep interiority and a freedom from external contamination, an intactness of the psyche that protects what is immature and unripe (Hillman 190). On the one hand, this condition supports the kind of aloneness necessary for self-growth and creative reflection; on the other, it can be so enclosed within itself that there is no adequate engagement with the world and no recognition, ability, or seeming need for relationship outside of herself.

Von Franz (38) speaks about the person who is pushed out of childhood too soon and crashes into reality, dropping the painful work of self-making because it seems too difficult at this time of life. This pattern is especially notable in the puella. She observes that analytic work takes much patience and tact because the unmasking of reality can be tricky due to vulnerability and repression. An inauthentic pose and accommodation to outer demands protects the terrified and precarious self that cannot face the world. A false self takes over, resulting in a loss of natural instincts; the real self remains walled off and silent. It becomes necessary to descend into the depths of the shadow and to abandon the false self for the real.

The paradox is that the puella is driven by desires to be seen, to excel, and to be loved but not to be known intimately. Her fantasy is that one day she will become this ideal self that she cannot achieve now because she flees from reality (Hillman 29). There is always a "but" preventing development or commitment because each situation is for the short term, and relationships are with others of similar bent. She becomes bored easily and feels trapped, unaware of her own lack of self-knowledge. Thus, her potential withers before it can ripen, because she has preferred the fantasy of perpetual youth to the reality of painful development.

The sense of fraudulence as an adult creates tension and dissatisfaction. She exudes a brittle, crystalline quality and an aura of aloofness behind which she exists in her own untouchable domain. She is vulnerable, a terrified child for whom physical existence is a trial because bodily sensations are denied or ignored in order to avoid feeling and to protect her from anything that is not part of her carefully constructed world. Because the puella feels undeserving of love, which can be painful, she avoids the possibility of that pain (von Franz 39). This avoidance results in a lack of engagement, a restlessness, depersonalization, and inability to inhabit the present. It is no surprise that the puella type experiences an inner emptiness that adds to the craving for acceptance and adoration in order to fill that void. A passage from the Journal of Sylvia Plath expresses this:

> You have had chances; you have not taken them, you are wallowing in original sin; your limitations. You have lost all delight in life. You are becoming a neuter machine, You cannot love, even if you knew how to begin to love . . . You want to go home, back to the womb. . . . You have forgotten the secret you knew, of being joyous, of laughing, of opening doors. (*Journals* 62)

The wounds the puella feels, such as Plath's, arise from early losses, rejections, and lack of nurturing, all of which result in a sense of inadequacy. This keeps her moving and doing but not being or evolving. She enters analysis because "there is something [she] cannot forget, something [she] cannot stop telling [herself], often by [her] actions, about [her] life. And these dismaying repetitions . . . create the illusion of time having stopped" (Phillips 15).

This emotional arrest keeps her behind glass, removed from her existence and the world. She sidesteps the dark aspects of the self, which are threatening to her fragile sense of identity (Schwartz-Salant 22). But the shadow exerts itself in the puella woman; she looks a part and functions well according to others, but she feels nothing is meaningful, and without meaning the experiences are nothing (von Franz 148). To make sure neither she nor anyone else discovers this, she feigns confidence and composure that might come across as exhibitionistic and grandiose, self-centered, even mean-spirited, narrowly ambitious, and envious. This façade can seem harsh, for it conceals the lack of capacity for intimacy and reciprocity in relationships. Without a favorable image of herself, she has little basis for understanding others. She has trouble giving because she feels she has nothing worthwhile to give, and she is unable to take a step back and respond with flexibility to other people's behavior.

The puella needs love and attention, yet she engages in deception of herself and others by putting on a performance and acting "as if" (Solomon 639). She feels unlovable and experiences shame, vulnerability, and fear—all based on a conviction of not being good enough. The lack of basic trust and security leaves her chasing an ideal, through cosmetics, body reshaping, and other compulsive and negative thoughts and behaviors. This self-absorption, however, is actually a defense against self-intimacy and self-reflection. Preserved in a state of suspended animation, the puella is not present for the moments or the hours of her life. Rather, she is absorbed in watching the weight-scales, her hair, the wrinkles, and the imperfection of her work. How can she find her ground of being when this is the very thing she avoids? The self-denial renounces identity, eating her up from within and cutting off her feminine spirit from its innermost recesses. She endures an unending war between parts of the self, a victim of sadistic and unrelenting internal voices.

Many women in consulting rooms today remark about these inner forces; limitations based on sexual stereotypes, social and family pressures, all attempting to crush their bid for selfhood. Here are some of the shadow voices interceding in the psyche of the puella: "I do not like the physical reality of getting older with my dry and wrinkly skin. I hate what I see in the mirror. I cannot accept the fact that I am who I am. My work is not good enough. I do not remember what I did, felt, or thought yesterday." Even though it hurts, she returns to the negative self-images day after day, age coming to her like a disaster, not a celebration. Without an accurate inner mirror, she assesses herself secretly as either inferior or superior, an object fashioned for the adoration of others, the inside and outside worlds disparate and unrelated.

The puella character is not easy to pin down because elusiveness becomes reinforced as part of her charm. For years she hardly notices who or what she is, floating through life with her head in the clouds. Daily she dresses a mannequin, but she selects only a part, or the effect, or the image, set for the occasion. Because she lacks a capacity or desire for realistic self-reflection, her image is distorted by the inability to connect with her core. A dark shadow envelopes her creativity and expressiveness so that they can go nowhere; thus, while the shadow is seen as frightening and not herself, it also contains the parts she needs to gain self-fruition. The problem is that when the potentiality of the psyche is not used it becomes perverted (Leonard 89). Wrapped in self-denial, she cannot access her own natural gifts. Needing approval from others drives her competitive nature, but she must not threaten or surpass them as she fears being hated or excluded. Therefore, she diminishes herself by holding back in one way or another that perversely supports the cultural bias against women who are healthily competitive and strong.

The hallmark of the puella is that she lives provisionally by hiding in the shadows of disconnection, self-loathing, and disavowal of self-expression. Although she is self-absorbed, she needs others to reflect back to her and to witness her life. She wastes time thinking about the pounds she wants to lose and never does the thing that is always in the future, when the time is ripe.

Daddy's Girl

Typically, the puella is described as a daddy's girl who is special in his eyes as the one who understands and gives to him. Father and daughter are emotionally attached in her serving his needs so that she can obtain love. This father loves her when she is a child, but as she grows older he detaches, and she feels his absence, neglect, or abuse. The father who denies his daughter's essence restricts her to a half-dead life, while she remains bound to him. His unavailability entangles a daughter in overvaluing him and other males and denigrating femininity. His fathering and the nature of their bond, whether in overt or covert forms, affects her ability to love or express herself and brings about reactions ranging from melancholy to self-destruction. She may internalize a persecutory father figure and develop a hostile inner world; she may feel rage or numbness while she obstructs her own inspiration and arrests her own self-integration. Acquiring such patterns and behaviors, she grows more and more lost.

The puella learns to remain helpless to the father and other masculine aspects personally, culturally, and relationally. The daughter/father problem reaches to the intrapsychic depths and archetypal roots—to issues of self and culture wherein lie the complex aspects and the patriarchal biases that many daughters are raised on. For many generations of Western culture, a daughter was regarded as the least important member in the family. The daughter/father issue remained a dark terrain, and their relationship was relegated to the shadows. Cultural biases kept daughters docile and fathers unapproachable, as if they were not present in their children's lives. In fact, a father wielded so much influence that a daughter did not question her role with him and instead projected her disappointments and difficulties onto her mother, in yet another diminishment of the feminine.

A daughter naturally goes through a stage of idealizing her father. But, if he stays ideal, for whatever reasons, a daughter cannot gain a realistic sense of either of them. By default, she falls into the male-defined ideal, the woman who buys the myth of being an object of perpetual youth, docility, and sexual allure—all experienced as if at a distance. As such, she is a personification or reflection of the passive servant, an object helplessly absorbed into the other:

> The daughters of such fathers often arrive in analysis with a façade of self-sufficiency. They despair of earning their father's attention except temporarily and unconsciously, often as a sexual object, and they are caught in having to defend themselves while trying to prove themselves equal and worthy of their father's praise. They split off their sensuousness, capture men and/or accomplishments, but feel no tenderness and little self-regard. They are focused forever on seeking the father's blessing and personal attention. (Perera 66)

Father-dominated, the puella woman cannot access the feminine and therefore cannot find who she is.

Sylvia Plath and the Destructive Side of the Puella

Sylvia Plath's life and work expose the many facets of a dark shadow father bond, a yearning and adulation for him mixed with distance from mother. Her poems describe emotional distress in relation to both mother and father and parental relationships that have damaged attachment to self and others. Marking an unfinished area of the personality and originating from early trauma or emotional neglect, negative parental complexes harm a daughter's confidence, promote idealization of others, and destroy initiative while feeding an internalized cycle of self-hatred, oppression, and revenge. From the absence of her father a woman can develop a father complex that becomes like a demon holding her in its clutches (Leonard 88).

For Plath, part of the internal disconnection came from a father who was unapproachable, surrounded by silence, and then died when she was ten years old. She wrote in her Journal about the image of her father in childhood: "You remember that you were his favorite when you were little, and you used to make up dances to do for him as he lay on the living room couch after supper. You wonder if the absence of an older man in the house has anything to do with your intense craving for male company" (*Journals* 26). Plath developed a phantom relationship with her father epitomized by

> the power of the fathers: a familial-social, ideological, political system in which men—by force, direct pressure, or through ritual, tradition, law, and language, customs, etiquette, education, and the division of labor—determine what part women shall or shall not play, and in which the female is everywhere subsumed under the male. (Rich 57)

Given all this, it was not surprising that Plath fell into the arms of Ted Hughes, who had affairs with other women and eventually left her. In her Journal, Plath recounts,

> I dreamed the other night of running after Ted through a huge hospital, knowing he was with another woman, going into mad wards and looking for him everywhere: what makes you think it was Ted? It had his face but it was my father, my mother. I identify him with my father at certain times, and these times take on a great importance: e.g., that one fight at the end of the school year when I found him not-there on the special day ... Isn't this an image of what I feel my father did to me? ... Images of his [Ted's] faithlessness with women echo my fear of my father's relation with my mother and Lady death. (*Journals* 279–80)

The exit of Plath's husband aroused feelings similar to the isolation and abandonment following her father's death. Although her journal includes many dreams like this one, she writes few associations. Perhaps Ted, father, and mother are all connected with the mad, wild, unconscious parts of herself she refers to in the poem "Elm":

> I am terrified by this dark thing
> that sleeps in me;
> All day I feel its soft, feathery turnings, its malignity.
> (*Collected Poems* 192)

Plath's father and his image inside her became an impetus for her writing—a nonrepresented and unspoken figure from which she paradoxically drew information (Greene 69). His absence influenced the formation of destructive inner figures; like the puella woman, Plath grappled with the ordeals of feminine identity and estrangement, discordance and disunity. Plath's childhood paradise was too early destroyed, and the whole thing became a crime against her, imposing on her the role of a vengeful victim. As a result, Plath deadened herself and her psyche due to the deadened object within (Bollas 74). Its detritus haunted her, and, like the dark side of the puella, she suffered symptoms of depression, depersonalization, despair, anxiety, and disturbed connection to self.

The psychological process of canceling the dark shadow of the personal father's claim on a daughter's spirit—as well as the claims of general patriarchal attitudes—requires becoming close to him. This is a dance between keeping an eye on him, becoming absorbed in him, and incorporating the forces related to him, without being destroyed in the process. In the poem "The Jailer," Plath writes about the dead father who remained psychologically alive within:

> I imagine him,
> Impotent as distant thunder,
> In whose shadow I have eaten my ghost ration.
> (*Collected Poems* 226)

Plath used her poetry as a catharsis to express rebellion against personal and cultural constraints. Through her poetic visioning, Plath tried to slough off the old, ill-fitting roles and gain freedom from being the girl-toy of the male. She wrote in language inflamed against males whose attitudes exclude the feminine, and she angrily pricked at the cultural images of the blind adoration of women toward men. She comments in her Journal: "The worst enemy to creativity is self-doubt. And you are so obsessed . . . to face the great huge man-eating world, that you are paralyzed" (*Journals* 85). Plath tried to extricate herself from the psychological agony and to break the narrow, cultural scripts of the daughter who is merely sweet and pretty. After all, the brightest women of Plath's era were channeled toward menial roles, their futures relegated to being satellites to powerful men—a pernicious societal attitude, with similar disastrous effects on women and men, that continues to this day.

Plath's poetry expresses a psychological journey in which she attains power not through following the dream of marrying a prince and then denying herself but through appropriating her own energy and position. Plath and the puella woman share the same responsibility: they must avoid sinking into a wrongly conceived fairytale image of feminine passivity. This path is too unconscious, and it sidesteps dealing head on with the issues concerning the roles of women and the constructive use of her energy. Otherwise, "she is sentenced to live her daughterhood as a father's priestess, votary, bride and queen" (Kroll 83).

It is interesting that the popular image of Plath is that she wrote poems of aggressive threat and power; this is misleading. These aggressive poems are actually relatively few among her works. Far more of the poems present the protagonists as basically passive, depersonalized, helpless victims—the female serving the male torturer whose perverse needs bring women to submission. They contain images of the woman who animates and becomes animated in the mirror of a male-inscribed text. Masochism, loss of will, and the woman controlled by the man are tortures suffered by her heroines. Her poetry also enacts the masculine castration that results in the women's turning the aggression against themselves and sacrificing the feminine, which evokes connections with the shadow side of the puella.

A Refusal of Mother

Becoming conscious of how mother and daughter images live inside her helps a woman manifest her life. She becomes centered on her own axis and expresses the autonomy of her body and psyche, remaining unswayed by cultural dictates. However, a puella woman often feels the wounds from her mother's ignored and betrayed creativity and the insufficient use of female potency. This pits her against her mother, and she ends up not accepting or not knowing how to access her own feminine qualities. The emotional distance, disapproval, or blame of mother forms a vacuum of intimacy between them that is compounded by the cultural lack of favorable feminine images.

Unable to appreciate the maternal, a daughter feels unlovable about herself, and this attitude alienates her from her body and the earth; it can escalate into a hatred of life: "She started out in the world with averted face . . . and all the while the world and life pass by her like a dream—an annoying source of illusions, disappointments, and irritations" (Jung, *Archetypes* para. 185). When the instincts are injured, she may experience problems with her female organs, remain unconscious of her ability to conceive or be creative, and repudiate or rebel against her feminine nature. A rage toward her mother can also result in self-inertia and low self-worth. The mother complex in this type of woman is manifested in depressive moods, constant dissatisfaction with herself and with the whole of reality (von Franz 126).

Sylvia Plath describes a feeling of crushing maternal self-annihilation and a mother's guilt-inducing refusal of her daughter's autonomy through the medusa image in her poetry. In her Journal, Plath wonders what the gods ask and wonders about herself, as well: "Am I living half alive? . . . I feel in a dream, a fog" (*Journals* 324). Her poetry reveals a disturbing netherworld of psychological oppression and need for release from the mutilations acquired from marriage and mothering. She mentions Jung in her Journals—his references to parents who do their best and who live for their children. Pressure to achieve, especially for her mother, is manifested as a distorted mirroring she turned onto herself.

In her Journal, Plath attributes her suicidal tendencies to "a transferred murderous impulse from my mother onto myself" and blames her rage on fear of her mother's appropriation of her writing (*Journals* 280). Feeling doomed to be enveloped in her mother's dark shadow, Plath writes about this conundrum: "How can I get rid of this depression: by refusing to believe she has any power over me, the old witches for whom one sets out plates of milk and honey?" (*Journals* 280).

The Shadow of Her Body

Operating in the tradition of feminine passivity, many puella women stay dependent, immature, and unaware—not knowing what they want or do not want and wondering if they will be loved or hated. The puella lives as if life goes on forever, while she remains stuck on a treadmill of predicable responses, repetitive and self-deprecating behaviors and thoughts that include a disturbed relationship to her body.

About this, Plath opines that the exploitation of women is partly due to their compliance with demeaning roles. Her words put a visage on inner chaos, whereas if she remains mute, she will be mutilated by avoiding self-knowledge (Van Dyne 54). Her heroines endure physical dismemberment through mutilation, torture, and victimization. They act ineffectual and suppressed, cornered into immobility, the feminine ego wrenched from the true self. Like a puppet, deprived of independent action, the woman is vulnerable and then erased, unable to forge her own image. Self-hatred is at work in the desire to be rid of her body—because it is female. In the poem "Lady Lazarus," the woman is reduced, her body an object, doll-like and man's prey:

> I am your opus . . .
> You poke and stir.
> Flesh, bone, there is nothing there.
> (*Collected Poems* 244)

The puella is the woman unable to use her talents as she holds some internally imposed ideal, a feeling that frustrates yet has been with her for as long as she can remember. For the puella the pressure to be perfect means that unacceptable feelings must be hidden at all cost. She outwardly takes on the role of seeking to please others while inside are fears about showing her real self. A punishing core of "I don't deserve" creates an ever-present tension that cuts off pleasure in both mental and physical activities. This derives from the narcissistic wounds that create inertia and repress the aggression needed for entry into life. A sense of not being present promotes the continual search for the ideal rather than the real. This is a narcissism that has to do not with self-love but with self-hatred (Schwartz-Salant 24). Various modes of emotional protection and avenues of psychological escape are sought out as methods of defense that lead to an inauthentic existence. And, at the same time, she does not notice that the idea of an ideal life gets in the way of living it.

Much as she strives to ignore it, the shadow draws her to pay attention: "Closer examination of the dark characteristics—that is, the inferiorities constituting the shadow—reveals that they have an emotional nature, a kind of autonomy, and accordingly an obsessive, or better possessive quality" (Campbell 145). Raised to be aware of her background, looks, and the externals in life, yet equally trying to refuse any shadowy parts puts the puella in conflict.

The repressed natural body urges, instincts, and feelings fall into the unconscious. The writer Adrienne Rich, living in the era of Sylvia Plath, commented on this: "But the fear and hatred of our bodies has often crippled our brains. We have tended either to become our bodies—blindly, slavishly, in obedience to male theories about us—or to try to exist in spite of them" (Rich 284–85). Left with a split-off and unrealistic self-reflection, the puella woman needs a perfect body, but not one to enjoy. Denying the body leaves a woman without desire, and the dispossession of her body means a bulk of her libido is devitalized and scattered. Likewise, Plath's poetic imagery of dismemberment suggests physical alienation and fragmentation as well as thwarted longings for emotional relatedness and the struggle to reconnect the personality. Jung says that the body depends on the psyche just as the psyche depends on the body. Bodily experiences bring one into the here and now, and, "The hole which one falls into is through the body and the body says 'but this is you'" (Jung, *Symbolic Life* 209).

Summary

The puella represents one of the dis-eases of our era—she does not breathe deeply; she fears being emotionally touched and does not know how to be present to the basics of life. This is a collective discomfort, and Jung says, "The fear of life is a real panic . . . It is the deadly fear of the instinctive, the unconscious, the inner [woman] who is cut off from life by [her] continual shrinking back from reality" (*Symbols* 298).

The task of the puella is to become real, no longer relying on outer adulation or putting on masks but accessing the spark within. This involves engaging with the wounds, reclaiming the damaged parts, integrating the shadow by breaking down the ideal, and openly acknowledging her strengths. However, for Plath—again, as an example of the extreme—the liberation from internalized captors and their devouring aggression against her did not happen. Although she expressed desire for reconstruction, she could not hold the weight of the conflicts, and she took her life—after writing what became some of her most well-known poetry.

For the puella, the shadowy recesses reveal the parts calling for re-cognition—accessing her feminine core, resolving the yearning and melancholy, creating support and feeling from within—so that she can be present to her individuality and creativity. The girl becomes a woman through accepting the shadow, acquiring patience and healthy regard for herself and for others.

In the process, she discovers the meaning in her personal drama, and this is a step toward healing the collective attitudes that limit the feminine. As Jung said, "Woman today . . . gives expression to . . . the urge to live a complete life, a longing for meaning and fulfillment, a growing disgust with senseless one-sidedness, with unconscious instinctuality and blind contingency" (*Civilization* 130).

Works Cited

Baumlin, James S., Tita French Baumlin, and George H. Jensen, ed. *Post-Jungian Criticism: Theory and Practice*. Albany: State U of New York P, 2004.

Bollas, Christopher. *Cracking Up*. New York: Hill and Wang, 1995.

Greene, Andre. *The Tragic Effect*. Cambridge: Cambridge UP, 1979.

Harvey, P. Personal communication. October, 2005.

Hillman, James, ed. *Puer Papers*. Irving, TX: Spring, 1979.

Kroll, Judith. *Chapters in a Mythology*. New York: Harper and Row, 1976.

Jung, C. G. *The Archetypes and the Collective Unconscious*. New York: Pantheon, 1959.

———. *Civilization in Transition*. New York: Pantheon, 1964.

———. *The Portable Jung*. Ed. Joseph Campbell. New York: Viking, 1971.

———. *The Symbolic Life*. New York: Pantheon, 1954.

———. *The Symbols of Transformation*. New York: Pantheon, 1956.

Leonard, Linda Schierse. *The Wounded Woman: Healing the Father-Daughter Relationship*. Boston: Shambhala, 1982.

Perera, Sylvia Brinton. *Descent to the Goddess*. Toronto: Inner City, 1981.

Plath, Sylvia. *Collected Poems*. New York: Harper and Row, 1992.

———. *The Journals of Sylvia Plath*. Ed. Ted Hughes. New York: Dial, 1982.

Phillips, Adam. *On Flirtation*. Cambridge: Harvard UP, 1994.

Rich, Adrienne. *Of Woman Born*. New York: Norton, 1986.

Schwartz-Salant, Nathan. *On Narcissism*. Toronto: Inner City, 1982.

Solomon, Hester. "Self Creation and the Limitless Void of Dissociation: The As If Personality." *Journal of Analytical Psychology* 49 (2004): 635–56.

Ulanov, Ann Belford. *Receiving Woman*. Philadelphia: Westminster, 1981.

Van Dyne, Susan. *Revising Life*. Chapel Hill: U of North Carolina P, 1993.

von Franz, Marie-Louise. *The Problem of the Puer Aeternus*. Toronto: Inner City, 2000.

Provincials in Time

The Provisional Life

MARITA DELANEY

A scene in *Dr. 90210*, a popular television program about plastic surgery among the Beverly Hills population, shows a physician looking at a photograph of the distended abdomen of a pregnant woman and commenting on how terribly pregnancy ravages the body. His colleague nods solemnly in agreement. The young woman, who has come to these physicians to have her abdominal scars removed, looks on. These men make it their life's work to reverse the shaping influence of age, gravity, and heredity on the flesh. Unspoken, on the television program and in life, is the truth of the body that says, *So does life ravage the flesh, and it is inevitable that it do so.*

At midlife, we develop a heightened awareness of the temporality of the body, either through the creeping ache of sore joints and muscles or the shock of chronic disease that jolts us out of midlife slumber. The persistent drive to reject this inevitability is a manifestation of puer psychology in which commitments are easily undone, and we can remain young and beautiful, and—above all—unmarked by time. The physicians who display themselves through the video screens of America are priests of a new religion in which the body is no longer a vessel of spirit—it is the agent of the transformation of consciousness. Even those far from Hollywood, viewing these transformations in living rooms of rural America, are part of the collective consciousness that is changed by these rituals.

Contemporary American life is dominated by a puer psychology that is characterized by being simultaneously grandiose in personal expectations and intolerant of the suffering of others. The roots of this complex lie deep in the collective unconscious. Before there were scientists and computer technicians, there were alchemists and magicians who pursued the mastery of nature. The same urge for mastery and transformation that nourished the work of early magicians also feeds scientific and technological ambitions today. Human grandiosity is seen in the particular manifestation of consumerism that increases luxury items, creates communication innovations, and mobilizes air travel and cosmetic innovations. Rather than addressing distribution of food, economic development, or dispersal of medical care, consumerism fuels grandiose personal ambitions, thereby obscuring awareness of uncomfortable realities.

We are provincials in time, as poet Allen Tate called contemporary men and women:

> The regional man . . . extends his own immediate necessities into the world, and assumes that the present moment is unique; he becomes the provincial man. He cuts himself off from the past, and without benefit of the fund of traditional wisdom approaches the simplest problems of life as if nobody had ever heard of them before. (Tate 539)

We live without awareness of past and future, and a deep forgetfulness characterizes the present moment. This is both the wealth and the curse of the *puer aeternus*. The puer psychology of our time encourages the obliteration of the everyday, the cyclical, and the regular aspects of human life in favor of the cultivation of that which is unique and extraordinary.

The puer is described in the Jungian literature as living a life that is characterized by significant potential yet ultimately immobilized in creative pursuits because still bound to the mother world (von Franz 7). The puer does not have to fend for his needs because Mother—or Father, or God—cares for him or her wholly. The rent is not paid, the credit card bills pile up, and the car breaks down. All the details of life are too much, and goals are never met because of these constant impediments to creativity and freedom. Like an adolescent, the puer is bound to parents and parental complexes yet maintains a conscious attitude of freedom from them. Under the weight of this ambivalent psychic complex, life is an incoherent struggle that often leads to depression. Turning potential into real accomplishment involves willingness to experience painful losses—loss of freedom, loss of creative spirit, and loss of spiritual dignity that may never be recovered. The inflation that characterizes imagined creative skills often collapses in the face of hard reality.

Youth and the Puer Aeternus

Puer aeternus possession results in a temporary approach to life and a sense that no decisions are final, but sometimes reality intervenes in a traumatic event. An unplanned pregnancy occurs, and a young woman's life is irrevocably transformed. A skiing accident shatters a leg of a hotdog skier. A car accident leaves a young couple overturned on the side of the road. And with each of these events, a sense of mortality is born.

The breaking of the body is sometimes a psychological necessity, and the physically or psychically dismembering accidents of youth are initiation into a new maturity. As Jung commented, "If the demand for self-knowledge is willed by fate and is refused, this negative attitude may end in real death." (*CW* 14: 675). Accidents, illness, and death are expressions of the sometimes irresolvable split between spirit and nature. The tragic divide of human nature is one in which the individual is both apart from nature and helplessly bound to it. Ernest Becker identifies how the psyche copes with this paradox and maintains a sense of personal invulnerability: by forming a hero project and striving to overcome nature, one gains a sense of divinity through identification with something "other," such as nationalism, fame, success, beauty, or religion (26).

Here the plastic surgeon/priest steps in to bridge the gulf between aspiration and reality by transforming the body into the semblance of youth that supports the fantasy of immortality. Drawing close to death under general anesthesia, one is lifted from bodily limitations. It is the puerile impulse for ascension and flight from limitations that Marie-Louise von Franz points out in *The Problem of the Puer Aeternus*, when she notes that the puer is known for fascination with planes, mountaineering, rock climbing, any endeavor by which one leaves earth's limitations (8).

Flight of the Puer

In his phenomenology of mythological symbolism, Mircea Eliade says that "the symbolism of ascension always refers to a breaking-out of a situation that has become 'blocked' or 'petrified,' a rupture of the plane which makes it possible to pass from one mode of being into another" (118). Flight is associated with spiritual adepts, such as the shaman or the yogi who embark on spiritual journeys. Birds and other winged creatures symbolize spiritual aspiration. Their movements are sudden and swift, like those of the sky-gods. The image of flight signifies a rupture in the plane of experience. Transforming psychic experience often occurs as a rupture, a breaking forth or breaking into a new state of being.

The transcendence of bodily limitations offers a kind of freedom. For some *Dr. 90210* patients it is economic freedom, for their livelihood depends upon their looks, while for others it is freedom from a debilitating self-consciousness. Never mentioned is the rare and tragic death that occurs to an individual undergoing a cosmetic procedure, for not only would that blemish the entertainment value of the program, but it would break the hearts of the viewers, who derive a surrogate pleasure from the lives of others more privileged and more overtly desperate to transform themselves. The literal transformation of the flesh carries a symbolic import in the minds of the viewers as they see mortality defeated before their eyes. Following the surgery, *Dr. 90210* clients go to a luxury hotel where nurses assist them in their recovery. It is perhaps an unmet need for psychological initiation that is exercised in these activities. Psyche hungers for ritual to acknowledge the serious and deep changes that occur in the course of a lifetime.

Psychic Energy and Midlife

Psychic energy is inherently dynamic and will fluctuate between polarities—any extreme stimulates a move toward its opposite. Therefore, in the life of the average person, the very impulse for transcendence brings one back to earth. With the onset of midlife, even those fortunate enough to avoid serious disease experience limits to their energy and to stamina. Midlife health problems are initiations into a new psychological status. It is how we are transformed psychologically into mature adulthood. During this period, individuals also may begin taking medications to prevent osteoporosis, lower cholesterol, or deflect whatever genetic vulnerability is present. Our inherited weaknesses represent the family unconscious, which comes home to rest in our bodies. We put on reading glasses for the first time and we often feel that we are turning into our parents.

At this juncture, in the more prosperous communities in the United States, individuals may voluntarily seek a midlife initiation through cosmetic surgery. From the point of view of the unconscious, to go under the knife for cosmetic reasons is not intrinsically different from any cultural initiation involving slipping into unconsciousness, being acted upon by the larger forces of the culture, and then awakening transformed. One must retreat from the demands of the world during the healing process, like an initiate into a newly formed religious sect—the Order of the Transformed Body. The credo that youth must be preserved at all costs is supported by the puer psychology of the culture, and thus we take solace in the fantasy that loss and deterioration are what happen to someone else.

Cultural Psychology of the Puer

Von Franz describes the puer as a man who has a pronounced mother complex and a pattern of behavior in which he is unable to commit to any situation or person (7). He is impatient and resists hard work. Hard work is in fact, according to Jung, the cure for puer psychology: "[W]ork is the one disagreeable word which no *puer aeternus* likes to hear," says von Franz, "and Jung came to the conclusion that it was the right answer. My experience also has been that if a man pulls out of this kind of youthful neurosis, then it is through work"

(10). Although the puer can work when in a state of great enthusiasm, what "he cannot do is work on a dreary, rainy morning when work is boring and one has to kick oneself into it" (von Franz 10). The self-discipline, ego strength, and the directed will are qualities that the puer lacks, but the cultivation of these skills allows a maturity to unfold. The puer tends to suffer when authentic creativity is called for, because his uniqueness is best recognized in potential. Von Franz refers to the term *provisional life*, which she states was coined by H. G. Baynes (8). To live a provisional life is to live as if life choices are temporary as to job, partner, home, or locale. The concept of commitment is innately paralyzing to the puer. To have a spouse, a dog, a house—to be ordinary—is anathema to him, because that is to be like everyone else.

Some of these characteristics manifest themselves on a collective level when difficulty in maintaining relationships on an individual level is mirrored in a societal inability to sustain relationship with the earth and its inhabitants. We exhaust fossil fuels that run our industries and automobiles, and we deplete the ozone layer as if it were just a conditional choice that has no impact on the future of the earth and its inhabitants. Since it is all temporary, there is no reason to commit to the health of future generations. The provisional life on the collective level has as its shadow the destruction of earth. To live without limits, without mindfulness in relationship to boundaries, and to focus always on the bright star of possibilities has a way of constellating a painfully dark shadow. The breakdown of economies based upon limitless consumption and the violence connected with oil reserves and oil production are dark shadows of the search for limitless human productivity and creativity. We exhibit a collective reluctance to acknowledge the limitations of humanity and of the ecosystem. It is typical of the puer to hold on to feelings of privilege that are typical of youth long after youth is over. The United States of America is like a youngster who is saddened when no one understands how extraordinary s/he is. The psychological shift from a young nation that offers a beacon of light to the world for religious freedom and economic opportunity to a mature nation is a difficult one. We continue to feel unique, but emptiness characterizes our relationship with the world and with ourselves because we cannot see the narcissistic wound that is startlingly visible to the outside world.

Developmental Pathways to Puer Psychology

Jeffrey Satinover has outlined the developmental pathway to becoming a puer, and it is largely indistinguishable from the development of the narcissistic personality. Either the environmentally deprived child or the grossly overin-dulged child can develop a personality flavored with grandiosity, since both parenting methods miss the child's developmental needs and the Self must cope with the inadequacies of the environment. Normal childhood development involves a grandiose enlargement of identity. Imagination opens the child to the world of ultimate possibilities and childhood games of superheroes, kings, queens, and various types of world creators (Satinover 91). As grandiose fantasies encounter reality, frustration grows; the management of this frustration by the child and by the environment becomes the source of puer psychology. The environment excessively frustrates one's sense of being special, which leads to fragmentation of the developing Self. Alternatively, the child may be sheltered from forces that challenge the grandiose self, and thus the child never encounters a psychological challenge to grandiosity. Either developmental pathway may lead to a cycle between grandiosity and despair that typifies puer psychology. This narcissistic sense of specialness that derives from either developmental pathway has as a consequence the development of depression. Problems arise in both love and work because of this cycle of grandiosity and despair. Actual achievements never live up to the fantasy of the childhood Self:

> Barely to pass the crucial exam, but without any preparation, is a more prodigious feat than to turn in an excellent performance due to strenuous effort. The Puer prefers to be known, and to know himself, as brilliant if erratic, rather than as a successful drudge. He prefers his fantasied potentials to his actual potentials because the former better evokes the glory of the childhood Self. (Satinover 96)

In love relationships, the puer seeks reflection of his greatness through relationship with another. Satinover has suggested that the preoccupation with "superstars" and the cult of personality that defines the entertainment business is a manifestation of the puer psychology that dominates the culture (98). Indeed, we build up megastars and then dismember them repeatedly. The hero cannot remain a hero, because it is too painful to see a display of greatness in someone who is not ourselves.

Grandiosity and Despair

The cycle of grandiosity and despair can be seen in the dynamics of cultural evolution. Joseph Campbell suggested that the tallest building in a city reflects the supreme values of the culture. In the medieval European town, it was the cathedral. In contemporary New York, it was the World Trade Center, where finance is the dominant force. If, as Jung suggested, the unconscious is lived out in world events as much as it is in the life of the individual, then the devastation of the World Trade Center signaled collapse on several levels: collapse of America's self-image, collapse of a sense of safety on this continent, collapse of the sense of entitlement that we need not be affected by the deep discontent of others. We grieved deeply the loss of our self-image. An inflated sense of self-esteem is evident in our sense of entitlement to intervene when and how we choose, as well as in the conviction that might makes right in international relations.

Is it no wonder, then, that depression is endemic in American culture and that antidepressants are the most prescribed medications in the United States? We are arguably the most depressed people on the earth. Our depression masks a deep sadness that we are mortal and are beset by mortal limitations. Distracting strategies, such as consumerism or plastic surgery, deflect this from our awareness. Sadness resolves, but repressed sadness is not permitted to resolve because it is linked to deeply formed personality dynamics that evolve into depression. If we could acknowledge unconscious sadness, we might be liberated from the disenchantment that characterizes depression. A compensatory mania for buying helps soothe the lack of pleasure we feel in objects. A deeply held ambivalence characterizes our relationship to the world of things; they simultaneously soothe us and threaten us as their production consumes the finite resources of the earth.

Solution to Puer Psychology

The answer to the puer's dilemma of having potential but being unable to commit to the humbling work of creativity or relationship is hard work, according to Jung. It is hard work to recognize limits of human life, respect boundaries of nature and resources, and dedicate ourselves to self-knowledge, rather than self-aggrandizement, but if we do so, we may move to a new psychological station. This requires that we refuse to project our soul outward into the heavens, or onto one another, but hold it within ourselves and own the complexities of human life by integrating them into our human consciousness.

If we take up the ideal of being servants of the world, rather than creators, we may find a path toward self-knowledge and a middle way that serves all of humanity and the earth's inhabitants. We may not be "great" in the sense of superiority to others but rather in the humble greatness of openhearted relationship to the world and search for self-understanding. Tempting though it is to our literalistic souls, no amount of consumerism will fill the void within us. Understanding technology and the excessive reliance on rationality will never replace the deep human hunger for meaning. We mourn a world that does not encompass us anymore. And if we try to remake it in our image, we are doomed, like Faust, to tragic devastation but without the descending angels to rescue us. Simply to be human, no more and no less, to be bound to our own creative lives, to acknowledge the impulses that arise in us for mastery and dominion, but not to be controlled by them—that is a true greatness that has thus far eluded us. To devote our imagination to the service of others, to acknowledge the importance of other earth inhabitants is deeply worthy psychic activity.

The modest impulses of the magical tradition of the alchemists—to relieve suffering, to prolong life, to cure disease—are still our humanistic goals. Realization of these goals requires that we not be bound unconsciously to Mother, like the puer, but bound with conscious awareness of our needs and responsibilities to earth. To give up our provincialism is to enter into connections with currents outside of our understanding and to know there is something that must be served for the realization not of the individual personality but of the collective life of the psyche. We are asked to take up our wounds, our puerile impulses to favor ourselves too deeply and unconsciously, and to transform them into a broader human consciousness, a consciousness that celebrates not the greatness of individual achievement or of personality but encompasses the complex and mystifying greatness of the earth.

Works Cited

Becker, Ernest. *The Denial of Death*. New York: Macmillan, 1973.

Dr. 90210. E! Entertainment Television. 2004–present.

Eliade, Mircea. *The Sacred and the Profane*. New York: Harcourt Brace Jovanovich, 1958.

Joseph Campbell and the Power of Myth. Vol. 1, "The Hero's Adventure." Videocassette. Apostrophe S Productions, 1990.

Jung, Carl. *Collected Works of C. G. Jung*. Princeton: Princeton UP, 1969.

Pico della Mirandola, Giovanni. *Oration on the Dignity of Man*. Trans. A. Robert Caponigri. Chicago: Henry Regnery, 1956.

Rees, Graham Charles. *Francis Bacon's Natural Philosophy*. Diss. U of Birmingham, 1970.

Rossi, Paolo. *Francis Bacon: From Magic to Science*. Trans. Sacha Rabinovitch. Chicago: U of Chicago P, 1968.

Satinover, Jeffrey. "Science and the Fragile Self: The Rise of Narcissism, the Decline of God." *Pathologies of the Modern Self: Postmodern Studies on Narcissism, Schizophreni,a and Depression*. Ed. David M. Levin. New York UP, 1987. 84–113.

Tate, Allen. "The New Provincialism." *Essays of Four Decades*. Chicago: Swallow, 1968.

von Franz, Marie-Louise. *The Problem of the Puer Aeternus*. Toronto: Inner City, 2000.

List of Contributors

Tita French Baumlin is Professor of English at Missouri State University. A specialist in Shakespeare and Early Modern drama, she was editor of the scholarly journal *Explorations in Renaissance Culture* for ten years and co-editor of *Ethos: New Essays in Rhetorical and Critical Theory* (with James S. Baumlin; Southern Methodist UP, 1994) and of *Post-Jungian Criticism: Theory and Praxis* (co-edited with J. Baumlin and Jensen; State U of New York P, 2004). She has co-authored two post-Jungian articles: "Revisioning Feminine Archetypes through *Jane Eyre*" (in *Post-Jungian Criticism*) and "*Chronos, Kairos, Aion*: Failures of Decorum, Right-Timing, and Revenge in Shakespeare's *Hamlet*" (in *Rhetoric and Kairos: Essays in History, Theory, and Praxis*, ed. Sipiora and J. Baumlin; State U of New York P, 2002).

A thesis and research director, **Craig Chalquist** also teaches depth psychology, ecopsychology, social science research, history of psychology, mythology, and related topics at four Bay Area schools, including Sonoma State University and John F. Kennedy University, a school dedicated to global transformation. He also works as dissertation coordinator for Pacifica Graduate Institute.

Marita Delaney is Associate Professor of Counseling and School Psychology at Western New Mexico University, where she is coordinator of the Masters in Counseling program at the Gallup Graduate Studies Center. She is a licensed psychologist and certified as a supervisory-level school psychologist. Her interests include Jungian psychology and community mental health. She has worked as a clinical psychologist in schools on the Navajo reservation and community mental health centers in northwest New Mexico for the past ten years.

Darrell Dobson was the founding editor of *JUNG: the e-journal of the Jungian Society for Scholarly Studies*. He is vice president of that society. His doctoral research is an inquiry into the professional knowledge and reflective practices of four teachers who use analytical psychology and the arts to promote transformative learning. He lives in the Canadian forest with his wife and two sons.

A recent recipient of his Masters degree from Pacifica Graduate Institute, **Dustin Eaton** is now a doctoral candidate in the Religious Studies department at The University of Iowa.

Chaz Gormley is an independent scholar living in Santa Fe, New Mexico. He is completing a Master of Arts degree in Depth Psychology from Sonoma State University and has long had an active interest in exploring Jungian and archetypal material. He has given numerous papers at national and regional conferences. He has taught at the university and community college level, edited journals, and continues to facilitate local groups pursuing mythological studies.

John Gosling is a psychiatrist and Jungian analyst. He completed his training as a Jungian analyst at the C. G. Jung Institute of New York in 1994. He spent twenty years living in Manhattan where he maintained a private practice while serving on the Board of the C. G. Jung Institute of New York where he also taught and supervised analysts in training. Three years ago Dr. Gosling returned to South Africa, where he was born and raised, and he currently lives in Cape Town. He has presented seminars and papers on a variety of topics both nationally and internationally. He is a member of the Southern African Association for Analytical Psychology and is actively involved with the C. G. Jung Centre in Cape Town. He is a member of the International Association of Analytical Psychologists.

Luke Hockley is Professor of Media Analysis at the University of Bedfordshire, England. He was elected a Fellow of the Royal Society of Arts in 2003. Dr. Hockley has lectured widely on Jung and cinema in the United States, U.K. and Europe (including the C. G. Jung institute in Zurich). His most recent book is Frames of Mind: A Post-Jungian Look at Cinema, Television and Technology (Intellect Books, 2007).

George H. Jensen is Professor of English and Chair of the Department of English at the University of Arkansas–Little Rock. Dr. Jensen's numerous Jung-related publications include *Identities Across Texts* (Hampton P, 2002); *Personality and the Teaching of Composition* (Ablex, 1989) and *Writing and Personality* (Davies-Black, 1995), both co-authored with John K. DiTiberio; along with *Post-Jungian Criticism: Theory and Praxis* (co-edited with J. Baumlin and T. Baumlin; State U of New York P, 2004).

Anodea Judith is a former therapist, a worldwide teacher, filmmaker, and author of several books, including *Wheels of Life* (Llewellyn, 1987), and *Eastern Body, Western Mind: Psychology and the Chakra System as a Path to the Self* (Celestial Arts, 1996). Dr. Judith's book with Tara Lynda Guber, *Contact: The Yoga of Relationship* (Insight, 2006), won the 2007 Nautilus Award for best book in Yoga/massage/movement and the Independent Publisher Awards Gold Medal for 2007 in the category of Sexuality/Relationships. Her chapter, "Culture on the Couch," reflects her most recent book: *Waking the Global Heart: Humanity's Rite of Passage from the Love of Power to the Power of Love* (Elite, 2006) won the 2007 Nautilus Book Award for best book of the year in the category of Social Change/Current Events/Activism, and the 2007 Independent Publisher's Awards Silver Medal in the category of Mind/Body/Spirit. For more information regarding Dr. Judith's many programs and activities, go to: <www.wakingtheglobalheart. com> and <www.sacredcenters.com>.

Keith Polette is a Professor of English and the Director of the English Education Program at the University of Texas at El Paso. His most recent article on Jungian theory is "Airing (erring) the Soul: An Archetypal View of Television," which appears in *Post-Jungian Criticism: Theory and Praxis* (ed. J. Baumlin, T. Baumlin, and Jensen; State U of New York P, 2004). He has also authored *Read and Write It Out Loud: Guided Oral Literacy Strategies* (Allyn and Bacon, 2005) and *Teaching Grammar Through Writing: Activities to Develop Writer's Craft with All Students* (Allyn and Bacon, 2008). And he has recently written three children's books: *Isabel and the Hungry Coyote* (Raven Tree, 2004), *Paco and the Giant Chile Plant* (Raven Tree, 2008), and *The Moon over the Mountain* (Raven Tree, forthcoming). He is currently working on a book that will cross-thread Jungian theory and literacy pedagogy.

Sally Porterfield is retired Director of the A & S Drama Program at the University of Hartford. She has applied Jungian theory to her work as actor, writer, teacher, and director. She is currently president of The Jungian Society for Scholarly Studies and a member of the International Association for Jungian Studies. Dr. Porterfield's other publications include *Jung's Advice to the Players: A Jungian Reading of Shakespeare's Problem Plays* (Greenwood, 1994) and a chapter to the collection *Post-Jungian Criticism: Theory and Practice* (ed. J. Baumlin, T. Baumlin, and Jensen; State U of New York P, 2004).

Susan Rowland is Reader in English and Jungian Studies at the University of Greenwich, U.K. She was also the first chair of the International Association for Jungian Studies 2003–06. Dr. Rowland is the author of three books on Jung and literary or gender topics as well as numerous articles, including a chapter in the collection *Post-Jungian Criticism: Theory and Practice* (ed. J. Baumlin, T. Baumlin, and Jensen; State U of New York P, 2004). Recent books are *C. G. Jung and Literary Theory: The Challenge from Fiction* (St. Martin's, 1999), *Jung as a Writer* (Routledge, 2005), and *Jung: A Feminist Revision* (Polity, 2002).

Susan E. Schwartz is a Jungian analyst trained at the C. G. Jung Institute in Zurich, Switzerland; she also has a doctorate in clinical psychology. She is a senior analyst, teacher, and member of the New Mexico Society of Jungian Analysts. Dr. Schwartz gives lectures and workshops on various aspects of Jungian analytical psychology worldwide and maintains a private analytical practice in Phoenix, Arizona.

Rinda West is the author of *Out of the Shadow: Ecopsychology, Story, and Encounters with the Land* (U of Virginia P, 2007). She earned her PhD at the University of Leeds, England, has taught at the University of Chicago, Oakton Community College, and Christ Church University–Canterbury, and has served on the board of the Jung Institute, Chicago. Currently she is a landscape designer in Chicago, where she negotiates with soil and climate as encounters with shadow and the Self.

Index